60

FARRAR
STRAUS
GIROUX

SOCCERHEAD

SOCCERHEAD

AN ACCIDENTAL JOURNEY INTO THE
HEART OF THE AMERICAN GAME

JIM HANER

NORTH POINT PRESS

A DIVISION OF

FARRAR, STRAUS AND GIROUX / NEW YORK

NORTH POINT PRESS
A division of Farrar, Straus and Giroux
19 Union Square West, New York 10003

Distributed in Canada by Douglas & McIntyre Ltd.
Printed in the United States of America
Published in 2006 by North Point Press
First paperback edition, 2007

The Library of Congress has cataloged the hardcover edition as follows:
Haner, Jim, 1957–
    Soccerhead : an accidental journey into the heart of the American game /
Jim Haner.— 1st ed.
        p.   cm.
    ISBN-13: 978-0-86547-694-3 (hardcover : alk. paper)
    ISBN-10: 0-86547-694-2 (hardcover : alk. paper)
    1. Soccer—Coaching—United States.   I. Title.

GV943.8 .H36 2006
796.334'07'7—dc22

                                                                    2005006798

Paperback ISBN-13: 978-0-86547-733-9
Paperback ISBN-10: 0-86547-733-7

Designed by Gretchen Achilles

www.fsgbooks.com

1   3   5   7   9   10   8   6   4   2

FOR DONNA, BEN, AND SAM,

WHO BROUGHT ME HERE

CONTENTS

CONTENTS

SOCCERHEAD

PROLOGUE

It was a night made for werewolves and stickup men—one of those airless southern summer evenings—the sort of swampy half-moon nocturne that can evoke a sense of anxiety all by itself. June bugs rattled in the canopies of the streetlights on Fifty-first Avenue. The smoke from my cigarette hung motionless in the air. Nearby, a freight train trundled by, bound for Washington, D.C., too slow to stir the torpid vapors. As I mounted the metal steps for Parents' Night, I was beset by dread.

"Soccer?" I asked myself again, flicking a smoldering butt down onto the parking lot. "What in the hell do I know about soccer?"

Oh, yes, I was familiar with the game. In my youth I had wandered the globe as a sailor in the U.S. Navy and seen rubber-limbed young men play on the beaches of Rio de Janeiro. I had watched school kids, in white shirts and ties, dribble the two-tone ball in London's Hyde Park, and I'd seen the game all over Italy and in the narrow cobblestoned alleys of the Plaka, in Athens. In Cairo, a gaggle of urchins tried to goad me and a gang of shipmates into a match by kicking a dusty goat bladder at our heads. But we knew trouble when we saw it. These experiences, however, had been half a lifetime earlier, and none seemed relevant as I climbed the stairs that moist August night to do my duty at the local chapter of the Boys and Girls Club in College

Park, Maryland, a leafy village of 24,657 souls on the fringes of the University of Maryland in suburban Washington, D.C.

My wife had seen one of the club's flyers somewhere in town, and our six-year-old son, Ben, had begun to express an interest in sports. So she called the number and signed him up to play whatever games were available—then shoved me out the door with orders not to come home until I had gleaned the details.

"It's a meeting about soccer," she said. "That's all I know."

"Soccer?" I asked. "Why not baseball? Or football?"

"Because it's soccer season," she said.

"Well, when's football season?" I asked.

"Six-year-olds don't play football."

"Why not?"

"Because they play soccer," she said. "Now go to the meeting!"

As always, I was paralyzed in the coils of her logic and no less troubled as I stepped into the club's official sanctum—a suite of two grimy, overused offices piled to the ceiling with boxes and duffel bags and racks full of sorely abused sporting goods. The place smelled of old socks, mildew, and dried grass, the locker-room funk of phys-ed classes and boot camp barracks. I resisted the urge to flee screaming down the stairs. Parents' Night had already convened. It was too late to make a break for it.

I was still a relatively new father at the time, and the memories of my gloriously rotted bachelorhood were raw enough to grate on my nerves on occasions like this. In the preceding five years I had gone from barely reformed juvenile delinquent to responsible citizen thoroughly enmeshed in parental obligations. As if a spring trap were snapping shut, I found myself with a mortgage, a car payment, and a platinum card, married, the father of two little boys, living in a three-bedroom brick Colonial with 2.5 bathrooms, commuting thirty-two miles each way to and from my white-collar job every day. In short, I was a walking decal for upper-middle-class America: college-educated, ten pounds overweight, a cable-TV subscriber, Starbucks coffee snob, and owner of a Homelite SX-135 Bandit weed whacker. God help me, I even drove a Volvo station wagon.

It was a comfortable life, but it had pruned my manly prerogatives to an aching nub. Gone were the pizza-box squalor and six-hour drinking binges of NFL Sunday with my "bros." Gone were the biannual fishing expeditions. Lost were my prized Led Zeppelin albums—disappeared in transit between Philadelphia, New Orleans, Miami, Manhattan, and here—and my wife's taste in music ran more to moody female folksingers. Pile on the lawn care, dirty diapers, and PTA meetings, and I had become as nervous as a gelded sled dog, craving once more to run with the pack but unable to get myself off the couch.

It was in this ambivalent state that I arrived at the Boys and Girls Club to find six women sitting around a battered conference table with anxious looks on their faces, listening to a spirited soliloquy from a middle-aged guy in faded khaki hiking shorts and contractor's boots. He was built like a mailbox and had metallic green-blue eyes, charcoal-black hair, and the metabolic rate of a lab rat in an antihistamine experiment. He stood up as I walked in, shook my hand with the grip of someone in the construction business, and introduced himself as the club's soccer commissioner. He said his name was "Olfky, call me Dave," then sat back down and resumed his sermon on the virtues of the game.

Soccer is safer than football, he explained to the anxious mothers. It's the easiest game for little kids to learn and the most beautiful game to watch at the professional level. It's economical because all you really need are shin guards and a sixteen-dollar pair of cleats. It's the only sport that's played everywhere in the world; kids in Africa do it barefoot, he said, with a ball of newspaper wrapped in masking tape. It's the most democratic sport on earth. Soccer kids aren't segregated by gender the way they are in baseball or football. Everybody can play soccer, almost anywhere, he said. You don't need a big, fancy field or an indoor court or six referees or perfect weather. You can play soccer year-round! Soccer is fun! The essence of being! Soccer had changed his life, he said, given him focus, added meaning to his relationship with his children. Finally, soccer is a unifying force for neighborhoods, schools, and communities—if not the entire universe from here to the Crab Nebula.

"Never mind what you hear on ESPN," he told us. "It's already the biggest thing to hit this country since . . . I don't know what. Maybe microwave popcorn. The point is, soccer is everywhere. You don't know it yet, but you will soon."

The man was clearly a zealot. To hear him tell it, soccer might well hold the cure for gout, planter's wart, impotence, illiteracy, racial intolerance, and global warming. At the very least, there was no question that it prevented youth crime, drug addiction, and teen pregnancy.

"But my son is only five!" one mother blurted. "I'm not sure he's up for all this."

"Mine too," another mom chirped in. "I mean, how safe can it be if they have to wear armor on their legs? And cleats?"

The commissioner addressed these and other concerns with the patience of a rabbi and assurances that the club's coaches would watch over their lambs like biblical shepherds. "Speaking of which," he said, "the club is always looking for parents who might be willing to help out on the field—you know, maybe even volunteer to be coaches, like, sometime in the future? Especially dads? Since some of our kids don't have dads. But we have moms who are coaches, too. So really it's anybody who might be looking for an opportunity to make a difference. But we could use some dads right now."

At the other end of the table, I was filling out the registration forms and waiting for my chance to bolt when I looked up to find Call Me Dave and all six mothers staring straight at me. "I, uh, oh, no," I said. "I don't know the first thing about coaching. I came here to sign up my kid, and that's all. I mean, I have this really weird job, strange hours, couldn't possibly. Uh-uh. I mean, it's just not, no. Not me, guys. No way. I suck at sports—maybe not at basketball or football, but definitely everything else. Got hit in the face with a hardball when I was eight, you know, and it changed me. I, um, I'm just not, can't, won't."

"How'd it go?" my wife asked when I got home that night.

"You won't believe it," I groaned.

In less than an hour I had been shanghaied into the service of the Boys and Girls Club and sent down the road with my car trunk full of two-tone balls, four orange flags, and a cracked plastic first-aid kit missing half its contents. In my shirt pocket I carried a folded sheet of paper bearing the names and home phone numbers of twelve little kids and their parents. It took at least five calls to get over the shock of people calling me Coach. For of all the titles I never expected to hold in this lifetime, it was way up on the list—not too far behind Your Excellency and Mr. President.

Then it happened. Not slowly or easily, gracefully or gently, but, rather, with the vertiginous swoon that attends the dizzy nosedive of love at first sight. After just a couple of nights on the practice field with my squad of little hellions, I was hopelessly sucked in. Soccer claimed my heart and my soul. It was to become, as the prophet Dave foretold, the organizing principle of my life, the essence of my being. It was a parallel universe of bizarre rituals, weekly tribal gatherings, and hyperventilating men with whistles who jabbered in a coded language that would take me three years to fully decipher—precisely the sort of baffling Masonic enterprise that guys are drawn to after age forty. On that score, soccer had it all: strange uniforms encrusted with runic badges, special shoes, the fraternal field yodels of a secret

Moose brotherhood, and, most important, sacks full of specialized equipment—different-sized balls, flags, charts full of columns, sideline markers, little tools for picking mud out of your cleats. Men crave this sort of thing—gear and lots of it, especially obscure and highly specific gear. Friends of mine took up fly-fishing, golf, or foreign-car mechanics. I became a soccer coach.

As I stepped out onto the rutted half acre of a municipal park to conduct my first practice on an overcast evening in September 2000, however, there were few charts for the terrain. My manic band of striplings tore hither and thither with feral zeal, colliding, tripping, falling, and running into the goalposts. We sustained our first bloody nose by the end of that week. A black eye quickly followed, along with contusions and abrasions too numerous to count. At any given moment, half the team members were certain to have their shoes untied, ensuring that even on our best days we would have trouble staying on our feet and out of our own way. Dubbing ourselves the Hornets, we amassed a dismal record in our first year: zero wins and thirteen losses, all of them hideous beatings, including a season-closing 15–0 blowout in which one of our own players scored four goals against us for the other team and won himself the nickname Wrong Way Carlos.

Attention-deficit/hyperactivity disorder, once known as rowdiness, was endemic on the team. Promising youngsters would suddenly abandon the ball in the middle of an offensive sweep and wander off toward the woods singing the theme song to *SpongeBob SquarePants* ("He lives in a pineapple under the sea"). Others would lie down on the field, roll over onto their back, and stare straight into the sun until they were temporarily blind. Picking grass bouquets was a hugely popular activity up and down the roster. And at some point during the season everyone came down with butterfly disease—a mysterious affliction in which kids with no prior history of psychosis suddenly begin hallucinating and spin off across the lawn grasping after invisible floating thingies. One little boy named Charlie added a variation to the syndrome by occasionally shoving his hands into his shorts and briskly tossing his privates to assure himself that they were where he had left them.

At first no one seemed to care that we were getting clobbered every Saturday morning, and that was good, because I didn't have the slightest idea what to do about it. But as the year wore on some of the kids began to take it harder. Tears would flow on the sidelines, and certain parents started giving me the dead-fish look—the cold marble eyeball of dashed expectations, the outward symptom of their dawning recognition that I was almost entirely clueless. Clearly, I was losing my grip on the reins of coachly authority.

This, then, was how I came to begin researching the tactics, philosophy, and history of this strange game. Books began to pile up on my bedside nightstand. Long into the evening I sat in my darkened living room after my wife and kids went to bed, watching how-to videotapes by famous British, Dutch, and Italian masters. Soccer sites proliferated on the Favorites list of my Web browser. I bought soccer T-shirts, hats, warm-up pants, and a fifty-five-dollar pair of Adidas Liberos, the standard costume of the amateur coach. I took daylong training seminars and I started watching games with my boys on the Telemundo network, even though I don't speak Spanish. I sat in corner bars with other coaches until midnight, discussing club politics, the fine points of the penalty kick, and the role of Jesuit missionaries in bringing the game to the Midwest a century ago—to St. Louis, of all places. Fitfully, I progressed from reluctant soccer dad to bumbling soccer coach, then to apostle of what one writer has described as America's new "secular religion," a phenomenon that is changing the nation in ways that social scientists are only beginning to comprehend. For this simple game, with its simple rules, is now a full-fledged revolution.

I didn't know it at the time, but on that hot August night I stumbled through the looking glass, into the future, and away from everything I ever thought I knew about life. After that, things got really weird.

1.

SHELBY AND GOLIATH

THE MOMENT OF TENSION

As the wolf pack closes in, the Mosquito lies in wait.

Shifting ever so slightly on the balls of her feet, she bides her time, measuring the ground between them—her ground. Closer, closer. The wolves are cocky. She has seen their kind many times before, all boiling with testosterone and bravado, jacked up on Frosted Flakes and Cocoa Puffs and Gatorade until their eyeballs jiggle in their sockets. God, what pathetic creatures. The thing she despises most about them, besides their utter lack of elegance and their cheesy boy smell, is their insolence.

"Look, a girl!" they jeered before the game. "They got a girl! We're gonna kill 'em! Yeah!"

As her coach, this was music to my ears, for nothing motivated her more than the loudmouthed derision of her opponents. And nothing was more damaging to the other team's morale than the moment when she reared up and kicked their sorry butts.

Four of them are now charging downfield, forming up around

a lead striker on the fly. He's a belligerent Sluggo, bossing and pointing and directing traffic as he pounds the ball forward over the smashed brown grass of Magruder Field and the bald patches of dirt where 10 million kickoffs and Saturday-morning scrums have killed every living thing within a nine-foot circle. Not even ants can survive out here.

Sluggo has a wild brown nest of hair on his bowling-ball head, a round face like a frying pan, and the black eyes of a cave boy. Big and fast as a wagon full of rocks rolling downhill, he's used to getting his way, intimidating everyone around him—and he's eyeing the Mosquito with a murderous gleam. Before him stands a pixie of a girl. Her teammates call her the Mosquito because she is the smallest member of the squad—and because she harasses opponents to their last nerve. She's eight years old. Thirty-six pounds soaking wet, with a ponytail dyed blue some days to match her uniform. Her name is Shelby Hammond. And she lives to play soccer. She is the star defenseman and the only girl left on the eight-and-under College Park Hornets in the soccer-crazed suburbs of Washington, D.C.

Her hero is Mia Hamm, three-time Olympic gold-medal winner, two-time Women's World Cup champion, all-star forward of the Washington Freedom, and the most recognized name among female athletes worldwide. Shelby dreams of being Mia. She has a Mia poster on her bedroom wall, wears Mia clothes (pale blue nylon warm-ups, Carolina blue Nikes on her feet, jet-black scrunchy around her ponytail), and even though she's only in the second grade she has already decided that she will eventually play for the University of Maryland women's soccer team, a fixture in this town where the university is the leading industry and the primary source of civic identity. And after that, Shelby says, she will make soccer her life's work.

The Hornets had been together for two years at this point—

roughly seventy-five practices and thirty-five peewee-league games, enough to learn the basics of the sport, enough for a few of them to demonstrate something that might be called "consistency." But none were yet as consistent as Shelby.

She is crouching low now, rocking from side to side. Her steel-blue eyes are unreadable—a strange, unnerving void. Sluggo hesitates in mid-rush, momentarily perplexed. He is closing fast, driving the ball in a bum's rush for the goal, but the Mosquito shows none of the customary signs of panic or submission. In fact, she appears to be grinning at him.

Closer . . . closer . . . closer . . . The relievers erupt on the sideline—"Shelby! Shelby! Shelby!"—as the rest of the Hornets on the field begin to wheel into position. It is the only thing I have managed to teach them in two years of coaching: the importance of orbiting in one particular spot on the field instead of chasing after the ball in a mob and kicking one another until they're black-and-blue.

Thomas Waring, the team's hard-hitting midfielder and the kid who usually runs to the rescue on defense, is shot. Twice the size of the Mosquito, he's caked with dirt, red-faced, and soaked from battling for the ball against his oversized rivals—thirty-seven minutes of Irish-style, lunch-bucket soccer that has earned him the nickname the Hammer. The sandy-haired bodyguard stands on buckled legs, hands on hips, panting, thirty yards away from the action.

Not so the Killer Bees—Ben Haner and Bryan Basdeo—two-thirds of the Hornets' triple-threat offense, who are rolling back across midfield, trailed by Kevin Guerrero, the team's leading scorer. Kevin—the Salvadoran Terror—is the son of a player, and his grandfather was a player, as was his great-grandfather before that. In Kevin's world, kids take their first steps on soccer fields and they get their first pair of shin guards when they're three. The game is the center of community life for Washington's Latino émigrés. There are matches every weekend and double-headers during holidays, and the women bring food, so there's no reason to go home before nightfall.

Ben, Bryan, and Kevin know it's now or never. The score is 3–2. Underdog College Park is down by one goal to the team from Beltsville, favorites to win the division and advance, as always, to the county league championship. One more score and the Hornets become just another speed bump in powerhouse B-ville's blitz to familiar glory.

"Shelby! Shelby! Shelby!" the relievers chant.

"Three minutes, Shelby!" I bellow across the ocher plain, my voice swallowed up by the gusting wind and the war whoops on the sideline. "Three minutes—and it's game over!"

"Don't worry none, Shelby's gonna take him," the Mosquito's father says in his lazy West Virginia drawl. "Shelby's gonna chew him up, y'all will see." Terry Hammond is a walking refrigerator, a cabinet installer by trade and a former high school jock who signed on as my assistant coach on a lark and quickly became absorbed in every aspect of this game that neither of us had ever played.

The big man watches expressionless as Beltsville's horde closes in on his only child, the little girl who changed him from a pool shark and a rabid football fan into a doting butler, chauffeur, and equipment manager to a junior soccer prodigy.

The attackers are twenty feet out, tearing toward the right side of the goal, when they begin their familiar death spiral. Their coach, a towering guy in his mid-fifties with a receded hairline and a sprig of mustache under his nose, has been teaching this maneuver to kids for more than a decade. His name is Dave Pinchotti. He is one of the most well regarded coaches in the county, a gracious sort, who never fails to congratulate opposing coaches after crushing their hopes.

With Pinchotti's alpha striker bearing down on the net, the rest of the wolf pack veers to the left and fans out in front of the goal. When Sluggo shoots, they will swarm the Mosquito, confusing her goalie, coming at the ball from all sides. That's their plan. But then Shelby makes her move. Facing her opponent like a basketball guard, she shuffles three steps to her right, taking away the inches that Sluggo needs to shoot to the deep-right corner of her net—the shot he wants. In closing his angle, she forces him toward the center, where her goalkeeper can better make a play if she falls down or falters. What's more, her move forces the rest of the pack to move left to open up space for their leader until they drift, one by one, out of the play.

To make sure they stay that way, the Hornets' number-two defenseman, an insubordinate little genius named Linus Hamilton, dashes in between them and the outside goalpost for the checkmate. No kid on the team has a better sense of the geometry of the game than Linus, and no kid is quite so adept at critiquing the coaches' performance.

"You might want to try this," he'd say, or, "Their forward looks small, but it's a mistake to underestimate him."

"Thank you, Professor," we'd tell him. "Now please sit down."

"Linus's problem is that he's smarter than us," I told Terry Hammond one day at practice.

In fact, they were all smarter than we were—more adaptable, more flexible thinkers for not having a lifetime of preconceived notions about sports and how they should be played. In my journey from bumbling Parents' Night draftee to ranting soccer freak and, finally, fairly able coach, I would learn most of what I needed to know from children.

It's one-on-one now, the Mosquito vs. Sluggo, and Sluggo is confused. His overwhelming advantage has dissolved, and this damnable girl has shown no sign of folding. There is no fear in her eyes, which are blazing, locked onto the ball and the movement of his hooves.

"There is no animal more invincible than a woman, nor fire either, nor any wildcat so ruthless," wrote the ancient Greek comedian Aristophanes. Sluggo is about to learn the truth of this.

In the aluminum bleachers on the other side of the field, the Hornets' parents rise to their feet, mouths open. It is "the moment of tension," as the Dutch soccer photographer Hans van der Meer once described it—that thin slice of a forty-, sixty-, or ninety-minute game when ten thousand variables converge to produce a flash point in which anything can happen. Whether professional or amateur, soccer is made up of such sudden happenings. Unlike American football, the clock never stops. There are no huddles or time-outs. Unlike baseball, there is no ritual adjusting of codpieces, no practice swings or conferences on the mound, no standing around in the outfield waiting for the next hit while the pitcher reads twenty-seven hand signs from a guy squatting behind home plate.

Soccer is distinct among all sports as a study in constant motion. Every second is precious. Every pass, shot, block, or steal has the potential to alter the outcome for good. Promising paths taken up or down the field expire in dead ends or defensive traps. Over and over. The power of a single star to drastically affect the ebb and flow of the action—the trump card in basketball, hockey, or football; the reason that Jordan, Gretzky, and Payton are modern folk heroes—is most often nullified by the capriciousness of the ball, the immense field, the sheer distances that must be traveled, and the limitations of human endurance and foresight. Above all, soccer is an ongoing exercise in discombobulation and perseverance. Teamwork. Trust. For more than two hundred years, these have been the only reliable routes to success in this game. And the Hornets trust Shelby.

Ben, Bryan, and Kevin are in position at midfield—ready to take the pass they're sure will come. None of them rush to help her.

"Shelby! Shelby! Shelby!"

The range is down to less than three feet when the Mosquito finally strikes. Back to the net, shoulders squared, she halts her ten-yard retreat and launches a sudden feint, a small lashing kick, then backpedals again to see what happens. Sluggo obliges her by overreacting. Already rattled by her unnatural composure, he pips the ball even farther to his left, his "weak side," attempting to evade a challenge that hasn't yet materialized. Now he's lost control of the ball, and he's off-kilter. He's also inside the painted white box in front of our net, not ten feet from our goal. If Shelby fouls Sluggo now, the referee will give him a penalty kick, a free point-blank shot at the net.

Watching the moment unfold, I realize that I'm light-headed, sucking wind as if I were the one doing the running. On my next breath Shelby counterattacks in earnest. She brushes the ball with the tip of her toe, drops her shoulder, and plants it in Sluggo's chest, then swipes him with her arm as she ricochets toward the meandering sphere. It's a circus move, straight out of pro wrestling or hockey, and the physics of it send the brute twirling. The sneer drops from his face as the Mosquito squirts away with the ball and 110 pounds of goalie named Edward Curry barrels into him. Edward is exceedingly large for an eight-year-old. His teammates call him the Rhino.

The karmic splendor of the comeuppance is lost on the Beltsville loyalists in the bleachers.

"Foul! Foul! Hey, Ref, where's the foul?"

They're up now, stamping their feet, and several are rushing to the touchline at the edge of the field. They're red-faced, throwing their ball caps, casting imploring looks across the turf at

Coach Dave. But Pinchotti is as unperturbed as ever, his gaze fixed downfield on the unfolding action. Oblivious to the outrage of his followers, he checks his watch: under two minutes . . . and counting.

It is at times like this that the cultural divisions in youth soccer are most keenly seen. For the howlers among the parents are, by a wide margin, American-born white suburbanites steeped in the familiar rules that govern basketball and football—where almost every form of touching can, in the name of fairness, be nitpicked into various forms of foul. Noticeable on such occasions is the relative calm of the Latino, African, Asian, and Indian parents. The Guatemalans and Hondurans. The Nigerians and Moroccans. The Vietnamese and Chinese and Filipinos. The Hindus, Sikhs, and Muslims. These ethnic groups have settled in the D.C. area in vast numbers in the past two decades, and they now make up about 20 percent of the population, transforming the Potomac Basin into a soup pot of ethnic assimilation third in size only to New York and Florida on the Eastern Seaboard.

These newcomers have been playing soccer all their lives, and they are accustomed to the seemingly whimsical officiating of their native game. Absent a clear showing of malice, most physical contact on the field is considered incidental to the kinetic forces that make soccer the "beautiful game": speed, agility, dexterity, flexibility, aggressiveness, power on the ball. To stop the action at every bump or jostle would carve out the very heart of the thing. Add the fact that the referees are sprinting much of the time and it's unreasonable to expect them to get a clear enough look at a crime in progress to make an arrest in the vast majority of cases. Nor would most fans want them to. For in this game, as in life, bumps and scrapes and setbacks are expected as cosmic forces unfurl, and the ethnic soccer fans seem to have faith that the leveling hand of God will set things mostly right in the end.

Not so their native-born neighbors.

Almost nothing about soccer conforms to American conceptions about sports—or life in general. For one thing, you can't use your hands, which makes everything else more difficult. For another, the familiar orderly echelons and grids and diamonds are nowhere to be seen on the field, because there's only so much you can do with your feet to make a speeding ball behave rationally. Efficiency and expediency, which may as well be lyrics in the national anthem, are stymied at every turn. By necessity, legality becomes a much more fluid concept, based on snap interpretations of seventeen bright line Laws—which date to the nineteenth century—by referees who are beyond the checks and balances of instant replay or umpire conferences. For Americans, with their vestigial Puritan morality and their ornate codes of conduct and their constitutional entitlement to be secure in their personal space, watching their kids play this immoral game can provoke a spontaneous infarction.

On the sidelines, they can be heard bleating at the absurdity of it all, especially the fathers. Men who have thrown, caught, hit, held, and shot every manner of ball will clench their fists and pound their thighs at the sight of their children spastically struggling to achieve with their feet and heads what they could do in half the time with their hands. "FOUL! God DAMN it, Ref! FOUL!"

Here is the sound of the old order dying, the anguished rattle of well-settled expectations shattering. It is the sound of the comfortable majority losing their grip on familiar and predictable entitlements. For them, this new game is like a plague, skimming off the cream of the nation's high school athletes and consuming vast tracts of land for soccerplexes; they see it vying for the affection of their children, 14 million of whom now play soccer in organized leagues. Yes, soccer is here to stay, and the weekend soccer dad knows it, and it's driving him out of his mind, because his kids love it and he doesn't know the first thing about it. Watching these parents squirm, I empathize. I was once among them, as mystified by the seeming lawlessness and hypnotic effects of soccer as I ever was by the byzantine mysteries of curling, cricket, or hockey. Football was my sport, the only thing I ever really cared about. I grew up playing smashmouth pickup games with my brothers on frozen back lots and tar-hot beaches in southern New Jersey until our lips and knuckles bled—back in the days when only the weak went home early. But I was won over by this new sport, which requires far more skill, and in which the violence is more discreet and less likely to be crippling, rules are less a constant factor, and arbitration has no place at all. Only later would I learn that it is not a foreign game after all, that it belongs to us by birthright, that we owned it a long time ago, before we started forgetting everything we ever knew about our own history.

"FOUL! Hey, Ref! FOUL!"

It is too late. The moment has passed. Sluggo is eating dirt somewhere beneath the toppled Rhino, and the Mosquito is on the move, trailed by the tattered remnants of Beltsville's barbarian legion. Whatever slim hope their supporters had of inducing the referee to grant the team a penalty kick is gone in less than two seconds. In two "touches"—two quick kicks of the ball— Shelby is beyond their immediate reach, bobbing and weaving toward the sideline. She gives a glance and finds her strikers exactly where she expects them to be, strung out in a line at midfield, spaced a nearly perfect twelve feet apart, poised like relay sprinters awaiting a baton.

She does not have much time for decision. The drum of footsteps behind her grows louder as the shell-shocked opposition get themselves organized in pursuit. In a matter of seconds, one of them will pull even to shoulder her off the ball while the other two tear ahead to block her passing lanes. These boys are bigger, faster, stronger, and she's tiring. The element of surprise is now lost. The time is now. The Mosquito wallops the ball upfield— WHUMP!—then slows and finally stops. Bending at the waist, hands on knees, she gulps air. Not even Mia could have done better, and Shelby knows it.

What happens next is almost hard to believe, and Coach Pinchotti is the only one who sees it coming. His team is now hopelessly out of position. His midfielder, Sluggo, is struggling to untangle himself from the Rhino's embrace. His three strikers are exhausted from the long charge downfield and the unexpected chase back the way they came. The ball is gone, moving away from them faster than they can possibly run. And it's heading straight for the Hornets' most proficient dribbler—the kid with the blond bowl haircut and the flying feet. The coach's kid. The lefty.

"Watch out for him," Pinchotti yells to his two defenders as they charge past. "That kid is dangerous."

If they hear him at all, they don't heed the warning. My boy is a blur now. He has always had a comically short stride on the run, and he moves so fast that it gives him an almost reckless appearance that worries opponents. He sweeps in behind Shelby's pass and pushes the ball out in front of him, away from the center of the field, in a wide arc that takes it very close to the right touchline. It's a practiced maneuver, designed to draw the defenders to him while cutting off their ability to move on the ball—because most young soccer players have no idea that it's perfectly legal to step out-of-bounds to make a play, as long as the ball stays on the field. Hemmed in against the line, they rush straight at him, shoulder to shoulder. They're falling for one of his best tricks.

It helps that Ben has been playing this game since he was old enough to walk. Before he could even speak in complete sentences, my son was being schooled in the basic mechanics of soccer by a West African nanny who would roll balls at him on the lawn and urge him in French to blast them to *la lune*—the moon, outer space, his destiny. Her name was Maggie Dahl. She was a political refugee from Togo who had fled under a death warrant for participating in a rural voter registration drive. An accountant by training, her English was not nearly serviceable enough to allow her to pursue her trade in the United States, so, like so many other immigrant women in the D.C. area—where industrial jobs are all but nonexistent—she sought work in childcare. When she moved in with us, in 1995, a great blessing was visited upon the future Hornet with the bowl haircut.

In her heavily accented English, Maggie pronounced her national game "sockair," and on warm summer nights, as Ben whacked a ball around in the yard, she patiently explained to me that it was not merely a game but, rather, "the Game"—so deeply ingrained in the fabric of everyday life in her country that it was in many ways the primary instrument of socialization for young children. How the game is played in one corner of the globe or another is seen as a manifestation of national character and identity everywhere else. And in learning how to play children internalize the traits that are valued in their society. Maggie insisted that these things were generally understood everywhere but here. Soccer was a way of life, she assured me, the one perfect metaphor for everything.

"In Brazil, oh!" she said. "It is *très* beautiful! They play such soccer there, it is like dancing."

As serious students of the game will tell you, it's all that and then some. The Brazilians play as they live, with a wide-open, unstructured style that gives free rein to individual flourish and feats of athletic heroism. They call it samba, after their national dance. It's high-risk, fraught with injuries, wild swings in momentum, and soaring scores in which a sociologist or economics professor might find many useful insights into the Brazilian way of doing things generally. The Dutch, in stark contrast, play a highly organized variety of soccer that features precision dribbling and close-quarters passing. The aim is not necessarily to score but to maintain possession of the ball until an opponent fades from exhaustion late in the game. It is soccer by geometric attrition, and it suits a lowland country where civil engineering is a religion and meticulous attention to detail is all that holds back the raging sea.

Among other notable styles of play, the Italians are stubbornly defensive on the field and famously voluble in the clutch. It is soccer as opera, second only to the Brazilian form for sheer dramatics. British teams, on the other hand, are highly regimented and play a breakneck offensive game that is more than a little violent. The Irish are just plain mean, masters of the "hard tackle" and the discreet elbow to the nose. And so on. And so forth. And all of these things are fairly well understood all over the world—except in the United States.

Thanks to his French-speaking, Togolese nanny, our Irish-Polish-German boy plays like a Brazilian, a seemingly improbable lineage that is increasingly common for young American soccer players, many of whom now have Latino coaches or team trainers. Or women coaches. Or multilingual coaches of uncertain ethnic origin. During the summers, they attend high-priced soccer camps that have become totems of middle-class arrival for an increasingly diverse white-collar workforce. They are the children of tech immigrants, African-American strivers, and newly minted professionals with no-collar roots—parents, like me, who made good on common stock upbringings and found ourselves pulled in by the almost irresistible gravity that soccer exerts in suburbia. Because of this game our kids know things about the world that we never imagined at such an early age; and thanks to the tutoring of foreign-born teachers, some of them have that rarest of skills: ambidextrous feet.

The Beltsville defenders rush in, and Ben suddenly comes to a dead stop in front of them, pooching the ball back toward the center of the field with the outside of his left foot. Both defenders fly past him, through the vacant space where the ball was supposed to be, in a classic case of overplaying and underestimating their opponent. Just as their error is dawning on them, Ben jukes left, pokes the ball with his right toe, and jets back toward his buddies at midfield with the prize.

The play is unfolding in picture-perfect form. Six of the seven Beltsville kids on the field are now out of position, trailing far behind. The Hornets are all holding their spots. Two minutes to go, with the score 3–2 in his favor, Pinchotti stands with his arms folded across his chest, beaming. Could it be that the runts from College Park might tie the score against his awesome juggernaut?

Ben nudges the ball once more, pushing it back on course, straightening it into a beeline toward the goal, then looks ahead to find his man. Sure as cornflakes in the morning, Kevin Guerrero is way out in front of him, smack in the middle of the wide-open field, looking over his shoulder on the fly, waving his right arm for the pass, yelling to his teammate, *"La pelota! La pelota!"* The ball. The ball. Give me the ball.

Streaming down the opposite touchline, Bryan Basdeo paces himself to be the second man at the net, the striker who cleans up any errant shots or fumbled saves by the goalkeeper. He is so good at these mop-up shots that he's the Hornets' second leading scorer, the one they call Bigfoot. More often than not, however, "The Ben and Kevin Show" leaves nothing to clean up. On his third touch, Ben's right foot explodes on the ball with enough torque to spin him bodily into the grass. The ball sails up straight and true. At its apex it seems to hang in midair for a small eternity before landing six inches in front of the charging striker. All the math is now in favor of the Salvadoran Terror. Momentum. Distance. Timing. Velocity. Kevin flicks out his right foot at a full run, cushions the ball's landing with his instep, pushes it out in front of him—and fires.

It's a head-high shot from close range, straight at Beltsville's goalie. Heeding a primal survival instinct, the kid squats to save his nose, shuts his eyes, throws up his gloved hands, and hopes for the best. The ball has other plans. It rockets over his outstretched fingertips and splashes into center net, untouched.

"GOAL! GOAL! GOAL!"

The Hornets go berserk on the sideline—Michael, Braulio, Robbie, all the relievers and coaches, leaping and tripping over one another. Shelby's father, Terry, grabs me in a bear hug and squeezes the air from my lungs, then drops me back into my shoes, wheezing. Ben, Shelby, and Thomas slap five at midfield. Kevin sheers away from the net and cuts a U-turn, flying back up the sideline, grinning his famous foot-wide grin, and pumping his skinny arms. His parents and grandparents, aunts, uncles, and cousins leap up from the island of blankets they have spread on the grass. His grandfather and family patriarch, Rafael Guerrero—soon to be my *padrino*, the man who will finally teach me this game—raises his arms in the air, yelling, "GOAL! GOAL! GOAL!"

"Kevin!" the old man yells to his grandson. The boy flies to him and leaps into his arms before charging back to his teammates forming up for the kickoff.

"Okay, guys, we got a little less than a minute to go, and it's their ball," I shout to the kids on the field. "They're going to come at us with everything they've got. So be ready."

If I had learned anything about coaching the game after dozens of crushing defeats and near-victories turned to ties by last-minute goals in an opponent's favor, it was this: the ecstatic moments after you score are when the other team is most dangerous. Your guard is down, and their fangs are bared. But Beltsville doesn't have much fang left. Sluggo and his Mongols mount a halfhearted attack that peters out in a defensive trap. The clock expires. The referee blows his whistle. Final score: 3–3.

In the traditional end-of-game ceremony, the two teams line up in columns, then run past one another, touching hands as they go, reciting "Good game, good game, good game" to each of their rivals. The Beltsville team is entirely male, mostly white and African American. The College Park kids are an amalgam of blacks and browns and whites—the offspring of laborers and lawyers, underwriters and mechanics, civil servants and journalists. When they reach the end of the line, the Hornets mob their three stars, cheering and slapping their heads. Shelby turns red. Ben flashes a row of teeth. Kevin pours water down his shirt.

Then Pinchotti—Coach Dave, the boss of Mighty Beltsville— walks over to congratulate them. "I've been watching soccer for a long time, and that was one of the most beautiful plays I've ever seen," he tells us. "You guys have done a hell of a job with these kids. If they're only eight now, imagine what they'll look like in another year." Pinchotti comments on the courage of the Mosquito, the skill of the left-footed boy with the bowl haircut, the intensity of the Salvadoran fireball. He credits Thomas Waring for holding down the middle of the field against his bruisers. "You all looked great," he tells the awestruck group, then walks away.

In the lore of the Hornets, this would be remembered as a defining moment—the Play and the Day. It would be discussed for months, even years, to come. They had gutted it out and stuck together to match the best team in the league. At eight years old they had built themselves a small monument. Whether they could preserve it was another question.

I didn't know it yet, but my education was just beginning. My already laughable absorption would only intensify. And the husk of my former self—the workaholic careerist who had forgone personal happiness for too long—would crack and fall away. It would take us two more years to get there, two strange and sometimes frightening years, but the Hornets' quest for a perfect season had begun.

2.

THE RISE OF THE TWO-TONE BALL

HOW A GAME ATE SUBURBIA

Eventually, as Dave Olfky had prophesied on Parents' Night, every new student of the game of soccer will come to ask himself how the game got so big, so fast. Soccer is now one of the defining experiences of childhood in suburbia—like Boy Scouts or Little League two generations ago, only much bigger—but it barely existed in most places as recently as twenty years ago. How did this sport overcome a half century of stubborn indifference in America, seemingly overnight, to take over our lives and put thousands of miles on our minivans and station wagons?

The question comes up a lot during the hours of idle sideline chatter at practices and team barbecues and club banquets, especially among the new parents. The recently arrived who drift into soccer thinking it's just a cute weekend diversion for their kids can quickly find themselves entangled in a subculture whose tendrils spread like kudzu vine. What begins as innocent recreation ends in the dendrite embrace of an all-enveloping fixation, until you look up one day to find muddy cleats heaped in your front foyer, ball dents in your car doors, and the telltale traces of jersey-matching Diablo-red hair dye in the bathroom sink upstairs. Only then do most soccer parents realize that they haven't been on vacation in years and that they've blistered their credit cards on mail-order purchases from outlet warehouses in Hillsborough, North Carolina, and Herzogenaurach, Bavaria, among other centers of soccer chic.

For me the moment of recognition dawned in 2001, as the Hornets' third season was winding down. I surveyed the wrecked interior of my car—the seventeen empty Gatorade bottles, the exploded first-aid kit, the collection of mismatched shin guards and desiccated postgame orange peels—counted the bags under my eyes, and realized that my life was out of control. Right about then a friend recommended that I read a little book called *The Tipping Point* by Malcolm Gladwell, a funny and often surprising look at the phenomenon of "social contagion"—how minor fads, fashion trends, and oddball movements manage to spike the fevers of popular interest and become full-blown cultural sensations.

Soccer, I thought, surely was one such virus, and I didn't need to look much farther than the nearest mirror to see the symptoms. But there were other signs that winter, too. For one thing, the College Park Boys and Girls Club's master roster had mushroomed to more than 230 kids, which was some kind of major record for soccer sign-ups in town. It was also way more than the available coaches could possibly manage, but we took them anyway, which is how I became the after-school warden to eighteen cavorting banshees.

When I asked around about the sudden enrollment bulge to find out how such a thing could happen, I quickly discovered that soccer had gone thermal everywhere else as well. From virtual nonexistence ten years earlier, it had become the most popular sport offered by the club and the number-one source of enrollment dues for chapters all over Prince George's County, Maryland. The inaugural Spring Sting Soccer Tournament the previous May was one of the most lucrative fund-raisers in the club's forty-year history. Most remarkably, soccer teams were finally allowed to play night games under the lights on the town's manicured Duvall Field. Named for a long-dead mayor, the field had been the resting place of College Park's civic soul since forever—the closest thing to a focal point in this bedroom community north of the nation's capital. Laid down at the intersection of six highways, two river tributaries, two commuter rail lines, and the ever-lengthening spokes of a thirteen-hundred-acre university complex, the town was less a town than a jigsaw collection of neighborhoods shoehorned in between. In other words, it was typical "first-ring" suburbia.

For those who grew up here, Duvall Field was their allotted acre of grass and the object of ongoing jealousies among boosters of one sport or another. As in most small towns, feuds over whose turn it was to use the field were legend, and football usually won. Ever the latecomer, soccer was "the ugly stepchild that everyone wanted to smother in its crib," as one longtime member of the club's board of directors described it. But by 2001 the football program had gone under and the orphan sport had grown into the biggest game in town.

Known for its towering oaks rooted in alluvial clay, the surrounding county was equally bound to its southern, working-class sports traditions—held fast by informal booster councils that guarded their facilities and their share of the county budget. Here, as most everywhere else, football was the eight-hundred-pound gorilla of the parks and recreation system, eating up more field time and generating more equipment, insurance, and maintenance expenses than any other three sports put together. Soccer could barely get a toehold. That is, until the money started rolling in.

The southern "tech boom" and corporate land rush that re-shaped Baltimore, Richmond, Charlotte, Atlanta, and New Orleans during the 1980s and '90s shifted the demographics here as well. Just as millions of white-collar families and billions of bio-medical, dot-com, and financial services dollars were migrating from north to south, the black middle class doubled in size and the Hispanic population burgeoned into view. In the Washington, D.C., region, Latino households surged by 346 percent—nearly a half million people, more Spanish-speaking residents than any city east of Dallas, north of Miami, or south of New York City.

The shift was deeply felt in Prince George's. The county had successfully thwarted school desegregation for twenty years after the U.S. Supreme Court's landmark *Brown v. Board of Education* decision. In 1974 it made headlines as one of the largest jurisdictions ever to fall under a court-ordered busing plan, and it continued to make headlines for police abuses long afterward. But busing and police reforms did little to disrupt a de facto system of separate swimming pools, segregated churches, and bisected neighborhoods. In short, it was not a place that embraced change easily.

But, willingly or not, change came to Prince George's, and today half of all households are occupied by comfortably middle-class African-Americans, including a sizable population of immigrants from soccer-loving West African countries like Nigeria. One out of ten residents is Hispanic, and then there are the un-counted Yankee transplants who poured into the county during the nineties to be near their jobs in Washington and Baltimore. During that decade the number of youth soccer teams in the county recreation league almost tripled, from roughly 50 squads in 1997 to about 125 today. Where once there was only one private soccer club, there are now four. Soccer enrollment has surpassed that for baseball and softball and is now closing in on football.

"Once soccer got started here, of course, everything else tipped in a matter of a few years," Renee Milligan, the president of the College Park Boys and Girls Club, told me shortly after my son signed up. "The budget tipped. Enrollment tipped. We started taking in younger and younger kids—boys and girls. The club now takes in more money from soccer than from any other two sports combined."

She said all of this in an effort to convert me to her religion. Milligan was a registered nurse by training, the mother of two teenage daughters who towed her into the sport when they were young. Eventually she was pulled in so deeply that she became a licensed referee and coach. It was Milligan who persuaded me to take my first certification course, the gateway initiation ritual of the soccer cultists. For this is the only sport in America that requires its coaches to secure more and more advanced "licenses" to coach at higher levels of the game. As peewee teams advance upward through soccer's interlocking leagues, the do-gooder moms and dads who in the beginning innocently agree to do little more than stand on fields and blow whistles are coaxed into a training and certification system that ultimately can take them years—and thousands of dollars—to complete. No matter how much a coach thinks he might know about the game, there is always another high priest to remind him that his education has only just begun.

Before long, I was under their spell.

It is beyond argument when the Quiet Revolution first became visible. There would come a day unlike any other that had come before in the history of modern soccer. It was July 10, 1999. The Soccer Nation was on the move, and on that day its members came—90,185 strong—in an armada of Cherokees and Aerostars and Taurus wagons, wending a course through the Los Angeles basin, thence to Pasadena and into the ninety-seven-degree Thunderdome of the Rose Bowl. They came from Pittsburgh and St. Louis, Chapel Hill and Washington, Portland and Dallas and Tulsa, and scores of outlying subdivisions with bucolic-sounding names that aren't yet shown on maps. All to broil in the California sun until the red, white, and blue greasepaint ran down their faces and their fervor simmered over into prime time.

What happened that day is now an indelible slice of popular history, the single most potent symbol of the power, reach, and dedication of a previously invisible American folk species. A soccer team composed of the best women players in the United States—arguably one of the best teams ever assembled in this country's long and tortured involvement with the sport—beat China in one of the premier events on the international soccer calendar, the championship match of the Women's World Cup.

American defender Brandi Chastain celebrated her winning goal by stripping off her team jersey and falling to her knees in nothing but a sports bra moments before she was mobbed by her ecstatic teammates. A time-honored victory flourish among male players, Chastain's impromptu doff brought gales of opprobrium from the uninitiated, including a feminist snit in *The Village Voice* condemning the chiseled fullback for "objectifying women." But soccer fans mostly cheered, giddy that one of their peculiar customs would cause such furor, triumphant that they had finally seized the national spotlight. Reveling in their display of raw numbers, they were downright mystified by the fact that the mainstream American media seemed not to have "gotten it" yet.

"I love this game because it's rough and intense!" an ecstatic fifteen-year-old fan named Alyssa Finkle told the Associated Press that day, her leg in a steel brace from a soccer injury. "My sister also plays, and she has a rod in her leg now instead of a bone."

Such is the warrior ardor of the Soccer Nation—and its expression at Pasadena brought social scientists and market-study researchers running to gauge its depth. What they found was a new American constituency, 78 percent of whom were younger than eighteen, nearly half from households with incomes above $78,000, according to the Soccer Industry Council of America. While other sports declined in popularity among this new generation, soccer has been expanding at an average rate of 8 percent a year for more than a decade. The Sporting Goods Manufacturers Association reports that there are now more kids playing soccer in the United States than any other team sport except basketball.

One year after Pasadena, the National Federation of State High School Associations conducted a nationwide study that measured the precise girth of the colossus and found that among high school students, involvement in the game grew by 65 percent between 1987 and 1999. Today, 6 million teenagers play in organized leagues, and soccer is being added to the athletic programs of more schools than is any other sport.

In 1972, only 800 schools in this country offered soccer; students can now earn a varsity letter in soccer at more than 8,000 U.S. high schools. Compared with just 50,000 kids then, 600,000 teenage jocks now wear their school colors on the soccer field. At the same time, high school football and baseball have stagnated. The number of boys able to get parental permission to play football "froze" at about the one-million mark sometime during the Nixon administration—just as some two thousand schools were dropping the sport from their athletic programs. As suburban parents grew leery of violent contact sports, the unquestioned orthodoxy of football took a big hit amid choruses of "Not my son!" And in the liability-insurance crisis of the 1980s, municipal governments gave birth to a new species of bureaucrat—the risk manager—and football went the way of monkey bars, teetertotters, and asphalt playgrounds in small towns and cities across the country. Participation in high school baseball endured a long slump before leveling off at around 450,000 registered players, but the sport's overall "net gain" since 1970 has been only about 90,000—or less than a third of the growth rate of soccer. Starved at the roots, Major League Baseball began "importing" foreign-born players at such a clip that more than half of minor-league prospects and almost a third of Opening Day starters are now from overseas.

Soccer, it turns out, is a communicable disease, a social contagion of epidemic breadth that has been spreading for three decades. In his 1998 soccerhead confessional, *Fever Pitch*, Nick Hornby writes that loyalty to the game "was not a moral choice like bravery or kindness; it was more like a wart or a hump, something you were stuck with."

In a minor feat of prescience one year before the Great Convergence in Pasadena, *Washington Post* columnist Steve Twomey dubbed soccer "the game that ate suburbia," and griped in November 1998 that its fissiparous growth was threatening the "Rockwellian" charms of Little League baseball. Soccer, he snorted, is an "insidious" sport played by prissy boys in kneesocks that is "smashing evolution's highest achievement, the human brain, into a sphere." For a writer in one of the nation's most fervid soccer strongholds, it was either an act of stupidity or an act of bravery. At any rate, the hate mail rolled in.

"Steve Twomey has once again displayed his ignorance," one soccer dad retorted in a letter to the editor. "Baseball and football cut out 50 percent of our population—our young girls, who do play soccer. Baseball is interminable and has nostalgic appeal to an elder, non-soccer generation. Football is so fraught with random violence that few parents want their kids to play. Hockey teaches that if you can't finesse an opponent, you beat him up.

Basketball is self-destructing, encouraging the flouting of author- ity and opponents."

When passions run this deep over anything in the United States, commercial marketeers usually aren't far behind. But even as soccer spread into the far corners of hometown America dur- ing the nineties, the nation's corporate fathers failed to catch on—until that day in Pasadena when the soccer legions revealed themselves in full regalia and the shirtless Chastain injected the media with an image that could finally be understood by balding white male suburban-dwelling news editors with golf bags in their car trunks and season tickets at the baseball stadium.

"Soccer is front-page news now," Jim Moorhouse of the U.S. Soccer Federation, the Chicago-based governing body of the sport, told me. "Just look at the coverage the game is getting. We're A-one news, with a front-page picture and two more pages in the sports section of *The Washington Post* and the L.A. *Times* and *USA Today*. Soccer is all over cable TV, and the big networks now roll out their satellite trucks for the bigger competitions like the World Cup. In terms of print and broadcast media, there's probably ten times the number of reporters covering the game today as there were just five years ago. It's long overdue, and it happened almost overnight."

Prior to Pasadena, soccer was a sociological redwood toppling onto the American scene and sending tremors around the globe— without making much noise in its own backyard. Aside from the odd newspaper column here or there, the sport barely registered in the media. Lacking for television coverage or the saturation ad- vertising that corporate sponsorships have brought to such sports as golf, tennis, and auto racing, soccer was all but invisible. It is telling that I knew almost nothing about the sport when I first be- came involved in it. I had been a reporter for twenty years, work- ing on the metro desks of major newspapers from Manhattan to Miami, saturated in information, plugged into the humming digital nervous system of the most voracious media complex in the world, at least nominally aware of every major commotion in the country. Or so I thought.

With almost no prior fanfare in the press and little backing from corporate sponsors, the '99 U.S. Women's National Team drew the largest number of spectators ever to attend a women's sporting event, attracted another 2.8 million cable-television viewers for the championship game, and finished their World Cup series with a higher TV audience share than the finals of professional hockey or basketball. Suddenly there was a soccer team on my box of Wheaties.

"It's great!" said fan Frank Quezada, of San Francisco, to the Associated Press at the time, resplendent in a full George Washington wig and costume—and blasting on a plastic horn. "I love seeing people get so excited about something that a lot of people haven't paid attention to before."

"There were no elaborate pre-game shows, no special newspaper sections," sportswriter Christine Brennan wrote in a widely quoted passage in *USA Today*, but "the minivan revolution was going on whether anyone paid attention or not." By "anyone" she meant, of course, the media barons and the boardroom swells.

Stiff-armed by network television and such likely potential sponsors as Coca-Cola and McDonald's, organizers of the Women's World Cup pulled off their marketing coup by appealing directly to the Soccer Nation—a tactic that has since become standard procedure for the sport's promoters. For two years leading up to the games, they pitched tents at suburban tournaments and soccer camps, handing out bumper stickers and T-shirts. They fired off direct-mail brochures to youth coaches in such "soccer capitals" as Washington and St. Louis, and they plied the Internet with family-friendly Web sites offering discount package deals on tickets. Brush up against the soccer world these days and your e-mail address, too, will quickly find its way into someone's database, because guerrilla marketing will continue to be the sport's lifeblood until the current generation of sports editors dies off.

"Huge papers, the *Houston Chronicle*, for instance, didn't send a staff writer" to the Women's World Cup, Brennan said in an online discussion for *Slate* magazine in 2000. "Another major metropolitan daily in the South told its reporter that it would not pay her airfare or expenses. Most sports editors refuse to notice. Don't these guys drive by soccer fields on their way to work?"

Caught flat-footed in Pasadena, meanwhile, manufacturers of food, drink, cars, cameras, and credit cards wised up in a hurry and began pouring millions into the game at every level. Even youth soccer clubs now boast of sponsorship arrangements with such corporate giants as Adidas and Nike. For some, this represents a troubling trend toward commercialization in youth athletics, but soccer organizers point out that they have been driven to it by necessity. Kept in a state of financial malnutrition by entrenched football and baseball boosters (who continue to command the lion's share of public money in local parks and recreation departments), soccer continues to lack for the simplest of things. Basic needs—such as fields and uniforms—have to be leveraged with private money, or the sport most assuredly would have died by now.

Two years after Pasadena, the sociologists Andrei S. Markovits and Steven L. Hellerman published a wickedly wry and exhaustively researched treatise on the growth of professional sports in the United States. In their book, *Offside: Soccer and American Exceptionalism*, they concluded that pro soccer would have a hard time surviving in a country already dominated by four major sports leagues. The two "soccerologists" became the instant darlings of doomsayers in the American sports media, quoted liberally in magazines and newspaper articles prognosticating the game's extinction. Absent from these obituaries, however, was any mention of the book's later chapters, in which the authors hedge their bets by remarking at some length on the "meteoric" growth of the sport at the grassroots level over the past twenty years. Says Jim Moorhouse, of the U.S. Soccer Federation, "The soccer-knockers go on saying it's a fringe sport that's only popular with a certain hard-core cult of fans, and I just have to laugh at this point."

True, he admits, basketball is still king in U.S. cities—where a shortage of wide-open spaces has so far hampered efforts to introduce soccer on a large scale—but he points out that places like Georgia and Texas, once considered invulnerable bulwarks of youth football, are now home to thriving soccer clubs and collegiate programs. Even the University of Alabama, home of the Crimson Tide and a temple of southern football culture, now has a soccer stadium.

"There isn't a small town in America today that doesn't have at least one dedicated soccer field with a couple hundred kids running around on it," Moorhouse says. "It's an army, and it's going to keep on coming, and the rest of the world knows it."

The advance guard hit the field in the early 1980s: Jeff Agoos, Michelle Akers, Paul Caliguiri, Joy Fawcett, John Harkes, April Heinrichs, Cobi Jones, Alexi Lalas, Tony Meola, Tab Ramos. The list is long, even if the names are not particularly well known outside the soccer intelligentsia. By the 1990s, however, the fever had swept virtually every major university in the country and that generation's players did manage to penetrate the national consciousness by turning the United States into a serious Olympic and World Cup contender for the first time: DaMarcus Beasley, Landon Donovan, Julie Foudy, Kristine Lilly, Clint Mathis, Tiffeny Milbrett, Brian McBride, Mia Hamm, Briana Scurry. In 1989 and again in 1994, the U.S. men qualified for the World Cup. By 2002, it was a foregone conclusion that the American men would make it. The women, meanwhile, were all but unstoppable.

Calculating the progress made in so few years, no less an authority than the head of youth training for England's powerhouse Manchester United team—the New York Yankees of international soccer—has predicted that the United States will win the men's World Cup before England does. There are simply too many kids playing the game, and too much money being invested, Les Kershaw told *The Washington Post* in 2003. In a rough reprise of Winston Churchill's famous description of the United States as "a sleeping giant," Kershaw said, "One thing about America, if it does something, it will research it fully and do its homework fully, and that is what has happened with its soccer."

That the giant has awakened since Pasadena is a point that even Europeans now must grudgingly acknowledge. More Americans—including English Premier League goalkeeping sensations Brad Friedel and Kasey Keller—have been signed by top-ranked professional teams in recent years than at any time in the preceding five decades. Three new Major League Soccer stadiums, the first of their kind in this country, have been built. And the mass marketing of the sport in videogames, magazines, soft-drink packaging, and children's clothing has made soccer ubiquitous in American pop culture. Three soccer movies have been produced, most recently *Kicking and Screaming*, an uproarious comedy aimed squarely at the youth market. From being nearly invisible when Chastain tore off her shirt in Pasadena, soccer has become a fixture in the lives of the College Park Hornets' generation. To escape the game, you almost have to crawl into an underground bunker.

By the time of the 2002 Men's World Cup, U.S. homes ranked sixth in World Cup viewership worldwide, and first among Western countries—even though most of the games being broadcast from Japan and South Korea reached North America in the middle of the night. At my kids' school, families gathered in the community room before sunrise to watch Cup matches together. Sports bars downtown locked their liquor cabinets at 2:00 a.m., fired up the coffeepots, and stayed open all night. While some in the media still tried to write off soccer as a stubborn fad, everywhere anybody looked the evidence belied the stereotype.

In the spring of 2003, while I was sifting through the data and mashing numbers on my computer, *Bend It Like Beckham*, a small independent film about two girls in England who defy their conservative parents to play the unladylike sport of soccer, opened in limited release in 484 U.S. theaters. The buzz grew swiftly in youth soccer circles, and in a little more than a month *Beckham* managed to gross nearly $11 million. By May, it had surged onto the list of the top ten movies in the country, and in August it went into wide release in more than one thousand theaters. By the end of 2003, the little movie had grossed $32 million in the United States for Fox Searchlight Pictures, the most surprising hit of the year. The movie's themes—perseverance, nonconformity, defiance in the face of authoritarian opposition—resonated with an unexpected audience of millions. To borrow a phrase from Gladwell's *The Tipping Point*, it had a quality known to marketing gurus as "stickiness." The American soccocracy made the movie a word-of-mouth sensation because they identified with the story line. They had lived it themselves.

Given everything I had learned by the time *Beckham* broke on the scene, I wasn't surprised to find that soccer had become a political cause. Frustrated by a lack of dedicated fields, affluent and politically active families formed powerful lobbies, leveraging county and municipal governments into building elaborate soccerplexes that dwarf traditional hometown athletic facilities. Major youth soccer complexes have sprung up in and around Albany, Philadelphia, Virginia Beach, Raleigh, Cincinnati, Des

Moines, St. Louis, Indianapolis, Boulder, Denver, Las Vegas, Sacramento, San Jose, and at least five other cities in California (which now claims more than 2 million registered players). In Salt Lake City, thirty-four thousand kids in shin guards campaigned door-to-door to support a $15 million bond issue for a 'plex of their own—thirty fields along the Jordan River. And lately the game has begun to appear in places where it was never seen before.

Little more than a twenty-mile stretch of farmland along Interstate-81 a few years ago, Loudoun County, Virginia, is now a fast-growing "third-ring" suburb of Washington, D.C. Its population has more than doubled, to 250,000, since 1990.

"On the list of least likely places where you might have expected a soccer boom ten or fifteen years ago, Loudoun would have been up there," observes Mark Gionet, a landscape architect who is assisting the county in building new athletic fields. "But Loudoun has followed a course that's fairly well recognized by now, at least in my industry. Look anywhere in the country where housing subdivisions are being built and you will find soccer fields somewhere on the planning maps."

A survey done by the county in 2002 found some four thousand Little League baseball players—and more than five thousand registered youth soccer players.

"If you look strictly at current usage, we could double the number of soccer fields we have right now and still not have enough," says county planner Bruce McGranahan. "When I look back just ten years ago, I have to laugh, because folks around here hardly knew what soccer was, and the few people who were involved in the sport would settle for a brown patch of grass in the end zone of a football field somewhere. Now they want lighted fields with irrigation and drainage, and bleachers for five hundred spectators." From "approximately zero" in 1990, the county's inventory of dedicated soccer fields now stands at around 110—and 150 more are planned in the years ahead. McGranahan adds that they will come in three different sizes ("full, medium, and micro") to accommodate players of every age and ability, because "kids aren't the only ones playing the game now—their parents are being sucked in, too."

Cindy Welsh, parks director for the county, says, "What's the surest sign of growth in soccer? Pregnant women. Just look at the birthrate and add four years, because that's when those kids will be getting their first set of cleats and shin guards. In the world of parks and recreation planning, soccer is the one sport where growth is almost assured. Some of those kids may drift on to other sports as they 'age up' through our system, but they will all start out as soccer players—because it's the one game that little kids can play. Way before they're coordinated enough for baseball, tall enough for basketball, and big enough for football, they're more than capable of playing soccer. And the ones who get good at it tend to stick with the sport."

Here in the verdant heart of Virginia's Baseball Belt, she adds, the number of youth soccer players is expected to more than double in the next ten years. "Where we once had a single soccer club, we now have three," Welsh says, "and they're all run like little businesses. That's probably the biggest change I've noticed. Unlike a lot of other sports, youth soccer is much more businesslike. The clubs have at least one paid staff person. They're very efficient. They come prepared. They know how to make their case."

Ken Wiseman, a principal with Cannon Design, one of the nation's largest architects of sports facilities, says soccer's growth is the result of a "happy convergence of good, clean fun, altruism, and, let's face it, money. The soccer people have political clout—they vote, they know how to organize, and they are very adept at getting what they want. There is a certain momentum to this sport that will not be denied."

Wiseman suggests, too, that in places like Los Angeles, Miami, Dallas, and Washington, D.C., the "happy convergence" also includes a lot of immigrants, especially Latinos, who are only now finding their way into the middle-class suburban club system. The most celebrated phenom to come out of U.S. youth soccer in recent years is, in fact, a West African immigrant who was nurtured in a private youth club in affluent Potomac, Maryland: seventeen-year-old Freddy Adu.

"A lot of people outside the game may just be waking up to it now because of the '99 Women's World Cup and some other major events, but the growth has been going on for a very long time and we see no sign that it has begun to peak," Wiseman says. "The constituency, if you will, is just too big now. And they're very committed. You'll hear this a lot: it's not just a sport to them."

It is this idea, this central truism, that any new student of the game must come to understand if he or she hopes to unravel the mystery of the Great Convergence in Pasadena and of soccer's seemingly inexplicable growth in America. As I ventured ever deeper into this world, the undercurrent of determination to make soccer a national sport was palpable.

"I just don't know how to describe it," says Herb Giobbi, the executive director of the U.S. Soccer Foundation—a $75 million trust headquartered in Washington, D.C. "It's almost a religious fervor. I see it all across this country. In fact, I'm still a little taken aback by it."

If anyone could illuminate the evangelism of the soccer movement, I thought, surely it was Giobbi. We met for breakfast in the gleaming white dining room of the Mayflower Hotel not far from his office. With its massive crystal chandelier and quarter acre of fresh linen and cut flowers, this hotel is a favorite meeting place of the nation's power elite, company he knows well. An attorney by training, Giobbi was the ideal face of the movement when he came to the foundation in 1998. He had been a Democratic Party organizer, a U.S. House of Representatives staffer, and a Washington lobbyist when he signed on to represent soccer in the halls of government. He is relentlessly upbeat, well-read on a broad range of topics, a gregarious conversationalist gifted in the lobbyist's art of genial small talk and gentle salesmanship. He also has a pin in his right shoulder, a memento of a hard tackle on a high school soccer field a long time ago.

"It may sound corny, but we really want to enrich lives through soccer," he tells me. "Yeah, we want to grow the sport. But we like to think we're doing something more than that. I just think it's a lot of people who have found something in this game that really clicks with them—and it really clicks with their kids."

As a father of three, Giobbi muses that we're living in a time when the happiness of our children is of "paramount importance" to us. To rear well-adjusted kids who post 1900 SAT scores and get into good colleges is the new definition of middle-class success, and athletic achievement on a high school transcript is definitely a leg up in the application sweepstakes. Sports do matter in the university acceptance calculus.

"Maybe that's it," he offers. "God knows, parents these days go to some incredible lengths to honor their kids' commitment to this sport. I'm sure our parents loved us, too, but the level of parental involvement in the lives of their children was nothing like it is today."

Giobbi's job is to make soccer their game of choice. He oversees a philanthropy that has underwritten some $30 million for soccer fields, new equipment, training, and youth-soccer expansion programs in cities and towns from inner-city Newark, New Jersey, to Indian reservations in Concho, Oklahoma. He is the bank president of youth soccer in America—its chief of diplomatic affairs and its master planner all in one.

The foundation has no true equivalent in the world of youth

football, baseball, basketball, or hockey. Over the years, those sports have been so heavily subsidized by the government and by professional leagues that they long ago lost any need for the services of a private fund-raiser or a central home office. "Those other sports got here way before us," Giobbi explains, "and their infrastructure—their fields and clubhouses and locker rooms, all their equipment—was mostly paid for with tax dollars by school boards and local recreation departments. When soccer first came along, it was forced to pay retail for everything. There wasn't any open land for fields in a lot of places, and what land there was cost a fortune."

It was the 1970s and '80s. The economy was dragging through serial recessions. Government funding was being cut by tax-slashing Republican administrations. And the U.S. Supreme Court was taking an increasingly restrictive view of eminent domain, the constitutional principle that allows local governments to seize privately held land for public purposes. This was the cause of the meanness between soccer and the more entrenched football and baseball factions in hometown athletic clubs. Money was tight, and land was tighter.

Few soccer organizers I met could explain their zeal, but a well-developed persecution complex is part of it.

"The baseball and football people saw us as a threat, no question," I was told by Gene Olaff, a retired state police superintendent who organized one of the first youth soccer leagues in southern New Jersey a decade ago. "They saw us as competing for the same kids and the limited supply of available public money. They didn't want us on their fields. They didn't want us in their clubhouses. They literally tried to run us out of town."

"It's all sort of comical to think about it now, but the football people threatened to have us arrested if we stepped on their field," recalls my friend Renee Milligan of the College Park Boys and Girls Club. She smiles thinking about the old power struggles, especially in light of the fact that soccer fees now generate more than half of her club's annual budget.

"We had to do everything on our own—or we'd still be waiting," says Len Oliver, a writer and historian who helped organize the Stoddert Soccer League, in Washington, D.C., three decades ago. "Football used to eat up so much of the local rec-league budget that there wasn't anything left."

Across the country, privately funded youth soccer clubs—as many as three thousand of them—sprang up during this time as refuges against indifferent and sometimes openly hostile rec boards and school athletic directors. Some, like the Stoddert Soccer League, were started when frustrated parents began meeting on playgrounds to vent about the lack of local soccer programs. From a nucleus of about seventy-five kids in 1977, Stoddert now claims more than five thousand dues-paying members and, with its own Internet Web site and a paid staff of five coaches and administrators, has raised nearly $1 million for capital improvements, half of which has been spent to upgrade neighborhood parks for use as soccer venues.

Who would have thought, back in 1977, that one day soccer would, as Oliver puts it, "finally move out of the shadows and into its own," or that soccer parents would be seen as a political bloc—a highly motivated constituency with money in their pockets and 2.2 home computers per household containing e-mail address books two hundred names long. Soccer, Herb Giobbi told me, "brings people together like few things in modern life, except maybe the church or synagogue or community mosque." He's right.

And who could have anticipated, as Oliver points out, that football would almost disappear in the District—at least "below the high school level because of all the liability issues." Or that baseball would decline because of a lack of interest among African-American kids. "Washington is really becoming a two-sport town, at least at the youth level," he says. "It's mostly basketball and soccer now."

At the Mayflower, Giobbi rattled off a long list of congressional leaders, presidential hopefuls, and influential political insiders in Washington who now have a stake in the game because their children or grandchildren play it.

"When you put ninety thousand butts in the seats for a soccer game, that's when people finally notice you," Oliver says. "That's what Pasadena did for us. But it was a long time coming, a lot longer than most people know."

3.

BAD NEWS HORNETS

MARKING THE BIG KID

He carried the names of two great kings on his impossibly broad shoulders and an expression of imperial implacability on a handsome, sculpted face: Malachi Alexander.

There was not an ounce of fat anywhere on the kid's body, nor a bead of sweat anywhere on his brow. The perfect aerobic machine, he covered the green turf of Schrom Hills Park as though he were on horseback, leaping over the pestiferous blue rabble of the College Park Hornets, taking the ball to our goal at will. Twice in less than fifteen minutes, Malachi ran from one end of the seventy-five-yard field to the other. Twice he flattened every defender who came near him. Twice he scored, emerging from our goal box afterward, through the mist of a foggy spring morning, like some celluloid vision of Hannibal in his youth, all cobalt sinews and bunching flexors.

Forty or fifty spectators gawked in silent amazement. It was March 15, 2003, opening day, the first game of our spring campaign. Another chance at a perfect season—and Malachi already had us in a 2–1 hole.

"We're bouncing right off him," the Mosquito gasped on the sideline, gulping water, her hair hanging in damp hanks across her reddened face. Even though she was our quickest defender, I had taken the drastic step of removing her from the field and substituting a bigger kid in her place in an attempt to check this marauder from the neighboring town of Greenbelt. Malachi charged downfield again, blowing by the sub and ripping a chest-high shot that only Edward Curry could have stopped.

"See," Shelby said, pointing to Malachi. "He's too fast, he's too big, he's too strong, and he's too good. . . . He looks like he's in high school. He could score fifty goals if he wanted to. He—"

"Dang, little girl, shush now!" Terry Hammond told his daughter. "The game just barely started!"

"Yeah, be quiet," I muttered, trying to keep my focus in a descending cloud of dejection. "You're depressing me."

"Well, just look at him!" said Nick Waring, the Hornets' second assistant coach. "He's built like freakin' Michael Jordan! There's no way that kid is nine!"

"They say he is," I replied.

The referee had checked both teams' ID cards during the standard pregame inspection, flipping through both coaches' stack of photo identifications, looking over each kid's "license" to play, making sure neither team harbored a ringer: a player older than nine.

"He must weigh ninety pounds!" Nick persisted.

"He's a hundred, or I'm a blind man," Terry said.

I was starting to get irritated. "What do you guys want me to do about it?" I asked.

Nick laughed. "I don't know what you *can* do!"

And therein lay the problem. Over the course of six seasons, this seemingly simple, beautiful game had steadily revealed itself to have more facets than a Rubik's Cube. After almost three years together, we were still reacting mostly on impulse and instinct from one week to the next. I had become a fairly good student of the history of the sport by then, but the tactics were still largely a mystery, in part because there was never enough time to study them.

Even at this subechelon of the game—nine-and-under, or "U9," recreation-league soccer—just keeping track of the unfolding dilemmas on the field was challenge enough. In a regulation game, there would have been eleven players for each team strung out over eight thousand square yards of space. I only had to keep tabs on seven kids on a rectangle less than half that size, and getting each of them to cover his four-hundred-square-yard share of it was like trying to nail Jell-O cubes to the side of a moving bus. Saturday afternoons found me prone on the couch, hoarse from yelling, completely spent.

Regardless of the final score, every goal "for" or "against" contained the highest of emotional highs and the lowest of lows, so the postgame crash was almost inevitable. As the games wore on, as the pitch of parental cheering and indignation rose, it was too easy to forget that these were only kids. Afterward, in the instant replay of fresh memory, I wondered how I got so far out of my own skin. Was it the nature of the sport, the unrelenting pace, as some coaches suggested? Or something deeper?

The preceding year had been full of rude awakenings.

The kids' reward for their surprising showing against the mighty Beltsville in the spring of 2002 was a 2-2-2 record—two wins, two defeats, and two ties—and a miraculous second-place finish in the Prince George's County league. This had won them the privilege of advancing in the fall from the AA division to the rarefied heights of AAA six months ahead of schedule. It seemed an honor to be invited to "play up," ratification of "our program." You'll hear a lot about "programs" in youth sports, because parents like the word. It implies prior planning, oversight, safety. The plain truth is that most programs are dreamed up by haggard fathers while they're driving home from work at eighty miles per hour trying to make it to practice on time. But all honor aside, Triple-A, as it is known, did not turn out to be about finesse or instilling sportsmanship in youngsters. Rather, it was the stomping ground of the county's biggest clubs—the land of red meat, thump-and-run, Irish- and Nigerian-style pummel ball. Critics of soccer who contend that African-American kids have no love for this game, that not enough has been done to reach them, obviously haven't been to P. G. County. The best squads the Hornets ever played were composed of black kids from the county's working-class communities. A sport is a sport, and soccer was better than most for honing the skills they'd need later to play football and basketball. In Prince George's, soccer is black, brown, white, ocher, and tan; brown-eyed and blue; the Afro-Euro-Latino game. The old stereotypes of American suburbia mean less every day.

Lacking the sophisticated tactics to solve a problem like Malachi, I tended to fret for a few minutes, panic, then start spouting traditional coaching slogans at the top of my lungs, like, "Somebody, *please*, stop that guy!" and "Oooooh, damn, not AGAIN!"

"Dad, all that yelling doesn't do any good," my son informed me as we drove home after a particularly animated display of such leadership. "Half the time we can't hear you, anyway. And you've never played the sport yourself, so you have no idea how hard it is to do what you're telling us to do."

"You think so?" I replied, eyeballing him in the rearview mirror.

"No, Dad," he said. "I know so."

He was already secure in his status as a star, and I couldn't think of a decent comeback, so I kept quiet and drove. Besides, I had to admit (if only to myself) that the kid with the blond bowl haircut knew a lot more about the game than his father the coach did. How he and his buddies had delivered the Hornets to the apex of the league was a continual marvel. I suspected it had less to do with me than with his ambidextrous feet. Contrary to what some soccer boosters would have you believe, not everyone can excel at the game; biology does matter. Yes, desire matters most of all, and yes, the annals of soccer are replete with tales of knock-kneed, pigeon-toed, bowlegged, skinny, misshapen kids who later emerged as superstars. Soccer is a lot like learning to play the guitar. Very few people come to it naturally, but almost anyone can do it if he's willing to suffer a little. That doesn't change the fact, however, that "natural lefties" have a huge advantage in the game.

Because of the overwhelming predominance of right-handers in the world, generally estimated to be around nine out of ten people, the action in sports tends to flow from right to left. So players naturally orient themselves along this pole, especially when they're young. This often produces farcical displays of overcompensation in youth soccer, among them the classic traffic jam in the corners of the field. The ball seems to have a mind of its own as every touch moves it farther and farther from the middle of the playing area and back to the same stubborn spots down by the corner flags. One kid with a hot left foot can change the whole dynamic. The lefty corrects the right-to-left drift of the ball and "spreads the field," and this can be enough to throw a youth-league defense into disarray. Havoc ensues and balls suddenly start appearing in an opponent's net for reasons that the untrained eye can't detect. It had taken me three years to figure this out—and it was just one of the many hidden variables embedded in the game.

The brain mechanism that controls this prevalence isn't well understood, but researchers have noted a long list of traits that are broadly associated with left-handedness. Among these are high verbal and math acuity, artistic ingenuity, superior coordination, and a certain intellectual anxiousness. Lefties are also more apt to develop that trait so prized in an athlete: ambidexterity. The three greatest players of all time—Pelé, Diego Maradona, and Johan Cruyff—were all lefties. None of them—as kids, or even as grown men, were much to look at. Pelé was a pipsqueak. Maradona, the eternal pride of Argentina, was built like a baked potato: lumpy and squat. The whirling Dutchman Cruyff was so skinny, he looked like a stiff breeze might carry him off. But they shared a special gift: by the time they were twelve, they were ambidextrous.

To be sure, not every lefty on a youth soccer field will grow to be great, and virtually every player who sticks with the game long enough will gain some facility in his or her "weak side" foot. But American youth coaches routinely spend countless hours with mind-numbing drills trying to teach kids to be ambidextrous, and 2 million years of human engineering aren't easily overcome. A lefty is a gift of the cosmos, the elders will tell you, and a coach who does not have one on the roster will get one sooner by praying than he ever will by drilling. And herein lies the next vexing verity of the game when it comes to kids: drilling does *not* work.

Had I known this sooner, I could have spared the Hornets hundreds of hours of boredom and frustration, but like most coaches I was a rube to the mechanics of juvenescent learning. Among the many epiphanies I experienced in the midst of the 2003 season, as I traveled around the country seeking insights into the ways of the soccerheads, was a chance encounter with a microbiologist and lifelong Baltimore soccer trainer named Mike Sidlak. He would eventually convince me that any improvement in my kids during the early years was largely a function of central nervous system development and that I, frankly, was just getting in their way.

"It can be painful for coaches when they first find this out," he told me.

It takes six, seven, or eight years for children's nerve branches to grow long enough to reach their fingers and toes, he said, which is why kids spill so much milk and walk like ducks when they're young. Once their extremities are all plugged into the main switchboard in the cerebellum, they begin to move in straight lines and gain control over their fine motor functions. And nothing a coach or a parent says or does before then can make much difference, except possibly to cause the sprites so much misery that they quit sports.

In Sidlak's construct, the law of averages is the prime force in youth soccer. If you take two teams of eight-year-olds and play one hundred games, each will win roughly thirty-three of them—and another thirty-three will end in ties—as long as one squad doesn't have more lefties or runny noses than the other, for the common cold is perhaps the biggest confounding variable in peewee soccer. The team that produces the least snot usually wins the one-hundredth game and takes home the two-dollar plastic trophies that parents value more than gold.

A year later, a coach can fairly well forecast how his or her season will turn out by looking at birth dates. If there are more "late nines" on the roster—younger kids with birthdays later in the year—the team is bound to struggle. The squad might surge late in the fall, when everyone's fingers and toes are wired up, but they will continue to have trouble tying their own cleats in the spring. I had tied approximately 1,275 pairs of cleats for the Hornets by that point, but I hadn't made the association. Later, reviewing old rosters, I could see immediately that Sidlak was right: the team's biggest stars were usually at least six months older than everyone else.

Of course, there are occasional prodigies who blow through the performance baselines, and every youth coach likes to think he's got one or two on his team until he finally meets a real one. He will make this acquaintance only if he sticks around the game for about ten years, because U.S. youth soccer is now so big that only about one of every nine hundred kids qualifies as a prodigy—and that's if you count the numbers generously. Many a lionized Hall of Famer will tell you that they are happy they played when they did, because they wouldn't have stood a chance today.

There's another thing I didn't understand when I began coaching: how much the presence of a single assertive little girl can shape the fortunes of a team; time and again, Shelby saved the Hornets in the closing minutes of a game by being in precisely the right place at exactly the right time to make the game-breaking steal, pass, or shot. She often lacked for physical presence among a thundering herd of boys, but she played smarter. She "got to the spot" before they did. Again, generally, brain researchers have established that intellectual capacity evolves differently—faster and more finely—in girls than it does in boys. They do not yet know precisely how this happens, whether it's chemical or structural, but it is an observable fact that girls are better at recognizing symbols, patterns, and external cues. Their memories and language skills are more acute. They learn quicker and retain more. Their abstract reasoning is far superior. Their "muscle patterns," the internal library of repetitive movements that are the building blocks of athletics, accrue more quickly. Boys, meanwhile, develop earlier in the frontal, "monkey" part of the brain. This gives them an edge at tracking moving objects and peeling bananas. Together with their higher muscle mass, their monkey brains make them better at physical tasks, but the job will get done faster if there's a girl around to get them organized. Fortunately for the Hornets, Shelby was one of those rare girls who could stand the smell of them.

It would be years before I figured out any of this—years in which I worked little kids to a frazzle, stood them in lines to take turns at kicking goals, had them dribble balls through bright orange cones, sat them in the grass and lectured them about the importance of passing. I coached soccer the same way I had been coached in football, basketball, and track. I drilled and whistled and yelled. I became my own worst nightmare, the bellicose coach of my distant childhood. Sidlak was too decent to say so, but the gratification I took from the Hornets' conquests over the years was delusional. In the 200-watt glare of perfect hindsight, the team's success could be traced to one lefty, a girl, a Salvadoran shooter, and a handful of kids with early birthdays and their collective good luck not to capsize in their own snot.

By reaching the AAA division ahead of schedule the previous fall, however, the Hornets were treated to a crash course in the reality of the game of soccer, for which they and their parents were completely unprepared. Stripped of their relatively slight advantages just as they were starting to find their legs, the kids arrived at the level of their incompetence overnight and were forced to persevere through the three long months of the fall season against bigger, older, and faster opponents whose coaches were far louder and more devious than I was. For the first time, rudimentary tactical shifts—subtle coaching adjustments to confuse or wear down an opponent—were coming into play. So was the "clean hit."

There are only seventeen rules in soccer, called "laws," and they barely fill two pages, a minimalist code of conduct so straightforward and generalized that it is almost beyond the comprehension of Americans. We are accustomed to all-inclusive regulatory schemes that require one of the largest law enforcement apparatuses in the world. As in our civic life, our traditional games are crawling with referees. In soccer, there is one. He has godlike power on the field—and, like God, he leaves the players mostly to their own devices. While refs may "call the game tight" in peewee leagues, they loosen up as teams rise into higher divisions of play. What was once a foul becomes fair play. For kids, this transition begins no later than age nine. Unfortunately, this is seldom explained to parents or amateur dad-coaches.

Among the most confounding rules for Americans is Law XII. It governs physical contact, and it is perhaps the most fluid of the laws in soccer's compact Magna Carta. It prohibits punching, biting, spitting, shoving, lunging, tripping, grappling, cursing, or hitting an opponent from behind. Hands should never be used except by a goalkeeper, or to protect your face or groin from an oncoming ball. Recklessness is also against the law. In the event of a minor infraction, the referee stops play, declares a foul, and awards the ball to the other team. If the contact is deemed serious, the ref writes down the violator's name in a black booklet and shows the player a yellow card. After two such warnings, the serial misdemeanant is shown a red card and tossed out of the game. In the case of a dangerous or malicious foul, the ref pulls the red card immediately, usually with urgent flourish. In either instance, the miscreant's team must endure the rest of the match one player short.

Much of the popular appeal that drove the youth soccer boom of the 1980s and '90s was fueled by Law XII; it seemed to address the long-standing concerns of Baby Boom parents about violence in sports. Soccer organizers seldom fail to point out that their game has an explicit rule against harmful, disrespectful, or off-color conduct. Unlike other sports, in soccer you aren't even allowed to argue with a referee. One peep of "dissent" and a player or a coach is subject to ejection.

"It was a big selling point and we sort of rolled with that right into the nineties," Sam Snow of the U.S. Youth Soccer Association (USYSA) told me. "It was also a source of some confusion as we went along, because a lot of parents didn't seem to make the distinction, and it's an important one: soccer is not a *collision* sport, like football, but it is a *contact* sport. We never said it was injury-free, but some parents still aren't prepared for how physical it can get as the kids head into puberty—particularly as the boys start to broaden in the shoulders and put on muscle mass. When the kids are little, there's not much danger of them hurting each other, but when they get older . . . soccer may not be for everybody."

What's more, "bookings" and ejections are rare as a practical matter because Law XII has more loopholes than the U.S. tax code. As long as a player doesn't use her hands to gain an advantage, or mow someone down from behind, almost all contact is legal if she appears to be "making a play for the ball" and isn't deliberately aiming to knock an opponent's block off. No one who ever has challenged Abby Wambach, for example, is unwary of her head. At nearly six feet tall, the forward for the U.S. Women's National Team soars high above most rivals in pursuit of "flighted balls"—those aerial passes that put a clutch in the throat of a true fan—and a tap from her noggin at any point along the way has been known to leave them unable to remember their home phone numbers. I have attended games where opposing coaches have complained bitterly about it to referees. But I have yet to see one prevail.

The best defense against a cry of "FOUL!" is to get a toe on the ball—the more firmly the better—before lowering a shoulder and detonating against your adversary. While it's no guarantee of immunity, for a cautious referee might still call a foul, he who last controlled the ball is presumed to be its rightful owner, and in soccer the owner is given wide leeway to protect his property. This is the marrow of the game's most devastating defensive stroke, the "slide tackle." It works this way: a defender waits for an onrushing attacker to look down at the ball or otherwise avert his eyes, then skids horizontally in front of him to form a human trip wire. As long as the defender spears the ball before making contact with the ball handler, the resulting collision is generally within the bounds of Law XII, even if it results in a bloody-nosed face plant.

Another permutation is that a referee cannot call a foul that he does not see, and since his attention is usually focused on the player with the ball, all manner of ruffian behavior may unfold behind his back and no amount of screaming from the bleachers will move him to issue a citation. These so-called "fouls off the ball"—the grabbing of jerseys, the well-aimed elbow to the ribs, the pushing and close-quarter tussling—are so much a part of the game that some players raise the practice to an art form. It is not at all unusual in Italian soccer, for example, for defenders to impede an opponent by clawing his shirt clean off his back.

For newcomers, the most mystifying exception to Law XII is that even when a referee does witness an infraction he may decline to take action if it doesn't result in a change of "advantage." So a one-hundred-pound defender can deliver a crushing shoulder blow on a sixty-pound forward with no consequences, unless the forward loses control of the ball and the mugger's team recovers it. A dangerous hit still might result in the defender's being "carded" afterward, but that rarely happens in the real world. At the age of nine, most kids understand the law intuitively, even if their parents and coaches don't—a fine point that I learned the hard way on a miserable day on a hilltop field at a place called Marlton Park. It was the last game of our ill-fated Triple-A season.

My mood was black to begin with. It was twenty-five degrees outside. Sheets of windblown sleet were coming in over the field. There were wallows of frigid water in front of both goals, and ice was forming on the nets. Dave Olfky, our club's soccer commissioner, had warned me from the beginning that the sport is an all-weather affair. Hence the adage: "It never rains on a soccer field." Matches are called on account of lightning, but don't be surprised if anything else is considered a sunny day, especially in higher leagues, and most especially late in the season, when calendars get tight between Thanksgiving and Christmas.

Cold, wet, and exasperated, I fumed on the sidelines as the sleet turned into a minor blizzard, and a pair of fullbacks from the town of Bowie systematically beat our forwards and midfielders black-and-blue. By halftime, Kevin and Ben were bruised all over, and Thomas was sitting on a gym bag, soaked to the skin with his head rolled back and a paper towel against his nose to stop the bleeding. "I don't want to play anymore," he told me, shivering. "I want to go home. This is *not* fun." By the start of the second half his nostrils had clotted and the Hammer reluctantly took the field again. He was promptly bullied back into the muddy ground. Terry and I beseeched the referee to call more fouls—only to have him reply, over and over, "No change of advantage" or "No reckless play" or "Fair possession," and, finally, the coldest cut of all: "You gentlemen really should learn the rules." I had *read* the rules, of course, and the dictionary, too, and I was certain that I knew what "reckless" and "dangerous" meant, and my kids were being recklessly endangered.

Then, it happened. Thomas, who had flecks of frozen grass between his teeth by that point, bore down in the middle of the field, beat Bowie's forward to an open ball, and leveled the smaller kid with a dropped shoulder before dumping a pass to Ben for an easy score. Seconds later, Shelby intercepted Bowie's resulting kickoff in the backfield, booted the ball down into their box, and Ben scored again as the ref was drawing breath for the final whistle. In less than a minute, they tied the game that would come to be known in Hornets' lore as "the Snow Bowl." In the car on the way home, Ben stripped off his soggy socks and shin guards to reveal lumps and cleat scrapes down the backs of both legs, then burst into tears, spluttering, "I can't believe we did it. We did it, Dad!"

"Yeah," I told him, "no thanks to the referee. You guys got beaten up pretty bad today."

"That's just soccer," he said. "That's what happens to forwards."

I was stunned, even more so when we got home and he ushered me to his PlayStation console, popped in a soccer disc, and proceeded to deliver an earnest clinic on Law XII by tackling, slashing, and muscling opposing players all over the TV screen in an attempt to draw fouls and cards from the electronic referee. "Legal," he said, after walloping one Brazilian player. "That's legal, too. So's this . . . and this . . . and this."

"So you think we were out of line today, arguing with the ref?"

"Probably." He shrugged. Smack! Down went another Brazilian.

Video games have achieved such a state of "situational realism" that panels of learned experts now convene at coaching conferences to debate which ones are the best "training platforms" for kids. However inept a coach may be, his players will absorb the fine points through electronic osmosis. One way or another, shouldering and tackling are main features of higher leagues, and unprepared players usually learn the limits of Law XII's protection the hard way.

"It can come as quite a shock," Sam Snow told me. "Especially for the parents."

Not once did I see it result in serious injury, but neither could I begin to estimate the bruises on the Hornets during that season at AAA. Most of the Hornets' moms and dads—and their coaches— went into those games still barely recognizing the game as anything more than a party lark, a slightly higher form of kickball. As far as we could tell, soccer required so little physical ability or real skill that our precious dumplings should be able to play it forever. But what was true in peewee league, where all the players were equally clumsy and the games dissolved into sticky-fingered, punch-guzzling social gatherings, ceased to be true in Triple-A. By the age of nine, much to our mutual dismay, the kids were expected to actually play *soccer*.

My home e-mail lit up like a distress flare that fall, and I was plunged into ninety days of more or less constant diplomatic negotiations. A little bumping and falling down were unavoidable, one concerned mother noted in a midnight dispatch, but deliberate aggression was another thing entirely. Weren't there rules against this sort of thing? Were the referees *blind*? That certain kids might begin to display athleticism and determination to win was, in a word, "appalling."

My own ambivalence on the question didn't go over well. Yes, the Bowie game was way more than I had signed up for, I replied, and there wasn't much question that our kids were in over their heads. At the same time, I was impressed by their tenacity. They were becoming a real team—more confident, more able to bear disappointment and setbacks. They had learned that they could "run with the big dogs" and still somehow win from time to time. Their losses had been glum affairs, shutouts mostly, but they finished the season at 3-3-2, firmly lodged in the middle of the seven-team AAA pack. Through their own grit, they had avoided automatic relegation back down the food chain to Double-A. But a cadre of persistent parents did not share my optimism, and they were burning a hole in my computer screen with demands for a southerly retreat. The faster and the farther down we went in the division rankings, the better.

Right about then, the jock parents weighed in. "The slow kids are killing the team!" one told me after a hard-rocking squad from the town of Oxon Hill destroyed us 6–1 and sent half the Hornets limping off the field. "You got to stop being so nice. Soc-

cer is no 'standing-around' game. . . . They have to be able to run."
Terry Hammond, the former basketball point guard turned doting soccer papa, became their chief spokesman—and I had no good
counterargument to give him. Too many of the kids missed practices, skipped games without notice, and quit from one season to
the next, then returned six months later, five pounds heavier, and
a mile farther behind. "How are they *ever* gonna get good at this
if they don't show up?" the big man asked me. "Your kid, my kid,
half the kids on this team haven't missed a single practice all season. And guess what? They can actually play. Funny how that
works, isn't it?"

Then there was Nick Waring—a competitive rock climber,
river kayaker, mountain biker, former Ultimate Frisbee player,
and one of the most physically fit forty-two-year-olds I knew.
When Nick was thirteen, his parents consigned him to a military
academy. When he was sprung, he grew his hair, bummed around
the country, got a liberal arts degree, and took up a solitary occu-
pation. He was a self-employed photographer with an almost
phobic aversion to bureaucracy, and the Hornets were beginning
to feel like one. "There's just too many of them," Nick said one
night over beers at the Town Hall, an off-campus watering hole
in College Park. "You have to start closing the roster sooner, because there's no way we can handle so many kids. . . . I'm starting to think you have a death wish."

Terry agreed. "There's too many for one team, and not
enough for two, and a whole bunch who aren't ever gonna be
soccer players."

At that point, the spring season was just months away. I had
already decided to bail out of AAA and regroup in the lower division. But for the first time the Hornets were divided. The mutually exclusive desires of the parents, and their competing visions
of what youth sports should be about, would test the team far
more seriously than any opponent on the field.

When the "echo boom" came to College Park—when the sleepy residential neighborhoods suddenly began to teem with new baby boomer families and their many offspring—no one really called it that. We treated it as if it were an isolated local event, something in the water, not noticeably connected to a larger national trend. The schools were jammed, trailers multiplying outside, buildings falling apart from overuse. On nights and weekends, the gyms and fields in town were overrun with kids. Then came the Latino population wave. Not even the U.S. Census Bureau had foreseen that one—not so soon, anyway.

A few weeks before the opening game of the new spring 2003 season, I was sitting in my doctor's office when I happened to pick up a copy of *National Geographic*. Inside was a two-page color map of the United States showing the distribution of Hispanic households. The Latino community had grown by 3.5 million people in just three years. The population in the Washington, D.C., region had more than tripled. The article did not mention soccer, but I knew from personal experience that the growth was contributing to the demand for roster slots. The teams above us in the Boys and Girls Club—the older kids just two or three years removed—had few Hispanics. I would eventually have five, plus two Nigerian kids.

In the county's "short-sided" league, where only seven kids could play at a time, managing a fourteen- or sixteen- or eighteen-kid roster on game day was a thankless assignment. Substitutions in soccer are allowed only when the ball is kicked out-of-bounds, a player is injured, or during halftimes. Long stretches of the clock disappear in this sport before a coach has a chance to change the lineup, and the opportunity lasts a matter of seconds before the ball is back in play. "It's hopeless!" Nick fumed one day, handing me his stopwatch and a sheet of squiggled calculations before stalking off the sideline. "I'm not going to be standing here when the parents start complaining."

We were so far beyond workable numbers, with such an odd group of kids and such conflicting demands from their parents, that it was impossible to please everyone. I learned from some grizzled veterans around the league that the quickest way out of the mess was through the familiar grinding process perfected by football—the "gassers" and "suicides" and "wind sprints" that cull the uncommitted. "Run them till they quit," one old warhorse cheerily advised. "When you're down to the number you want, stop making them run." This, however, required a certain reptilian guile, and I could never bring myself to be that cold-blooded. Here again, however, the demand for soccer conspires with other demographic realities to undo the most well-intentioned coach.

While most people are at least vaguely aware of the major adolescent health syndromes, the practical problems they present are not something we routinely contend with. Teachers and pediatricians do. Coaches don't, and soccer advocates seldom meet the question head-on, choosing instead to promote their sport as a game that anyone can play.

Among many unpleasant surprises as fall turned to spring were published reports that the death rate among juvenile asthmatics had risen by 78 percent over the past two decades. At least nine kids whom I had coached over the years were asthmatic. In two of those cases, I found out about their condition only when they started gasping for their inhalers. It is entirely possible for such children to safely play soccer—and sometimes superbly so, with proper medication—at the less aerobically demanding defensive positions. But it was most unsettling to be standing on a field with no medical training when a little wheezer suddenly declared himself by collapsing like a winged quail.

Overweight kids were another persistent challenge. Their

stamina faded more quickly, and their "productive minutes" in a game dropped accordingly. Opposing players also had a natural tendency to exploit them as weak links, which did not endear them to their teammates. While all of this might seem common-sensical, it is not easily acknowledged by anyone in youth sports. According to the Centers for Disease Control and Prevention, the prevalence of overweight kids has tripled in the past two decades, while asthma cases have increased by about 5 percent per year since 1980 to become the most common chronic disease among children. Soccer coaches are often the first to encounter these problems in youth athletics because it's the sport kids come to first. The game has become so ubiquitous that it constitutes a ready-made peer network for preschool children growing up in a culture of playdates and supervised leisure time, so parents often bring their kids for reasons that have nothing to do with athletics.

For children with physical limitations, soccer affords a two-or three-year period in which to develop the conditioning, di-etary restraint, and coordination necessary to hold their own in more demanding adolescent sports. It builds self-confidence and weaves them into a lattice of like-minded individuals who can buffer the relentless competitive jostling of their middle-school years. The "entry costs," both in real dollars and in emotional distress, are a pittance compared with nearly every other youth sport, most of which require more gladiatorial appliances and initial resolve than the average kid can muster. But soccer is not a free ride. At a certain point it morphs into a physically de-manding game, yet many parents fail to see the day coming, thanks in no small part to the creed of inclusiveness espoused by soccer advocates.

"Pelé did not become a great soccer player overnight," one mother lectured me after I substituted her son off the field when he stalled out, gave up two goals, and pleaded for relief after nine minutes of play. I was not well received when I told her that Pelé was never forty pounds overweight, either. Soccer has its share of wide-bodies, but they are goalkeepers, the one position on the field that 99 percent of parents do not want their children to play. Between Law XII, the echo boom, the errant marketing of the game by soccer advocates, and the health issues of modern kids, soccer can become a Catch-22 for all concerned. As Sam Snow of the USYSA told me, "Soccer coaches come in for a lot of heat."

This gathering constellation of concerns brought many corrective missives from the club's president, Renee Milligan, mostly urging us to rethink our misguided notions that youth soccer had all that much to do with sports. What youth soccer really is about, Milligan told me in one of our many exercises in pretzel logic, is "community development."

"It's about building better people," I countered.

"Well, how are you going to do that if you piss off parents?" Milligan protested.

"It's not about the parents."

"In soccer, it is," she said. "Peewee soccer was their kid's first social experience, and a lot of them have trouble ever seeing it any other way. They don't consider it a 'real' sport. It's much more important to them as a social network."

"Try telling that to a football coach," I said, laughing. "Football coaches don't even talk to the parents. You start bitching at a football coach and he'll run your kid into the ground."

"Football is different," she said with a sigh.

"Why's that?"

"I don't know why. It just is. Most of these parents wouldn't even think to take their kid to a football tryout."

"So here I am coaching a game that's five times more aerobically demanding, every bit as physical, without helmets or body armor—"

"I know," she acknowledged. "I know. I know. I know. It's crazy."

"And it's making me crazy," I said.

By opening day at Schrom Hills Park, we had returned to Double-A, but the game had changed even there. The division had filled up with losing teams from the higher bracket that had been tested, hardened, and stripped of any lingering illusions that soccer was merely a "social experience." The days of cakewalks and friendly rounds of nudge-and-waddle were over. We expected our first match of the new season to be a breeze, but Malachi Alexander was spinning our defenders into the grass with such gusto that they were losing their zest for the contest. We had taken a new kid onto the roster over the winter—a sweetly smiling, crew-cut bulldog named Matt Shade—and he was having some limited success against Malachi at midfield, but not nearly enough to stop the happy warrior from Greenbelt. Malachi soon discovered that Matt wasn't so easily spun and trampled, but Malachi was quicker, and he knew it.

After Matt, we were down to an odd assortment of haggard Hornets: dejected substitutes who had already been bested; injured first-timers who didn't know what had hit them; and gassed-out stars looking for the reserve tank they'd need to last the second half. As one jock dad described the team, shortly before evacuating his gifted son from our roster at the beginning of the season, the Hornets were the "Bad News Bears of P. G. County soccer."

There was no denying, however, that the ten or so Hornets who had managed to consistently make it to practice had gained a measurable mastery of the game. They not only had survived Triple-A but had managed to win a few times. They no longer wept over losses or complained about fouls. Their conception of the sport itself had been altered in the course of one miserable season.

"My favorite thing about soccer is that I don't even have to look anymore, because I know one of my friends will be there," my son wrote for a third-grade English composition.

Lately, that included a seven-year-old Guatemalan fireball named Braulio Linares who was simply too good to play with kids his own age. The youngest son of an immigrant tow-truck driver, the pint-size "Bee" joined us over the winter and became the cocksure badass that the Hornets never had before. "We gonna eat their LUNCH!" he would whoop before games. "We gonna take them to SCHOOL!"

At the end of the first half at Schrom Hills Park, the ones being taken to school were the Hornets. The 2–2 score was no measure of their progress, nor was it enough to remove the hangdog look of resignation from their faces as they straggled to the sidelines at the whistle. Malachi was killing them. "If they go into the second half looking like they do now, we're toast," Nick said. "Lemme go find Rafael and see what he says."

Kevin Guerrero's grandfather had only recently begun to counsel us, struggling to impart some of his fifty-two years of insight about the game to our addled Anglo brains. On the opposite sideline—where spectators were required to sit under a league rule designed to prevent parents from interfering with their kids during matches—I could see the Latino master instructing Nick, gesturing with his hands, sketching a plan in the air. Whatever it was, I needed it soon. The halftime break was only five minutes long, and the clock was winding down. Nick came sprinting back as if the keys to the universe were burning a hole in his pocket.

"He says 'mark' the big kid, like, cover him one-on-one," Nick said. "Raf thinks he's all Greenbelt has—cover him tight and they're done. Put somebody on him, somebody good, play him man-to-man, because we can't stop him once he gets the ball."

"So we should keep him from getting the ball in the first

place, right?" said a voice in the crowd of bedraggled Hornets splayed in the grass. It was Bryan Basdeo. I ignored him.

"Got any ideas?" I asked Nick.

"I'll do it!" Braulio piped up. "I'll kick his BUTT!"

I laughed. "Little man, he'd squash you like a bug."

"Anybody but Ben," Nick said. "He's our best shooter, and we need goals."

"Take me," Bryan volunteered.

"But you've never played defense a minute in your life," I said.

"I can do this."

"Like Brutus?" I asked skeptically.

"I can do this like Brutus."

"Okay, dog, you got one job."

"He doesn't get the ball," Bryan said.

"Thomas," I called out, "Greenbelt is gonna be looking to pass to that big kid at midfield, but Bryan isn't going to let that happen. So you gotta find the loose ball right away and pump it out to one of the wings—outside to Ben on the left, right? 'Cause they haven't been able to cover him all day."

"Yes, SIR!" Nick Waring's wiseacre boy replied, popping to attention and snapping an exaggerated salute. "Left, right?"

"Right, left," I said. "Shelby, you're going in at forward. Don't worry about the ball. Just get to the hole. Kevin, same thing. You're out on the right wing. Just get to the net and shut the back door. Don't hang around at midfield. The ball will be coming. One way or another, Ben will be sending it through the box. Got it?"

"Got it!" the Salvadoran Terror echoed.

"Ben? Where's Ben?"

"Over here," he said, raising his hand amid the throng. "I know. Shoot."

"Right away."

"Yep."

At that, the ref blew his whistle to start the second half, and the Hornets sprang to their feet, suddenly energized, eager to see if "the plan" would work, because we never really had one before. Here was something new, a chance we had designed together.

"On three!" I yelled.

Everyone crushed together in a tight huddle: three coaches, fourteen kids, and all our hopes for a perfect season. Every star and satellite bunched into a sweaty communal circle, hands piled on hands in the center.

"One. Two. Three," I counted.

"HORNETS!" they yelled, jumping out and away.

Within thirty seconds, it all came to pass exactly as the old master Rafael had foreseen. Then again five minutes later. Then once more before the final whistle. The mighty Malachi couldn't shake Bryan Basdeo. As the rabble from College Park routed Greenbelt 5–2, another prodigy was proved vulnerable to the game.

Beneath the din of victorious, tumbling kids and sprays of postgame Gatorade, Rafael appeared, shook my hand, and gently confirmed, "You did very good." My formal education had finally begun.

4.

IN THE BEGINNING

GRASSROOTS IN THE BADLANDS

When I began the first leg of my apostolic training in the soccer-head faith, in the fall of 2003, I truly had no idea what I was getting into. My motives were entirely innocent. All I wanted was to learn enough to coach my munchkin team to a county recreation-league championship. After our two years together, the Hornets were good and getting better, and I was running out of ideas for how to keep them improving.

As for writing a book about the experience, it had only recently begun to occur to me that there might be a story worth telling. We don't like to admit it, but most writers tend to approach every subject with an eye to the well-traveled, well-settled narrative path—the quickest route to an end product. No such thing really exists in this racket, but that doesn't stop us from sniffing for convenient story lines. Soccer seemed impervious: too recent a phenomenon, too new a trend to have much depth or texture.

If you hang around the American game long enough, however, you will eventually encounter the soccerhead persecution myth, and that's where things get interesting. Ask around about it a little more and you open up a king-size can of worms. The first time I talked to Len Oliver, I knew there was more to the story.

"The U.S. has a soccer history that's just as deep and rich as any country in the world," he told me on the phone. "It makes me a little bit crazy when I think about how much of that has been lost, or when I hear some jackass say that it's not an American game. . . . I can tell you this, it's a lot more American than baseball."

A couple of days later, I visited Oliver at his home—a stately, turn-of-the-century mission-style foursquare in Washington's Cleveland Park neighborhood—and found him waiting for me on his expansive front porch. Tall, with a full head of white hair, Oliver wore wire-rimmed glasses and a cardigan over a button-down collar. He was leaning against a column at the top of the stairs, smiling in that semi-bemused way that law school professors reserve for their precocious charges in the front row.

"How much time do you have?" he asked.

"All day," I said.

"Good, because I can talk about soccer all day. Just depends on how much you want to know."

"Everything," I said.

"Well, we'll see about that," he said, chuckling.

I had barely taken a dozen steps inside his front door before my misconception that American soccer is a "new phenomenon" fractured. A darkly wooded foyer offered views into two rooms and up a flight of stairs. Everywhere my eye settled, there was soccer memorabilia: framed black-and-white team photos from the 1940s; game-day event posters; silver trophies, gold cups, inscribed bowls, autographed soccer balls; letters of introduction, congratulations, and gratitude from clubs and teams around the world; a plaque announcing his 1996 induction into the National Soccer Hall of Fame in Oneonta, New York. Honorariums were piled up above the fireplace mantel, on the bookshelves in the living room, and on the side tables in his den: three-time collegiate All-American at Temple University (1951, 1953, and 1954); two-time NCAA champion (1951 and 1953); member of the 1963 U.S. National Team at the Pan-American Games, and again a year later at the Olympics in Mexico City. "How do you like your coffee?" he asked.

Upstairs in his third-floor attic belfry—a suite of three crowded rooms packed to the ceiling with what must be the largest private library of soccer books in the continental United States—the professor held forth.

"This game goes back, literally, two thousand years," he began, "and in the States, at least four hundred years. It's probably the oldest sport in North America, but you wouldn't know it from all the propaganda put out by Major League Baseball. When the Pilgrims arrived at Plymouth Rock, the Indians were already playing soccer—at least two hundred years before baseball was even invented."

The Native American tribes of New England called their sport *Pasuckquakkohowog*, and they played it with a deerskin ball. But the Pilgrims recognized it immediately as an unmistakable cousin of their own beloved "football," or soccer.

"Baseball likes to call itself 'the American game,'" Oliver told me. "But that's really a silly claim. In the seventeen-hundreds, right up to the early eighteen-hundreds, soccer was pretty much the *only* mass sport on the continent."

Oliver is among the last living links to a history that most modern soccer players, coaches, and fans know little or nothing about. Three decades seems to be the outermost limit of collective memory in this country, he said, the point at which popular recall fades to darkness and all that occurred before must be reinvented anew as if it never happened. Every generation makes the same discoveries and mistakes, and every cyclical boondoggle is sheepishly explained away as a novelty of the times. It's who we are, one of our most enduring, amusing, and maddening eccentricities as a people. But for the sport of soccer it nearly proved fatal.

In most modern accounts of the Great American Soccer Boom—and there haven't been many—the story begins with the arrival of a single luminescent figure, a Brazilian deity who streaked across American sports pages in the mid-seventies, forcing soccer into national consciousness and "glamorizing" it in the United States for the first time: Pelé.

The reason Pelé came, in 1975, was the upstart North American Soccer League (NASL), an audacious venture hatched by multimillionaire investors led by Texas oilman Lamar Hunt. One of the architects of the National Football League and the owner of the Kansas City Chiefs—among the most financially successful franchises in the NFL—Hunt was joined by a who's who of venture capitalists looking for a piece of the action in the rapidly expanding sports broadcasting business. They included Jack Kent Cooke, the flamboyant owner of the Washington Redskins, who was known to wear opera scarves to games; the swashbuckling Houston developer Judge Roy Hofheinz, who built the Astrodome over the protests of a city; William Clay Ford of the automaking family; and Neshui Ertegun of Atlantic Records, a subsidiary of what would become Time Warner Communications.

Other stockholders in the original twenty-two-team league came from construction, TV, and the front offices of pro baseball. But Hunt, Ford, and Time Warner would sustain American soccer for the next three decades. They were the long-haul investors who, like Nike founder Phil Knight, saw the shape of a coming boom. They bet, and bet big, that Pelé would be the dynamite cap on a powder keg of enthusiasm. Well past his prime, the

Brazilian was paid $4.5 million to play just three seasons for the New York Cosmos, an average of $70,000 per game, evidence of what soccer historian Roger Allaway has called "the most spectacular attempt ever made to establish a professional soccer league in the United States."

In due course, league organizers hired a dream team of the world's greatest players. No strangers to the opulent lifestyle of superstardom, they came because the money was extraordinarily good. Trading in the silks of some of Europe's oldest and most venerated clubs, they arrived "by the planeload," as Allaway put it, to don the cotton jerseys of such NASL teams as the Philadelphia Atoms, the Tampa Bay Rowdies, and the Denver Dynamos.

Franz "the Kaiser" Beckenbauer, two-time World Cup winner with the German National Team and the preeminent defenseman in the history of the game, joined Pelé in New York in 1976—followed closely by Italian marksman Giorgio Chinaglia and superstar Brazilian defender Carlos Alberto. Eusebio, nicknamed the Black Panther and heralded around the world as the greatest African player ever, came out of retirement to play for the Boston Minutemen. George Best, of the British juggernaut Manchester United, signed with the Los Angeles Aztecs and was soon joined by Johan Cruyff, the ballhandling dervish of the Dutch National Team, whose brilliant individualism helped Amsterdam's Ajax club revolutionize the game.

By 1977 the league had a broadcast contract with ABC and franchises in Atlanta, Chicago, Dallas, Fort Lauderdale, Seattle, and Vancouver, among other places. Average game attendance soared to almost fifteen thousand as fans flocked to see one of the greatest assemblages of soccer firepower in the history of the game. But it was Pelé, once famously described by a Brazilian team manager as the Shakespeare of soccer, who captured the imagination of the American public. With his daredevil playing style, he demanded the attention of American sports editors, who could no more turn away from the highlight photos and news tape than they could from the crash of a meteor.

In little more than three years he burned through the NASL, more than quadrupling ticket sales, drawing crowds of seventy thousand to Giants Stadium, scoring more than two goals per game, lifting the Cosmos to three national titles, and attracting such glitterati as Mick Jagger, Elton John, Paul Simon, and Henry Kissinger. And in doing all of that he sparked the wildfire of interest in youth soccer out in the sprawling, novelty-seeking suburbs of America.

"It says everything about Pelé's transcending genius that he was the one man able to set light to soccer in the United States in the 1970s," according to *The Ultimate Encyclopedia of Soccer*, which credits the Brazilian as the force that "firmly established . . . a grassroots American sport."

"Pelé made it cool to be a soccer player in the U.S.," recalled Roy Dunshee, a forty-four-year-old tavern owner and high school coach from Annapolis, Maryland, who took up the sport at the peak of the Brazilian's apotheosis. "I was just this skinny kid with zits from Neptune, New Jersey. And there was Pelé on TV, dressed to the nines, with the gold Rolex and everything. I remember thinking, Who wouldn't want some of that? Plus, I was way too small for football. All those guys with no necks running around smashing into each other? I would have gotten killed. And there were already something like, what, nine thousand baseball players in my hometown? What were my chances there? But Pelé, he showed you another way." His arrival immediately took our sport out of the margins. "He made you feel that soccer was better than other sports."

Fortunately, kids in North Jersey always had another way. You see, their backyard—best known as the proverbial armpit of the nation, the number-one Superfund region in the United States, notorious for its political corruption and gangster "Sopranos"—is also generally regarded as the cradle of American soccer. Here, where Frank Sinatra first rose to prominence as the Hoboken Crooner. Here, in the place that Bruce Springsteen would later call "the Badlands"—a place from which kids are *Born to Run*. Here, where the ghettos went up in flames in 1967 and black kids were railroaded off to jail by the vanload, Bob Dylan wrote, "In Paterson, that's just the way things go."

Here, on the banks of the Hudson River, is where the American game found its most fertile ground a long time ago; before the turn of the twentieth century—in fact, before the Civil War. As the story goes, soccer landed here before it ever got to Brazil, carried over by Irish, Scottish, and English immigrants, people who have never heard a story—especially a *true* story—that they couldn't improve over time.

Pelé may have set off a grassroots movement in the 1970s, but the roots had to grow in *something*, the immigrant elders are quick to point out, and the loam had been laid down thick and rich in certain parts of the country during the course of the preceding century. As I traveled through the northeastern homeland of the soccerheads, talking to the Hall of Famers and their heirs, I soon discerned the outlines of a great American saga as yet untold. The memories were so old that people could not easily retrieve them at first. But, as we talked and ate and drank and talked some more, the dam of memory broke and the tale poured out in waves.

"Aye, it was all so long ago, and only yesterday," Jake Bradley, of the venerable Scots-American soccer club in Kearny, New Jersey, told me one night at his kitchen table, as the clock edged toward 1:00 a.m. and the last of his beer supply drained away. "We had the Kearny Scots and the Kearny Irish, a couple of English clubs around. . . . Soccer was all ye did when ye weren't breaking your back for a dollar."

"The sport is all balled up with the history of these people who have been intermarrying and moving across each other's borders in Britain for a couple thousand years, fussing and fighting and carrying on," Len Oliver told me. "The Catholics hate the Protestants, and vice versa, and everybody hates the English. And about the only thing we all could agree on was our love of this game called football, which we now know in America as soccer, which was always more to the English and the Irish and the Scots than just a sport. If it wasn't for soccer, we wouldn't have had an outlet for all those ethnic and religious animosities, and we might have killed each other off a long time ago. And we wouldn't even be having this conversation right now, because I wouldn't be here. Anyway, it's all a glorious mess, and good luck figuring it out."

As in Italy and China and elsewhere around the globe, Oliver told me, various versions of soccer had been played for centuries both as a tactical exercise for military units and as a means to vent ethnic, religious, and regional rivalries long before the British started playing it in the 1300s and turned it into a flying rumble called mob ball or town ball. It was an ugly, nose-biting, ankle-twisting jolly-good riot of a pastime played by gangs of drunken young men kicking inflated sheep stomachs, pig heads, or balls of horsehair through the streets of London until they threw up their ale and collapsed from exhaustion. Florid deaths owing to trampling and suffocation were often part of the outing.

"It was a bloody affair, with broken limbs a regular occurrence," as *Newsday* sportswriter Pete Alfano described it in a monograph for *The American Encyclopedia of Soccer*. "Games matched town against town, married men against bachelors, parish against parish. Roads, trees, shrubs and buildings were used as boundaries. Needless to say, the sport did nothing to further the image of the English gentleman."

Under pressure from an emerging merchant class, who were fed up with having their storefronts staved in by drunken mobballers, Edward II eventually decreed, in 1314, that the game should be outlawed, proclaiming, "Forasmuch as there is great noise in the city caused by hustling over large balls, from which many evils may arise, which God forbid, we prohibit such game to be used in the city."

By 1600, and thenceforward to the nineteenth century, town ball was gradually wrested from the clutches of the working class and transported to the moss-draped campus of England's august Cambridge University. The peasantry continued to play in the countryside in accordance with local rules and local custom, until a famous meeting on October 26, 1863, at the Freemason's Tavern in London. Attended by representatives of the various English citadels of learning and the organizers of the nation's then emerging "football clubs"—as the reformed gangs of warring town-ballers had come to be known—the conferees finally codified a set of common rules for the sport. From that day forward, soccer began its inexorable spread.

Only in recent decades, however, has the game begun to shake off its past. Soccer's ulterior organizing motive as an alternative to mortal combat between tribes and nations, and as an outlet for deep-seated religious, ethnic, and class grudges, lives to this day in the rivalries between some of the world's oldest and best-known teams. Today, the United States is one of the few places in the world where the game is "just a game." But even here that was not always so.

As I drained my first cup of coffee in Len Oliver's attic, the professor was just getting started.

By the end of the nineteenth century, British schools had refined the sport of soccer, and British imperialism had spread a tidier version of it around the world. "Soccer was part of the colonial baggage," the historian Bill Murray notes in his book *The World's*

Game, "either as a leisure pursuit for the expatriates or as a means, along with the Bible, to accomplish their 'civilizing' mission . . . Christian missionaries . . . used sports to win the 'heathens' over." British-style soccer clubs were set up in China in 1843, Argentina in the 1860s, France and Portugal in the 1870s, Hong Kong in 1886, Singapore in 1889, Germany in 1892, Italy in 1893, Russia in 1894, and Brazil in 1898.

By then, European plantation owners had imported more slave labor into Brazil than into any other nation on earth—an estimated 3.5 million souls—to man their sprawling coffee, textile, and rail concerns in the South American country. When slavery was finally abolished in 1888, it coincided with the introduction of soccer by Charles Miller, the son of a Scottish railroad magnate who was returning home to Brazil from a stint at a British boarding school with a pair of soccer balls in his baggage.

"Many newly liberated slaves moved into the cities, creating a large impoverished underclass," Alex Bellos observes in his history, *Futebol: Soccer, the Brazilian Way.* And the game "spread rapidly among the urban poor. By the 1910s, football had become Brazil's most popular sport . . . both the private hobby of the rich and the preferred pastime of gangs of poor youths."

The class division flourishes to this day in the rivalry between Rio de Janeiro's Fluminense team—founded at the turn of the century as an exclusively white, European gentlemen's drinking and sporting salon—and the multiethnic, working-poor clubs like Vasco and Santos, which would deliver Pelé from the ghetto at the age of fifteen in 1956 and into the arms of the world. It also marked a sharp fork in the road in playing styles, between the punt-and-chase long-ball game that had been imported from Europe and the short-passing, razzle-dazzle, juggle-and-juke creativity that the street-ballers adapted for the confined spaces of the congested inner-city.

Wherever nineteenth- and twentieth-century European immigrants settled, soccer took root. By 1930, Scottish, Irish, and English newcomers had formed soccer leagues and associations in virtually every major American metropolis from New York to Salt Lake City, and in every outlying town engaged in their "native industries." From tiny burghs and boroughs in New Jersey to the modern-day Rust Belt hamlets of the Ohio Valley; from Pittsburgh to Baltimore; up into the Boston-area shirt-factory towns and down to the upholstery plants of the Carolinas; as far west as Chicago, Milwaukee, and Indianapolis—wherever people wove cloth, smelted steel, dressed beef, brewed beer, or worked on factory floors. Company sponsors went so far as to recruit better players from the British Isles, paying them to work no-show jobs in the plants and factories in order to satisfy immigration officials.

Industry magnates and their bitter rivals, the emerging labor unions, backed teams with names like the New Bedford Whalers, Boston Wonder Workers, Detroit Holley Carburetor, Chicago Bricklayers, Scullin Steel, Coca-Colas, JandP Coats, Indiana Flooring, Southside Radios, Todd Shipyard, Pullman Car Works, Wonder Bolts, Philadelphia Hosiery, and ONT, for Our New Thread. Named after the trademark of a North Jersey thread-and-fabric company transplanted lock, stock, and barrel from Scotland in the 1860s, ONT was the dominant force in northeastern soccer at the close of the nineteenth century, battling other textile teams from as far away as Massachusetts and Connecticut and winning four championship titles before relinquishing its grip on the American game to the mighty Beth Steel. Through a circuitous route, ONT and its sister companies in the old textile league would prove instrumental in the youth soccer boom of a century later.

"A lot of workers had no choice in the matter," Peg Brown, the wife of Hall of Fame forward George Brown and an archivist at the Hall, told me. "They showed up for work at the mill on their first day, and the foreman asked if they knew how to play football. If the answer was yes, they were hired on the spot. But if they got hurt on the field on Sunday they were out of two jobs. There wasn't any workmen's compensation or union disability fund. And, believe me, it was easy to get hurt playing soccer in those days. It was a rough, mean game." For players who went down, recalled Jake Bradley, sideline first-aid consisted of smelling salts and whiskey.

But if their less-talented brothers were careful not to get scalded, hauled into the machinery, or maimed in the mill during a typical six-day workweek, they would have a good game to watch on Sunday. For soccer had become a perk of the new immigrant worker's paradise. Appropriately enough, Sir Thomas Dewar—distiller of the Scots whiskey that still bears his family name—commissioned a seventy-eight-pound solid-sterling trophy in 1912 that would become the principal prize for all this risk and labor. Standing nearly three feet tall from base to gleaming peak, its four columns drip with carved silver bunting and end in a bouquet of finely rendered tea roses. Atop this pedestal sits a massive silver orb, a soccer ball bigger than a man's head, etched with the Dewar crest. And on top of that runs a lone silver striker pursuing a silver soccer ball. Standing in its presence in the archival vault at the Hall of Fame, I knew I shouldn't, but I couldn't resist: I ran my hand over the mystical silver ball that had been embraced by so many, now so long gone.

"Gently," Peg Brown said. "Veeeery gently."

With the introduction of the Dewar Trophy in 1912, Sir Thomas the Distiller gave American soccer a unifying focal point for the first time. The prize gave rise to a national final called the U.S. Open Cup, later renamed the Lamar Hunt U.S. Open Cup. At the time it was struck, the Dewar Trophy helped spark a movement to centralize soccer's far-flung and disconnected leagues and join together its two divided halves.

Until then, the eastern and western wings of the game—centered in New York and St. Louis—barely communicated, much less played together. The East was the land of big steel, textile, and manufacturing industries, the point of entry for the world's soccer-loving masses, the unrivaled hub of the American game. In St. Louis, which was heavily Irish-Catholic, the church became involved in the sport, launching what came to be known as the Saint Leo's, or "Monastery," League. "When we priests were ordained, we left the seminary with a Bible and a pair of soccer shoes," Monsignor Lou Meyer recently explained in a syndicated interview with *The St. Louis Riverfront Times*. "It's a cheap uniform sport. In the early days, we kicked soccer balls in tennis shoes, any kind of shoe. Soccer was such a cheap sport, it was natural for the parishes."

As a consequence, St. Louis soccer was organized and supported differently than was its eastern cousin. Traditional industry patrons—notably Miller Brewing Company and Anheuser-Busch, both of which sponsored teams, fields, and clubhouses—played their familiar role. But patrons of the church itself were more influential. Undertakers, car dealers, department-store owners, even a delicatessen operator, bankrolled prominent teams that would later win the national title. The Ben Millers, one of the most famous of these, was organized and funded by a hat company.

The Dewar Trophy helped to break this regional isolationism, coinciding with the establishment of the sport's first U.S. governing bodies and truly national leagues. The American Football Association, the American Soccer League, the American Amateur Football Association, and the all-important U.S. Football Association (USFA)—the forerunner of the current U.S. Soccer Federation—all came into being with the Dewar Trophy as their common annual quest in the U.S. Open tournament.

The USFA was birthed on April 5, 1913, at a meeting at New York's Astor House. It brought together regional soccer representatives from eleven U.S. states, including all the northeastern powers, the midwestern immigrant capitals of Ohio, Illinois, and Missouri, and the far-western mining center of Utah, which was just then being overrun by soccer-crazed Irish, Welsh, and Cornish diggers. In a 1996 treatise published in the *World Football Journal*, Roger Allaway, the prolific U.S. soccer historian, wrote that the Astor House gathering "holds a place in American soccer history not unlike the place occupied in English soccer by the famous meeting at the Freemason's Tavern in London" fifty years earlier. The results were no less profound.

After the Astor House meeting, teams from the nation's previously insular soccer regions began to play against one another; the best players from those teams formed traveling all-star squads and toured abroad; and three distinctive approaches to the sport started to converge into something that would one day be discernible as an "American style" of play. Following the Scottish tradition, the textile teams from New England tended to follow the Old Country way, with players closely supporting one another and moving upfield in triangle formations held together with short, crisp passes. Countless youth soccer teams are still taught to play this way today. But the St. Louis men followed a strategy popularized in Ireland, pounding the ball deep along the sidelines, flying after it, then launching spectacular cross-field passes and swarming an opponent's defenses with hard body contact and furious inside shooting. Boys became men in the goal box, and a thousand years of tribal slights were settled in diving midair collisions.

The third strain of the American game was more an attitude than anything else, an emerging tendency for gifted individuals to break away and forge ahead alone, relying on their own wits and on deft combinations of dribbling stunts to see them past the bruising defensive schemes of the soccer backfield. Many years later, this would become known as "the Brazilian way." The nascent trait defied all the orthodoxies of the British game, this cockeyed belief that one "superman" could prevail against three or four massed defenders if he struck when they least expected it and willed hard enough to succeed. It was to be the emblem of the American century, the daring frontal assault.

The early soccerheads found their greatest exemplar in a six-foot one-inch, 210-pound Portuguese gunner named Billy "the Big Bomber" Gonsalves, regarded by many as the Babe Ruth of American soccer. Olive-skinned and dark-eyed, Gonsalves began his career in the New England textile leagues in 1927 and went on to play professionally in six different states and four major cities—Boston, New York, Chicago, and St. Louis—absorbing every style then in fashion and incorporating them all into his own repertoire. With a booming shot that could tear the bark off a tree, he competed for the Dewar Trophy eleven times in fifteen years, and he won it a record eight times. "His power was murderous on goalies and anybody who got in his way," a former teammate once said.

"He was a gentleman," recalls Walter Bahr, who played with Gonsalves in the waning days of the Bomber's career and went on to inherit his mantle as the greatest American player of his age. "Even his hair was perfect. He combed it before every match, and combed it again at halftime. And he had that pencil mustache his whole life. You won't see many pictures of Gonsalves where he doesn't look just right."

Hall of Fame defender Harry Keough, who grew up watching Gonsalves play in St. Louis, says, "He had this one wicked shot where he'd hit the ball with the outside of his foot, and it would bend as it headed toward the net, then drop off at the end, like a curveball. First time you saw him do it, you might think it was an accident, you know? A lucky shot. But after you saw him do it for the twentieth time? There wasn't a goalie in the country who could stop that shot if Gonsalves got it off good."

Comparisons between Gonsalves and Pelé are obvious and numerous.

"There was only one Billy Gonsalves—and only one other who I can think to compare him to," says Gene Olaff, a Hall of Fame goalkeeper who played behind Gonsalves in the final years of his career in Brooklyn, before the Sultan of U.S. Soccer drifted into obscurity as a North Jersey bartender. "But the other guy is Brazilian. Billy was American."

It would take five decades and the arrival of the self-possessed Pelé and his multicultural New York Cosmos to finally fuse the three "American" styles into one spectacular working whole. And Gonsalves would die at his home in Kearny, New Jersey, before he got to see the resulting resurrection of his beloved game.

"A lot of the early guys wound up that way," Len Oliver told me, leaning back in a creaking desk chair in his attic offices. "They gave the best years of their lives to the game and never learned another trade. It was in the days before the G.I. Bill and government loans for college and all of that. They came off the field in their thirties, with their knees all banged up and their backs out of whack, and jobs weren't exactly easy to find. Some of them had their union cards and went on to live fairly comfortably. But there's an awful lot of sad stories about the guys who didn't make it." Because even as Billy Gonsalves's star was being launched in the 1920s, there were terrible times ahead for the sport of soccer.

The fingerprints of big-league baseball are all over the knife that cut soccer's throat. It's not the only reason for soccer's decline, but it's a leading factor. As the story goes, the Barnums of baseball and football—the larger-than-life hucksters of the nation's then emerging sporting industry—alternately exploited the game as a way to fill their empty stadiums during the off-season, then decried it as an "un-American" sport played by the immigrant dregs of Europe. Early owners of pro baseball teams in Detroit, Chicago, Milwaukee, Boston, New York, and Philadelphia, to name a few, lent their power and prestige to soccer one minute only to withdraw it the next.

One early flirtation imploded in 1894, when the overwhelming superiority of the Baltimore Orioles' soccer affiliate—which beat Philly 6–1 and shellacked its far prettier sister city of Washington, D.C., 10–1—brought rival fans and owners to complain that the team was composed of illegal aliens from Britain. When local newspapers lit up with thinly veiled partisan accounts of alien high jinks in Baltimore, the feds descended on the league. The entire operation folded within three weeks.

Following a secret meeting of the baseball owners at a New York City hotel, to which officials of the Baltimore Orioles were not invited, the barons of the hardball game leaked news to the *Boston Herald* that they had decided to cease operations for economic reasons. Soccer, they said, conflicted too much with the college football schedule to attract a large enough audience. Soccer would never survive as a fall sport, they concluded. The baseball owners admitted to not having planned well enough.

They apologized. They promised to reorganize the league the following spring. They never did.

"It was a specious excuse at the best," the late Sam Foulds argued in 1979 in his seminal book *America's Soccer Heritage*. Foulds pointed out that the coconspirators had scheduled their games during weekday gentlemen's hours, when the immigrant working stiffs who were soccer's biggest followers would not be able to attend. They failed to promote the sport. They did almost nothing to attract a broader class of fans. Similar ventures over the next thirty years ended the same way, with baseball owners duplicitously insisting that their genteel clientele had little affinity for the hard-knocks game of soccer, the natural inference being that it was a brutish proletariat pastime unfit for an American audience.

In short, at a time when soccer was the only other mass sport competing with baseball, Major League owners made sure to do it in. Basketball had only recently been invented, and pro football was barely in its infancy. I never understood it until I talked to the old-timers, but the vague animosity that exists to this day between soccer and baseball boosters is there for a reason. The soccerhead persecution myth has roots nearly a century deep. "The baseball guys convinced Anheuser-Busch to throw us out of the sports parks," Harry Keough told me of his younger years in St. Louis. "They said we were messing up the fields and their guys were getting hurt because of it. So as kids, you know, we wound up playing in the cinder lots down by the mills. You weren't allowed on the grass, because it was baseball-only. It's strange to hear that now, I know, because Budweiser is such a big supporter of our game, but that's the way things were back then."

What big-league baseball started, the Depression finished. Within two years of the crash of 1929, one-quarter of the American workforce was out of a job. Ninety thousand businesses closed their doors. Hundreds of banks went under. Soccer's half century of industrial patronage turned to dust in a few years. Indiana Flooring folded. JandP Coats of Pawtucket, Rhode Island—a Scottish thread manufacturer—folded. The New Bedford Whalers folded. The American Soccer League folded. Even the awesome Beth Steel team went black. Decades of soccer infrastructure lay in rubble, the crushed stone base upon which Lamar Hunt's North American Soccer League would rise fifty years later with the help of Pelé.

5.

I, COACH

I was up late on the night my father died. The heart attack struck him in his sleep, in the back bedroom of his house in the New Jersey pines, knocking him half out of bed. By the time the paramedics arrived, it was many hours too late. Looking back, my reasons for becoming a soccer coach were crystallized in the days of grieving and remembrance that followed that night.

As I would come to realize, it had something to do with what Herb Giobbi mentioned at the Mayflower Hotel: the part about "parental commitment" and how involved we now are in the lives of our children.

On the night my old man lay dying in New Jersey, I was at home in Maryland, feeling my way in the dark. Bearing toward the hack of my son's cough, I jammed my bare toes against the steel leg of the boy's bed. I was sure I had broken something, but I didn't have time for triage because Ben was in the throes of an upper-respiratory infection, and two-year-old Sam stirred in sync with his big brother. As every parent knows, the key to tending sick children is to quiet one down before the other wakes and sets off a chain reaction of moaning that might last till dawn. There wasn't a moment to lose.

My dad sired six kids and never lost a minute's sleep to strep, croup, measles, mumps, or diaper rash, because that was woman's work. If anything really bad happened, he was perfectly qualified to drive one of us to a hospital, but that was the limit of his caregiving. Born during the Depression, he was a boy from the Adirondack foothills, and he figured that no living creature was worth all that much trouble unless you could ride it, milk it, or drench it in gravy. To the best of my knowledge, no vegetable other than a potato crossed the man's lips in sixty-five years. His final meal, like every one before it, was a slab of red meat and a split brown spud drowning in a pond of butter—all washed down with a few stiff tumblers of Canadian whiskey. We worried about his drinking, but his doctor once told me that it was probably the only thing that kept the grease moving in my father's veins.

His interest in our recreational pursuits was minuscule—until, that is, I began to show some interest in the guitar. He had been a flash player as a teenager, and he made it as far as live country-and-western radio in Albany before enlisting in the Navy in 1953. When I was eleven years old, he gave me my first lessons, just before he and my mother broke up. In the tumult that followed, the guitar became one of the few constants in my world. It was something I could do fairly well that most people couldn't do at all, and that was a powerful reckoning in the life of a child. For if a boy could master such a thing, what else might he be able to do that no one thought he could?

So it was, thirty years later, that my ears were pulsing in time with my mashed toes as I rocked my five-year-old back to sleep on the night my father died. I had gotten home from band practice just a few hours earlier. The band didn't have a name, but

Mid-Life Crisis might have worked. We were three guys who met once or twice a week on the second floor of a vacant office building that formerly housed a driving school. Slightly doughy, lately graying, all married, we bashed out hybrid country-blues that we called amphetamine cowboy music. By daylight, the drummer was a librarian in a downtown law office. The bassist was a researcher for the U.S. Department of Agriculture. A news reporter by trade, I sang and played lead guitar. Our most inspired anthem was a savagely butchered, southern-fried version of Nancy Sinatra's timeless classic, "These Boots Are Made for Walking."

Within a year of that night, our trio had disbanded and the bass player and I had become soccer coaches—our boots drawn down new paths by our kids.

Standing on a striped field with a whistle around my neck, it struck me that there were few places less familiar. Growing up, I'd hardly known anyone who took part in organized sports. Despite an exploding youth population, interest in hometown athletic leagues had sagged in the United States during my generation's formative years. Sociologists would later ponder the paradox. Charting the decline, Harvard University researcher Robert D. Putnam observed in his 2000 book, *Bowling Alone*, that those decades coincided with the American tech boom, years in which televisions, personal computers, and other consumer electronics came within reach of millions of Americans. As the average number of video screens in U.S. households nearly tripled from 1975 to 1998, the amount of time that families spent basking in cathode rays rose to seven hours per day. Little wonder, then, that sports would suffer.

Still, while this was surely part of the explanation for a slump in youth athletics, it was not the biggest reason that my friends and I bailed out of basketball, track, or JV football. We split because our childhood games had been turned into boot camp maneuvers. Overseen by scolding gym teachers and war-veteran coaches intent on stiffening our moral warp and weft, physical education meant a never-ending regimen of laps, chin-ups, and rope climbs designed to ensure a future supply of able-bodied military conscripts.

Sports were also the principal device by which a minority of genetically gifted kids (known in my high school as "the pretty people") maintained a dynasty of privilege that would become one of the defining features of the American scholastic experience. The jocks turned third-grade dodgeball into a smash fest called Kill the Geek, which established the social pecking order for the rest of our adolescent lives.

Kids in North Jersey were already playing soccer by the time I got to middle school, in 1968. But a hundred miles to the south, on the other side of the trackless Pine Barrens that blanket the center of the state, the game did not exist. And the games that did exist were oversubscribed to the point of exclusion. There were at least twelve kids on my seventh-grade basketball team, and most of us played about ten minutes a game. Football? Forget about it. The one time I went to a tryout I left after the head coach pointed out that there were three kids vying for every position on the team. "Look to your left and look to your right, and know that two of you will be gone by the end of the month." We heard that sort of thing a lot back then.

In my freshman year of high school, I went out for basketball and persevered through three rounds of cuts—the heartbreaking weeding-out process that reduced a crop of some 150 wishful prospects down to a roster of 20, half of whom would barely get to play—before falling in the fourth. Ditto track. I had run respectably in the 220-yard, 440-yard, and mile races in the eighth grade but got smoked on day one of high school tryouts. "One cost of the crowded schools the boomers attended was reduced opportunity," as Robert Putnam found in attitude surveys of the time. "Boomers were less trusting, less participatory, more cynical about authorities." They became "highly individualistic, more comfortable on their own than on a team."

Not surprisingly, these were the years that saw the invention of the Frisbee and the skateboard, the introduction of rock climbing, and the cross-continental spread of the California surf scene to the shores of New Jersey and North Carolina. Rollerblades, mountain bikes, and snowboards, not to mention the lowly Hacky Sack, were not far off. And paintball, the ultimate renegade sport, arrived in 1981. Within two decades, it would claim 10 million players and annual proceeds of nearly $1 billion, according to *Sports Illustrated*.

These individual free-form sports took kids like me as far as we could possibly get from the fences, cages, grids, and statistical tyranny of America's traditional childhood games, where coaches ran players ragged, then benched them with impunity if their numbers slipped. It was the beginning of the "fun revolution," and there was no way to count the insurgents, because we didn't play in leagues and we weren't registered anywhere, and that was the whole point. We wanted to be invisible. A Red Cross T-shirt with the one-word legend "Independent" became the flag of the disaffected. We were streetballers, surf rats, prototypical "skate punks," unknowing pioneers of a movement that eventually leaped into plain sight in 1995 with the high-flying X Games. The annual Olympics of indie sports now draws 150 million viewers to ESPN and is said to have spawned a $2 billion indus-try. All we wanted at the time was to get away from the jocks and their potbellied handlers.

There was another factor at play, too. This wasn't simply a generation of rebellious kids who had lost their patience for male authority figures. This was a generation who had literally lost their male figures altogether. Divorce rates soared; cultural analyst Susan Faludi would later call the 1970s the time of "the vanishing fathers." Once my folks broke up, I didn't see my own father much at all.

When the fathers vanished in the millions—and growing up I may have had three friends who hadn't lost their old man somewhere—drugs and drug-induced stupidity began to cull the stooges from the pack. In my hometown, the less wary wound up wrapped around marina pilings in wrecked boats or killed in stolen cars or shipped off to "reform school." One died in a prank involving too much marijuana and a gallon jug of gasoline. Sometime around Christmas of 1973, the police found my sister's ex-boyfriend dead of a heroin overdose behind the wheel of his father's car. He was seventeen years old, the son of a prominent Philadelphia attorney. Such were the times. No one was immune.

The Atlantic City island where I grew up, with its four contiguous municipalities, was way past its prime as the self-proclaimed Playground of the World—a motto that jeered at us from tattered billboards riddled with shotgun pellets in the marshlands outside town. The stucco icing fell away from the wind-sheered facades of the city's empty grand hotels. The glimmering ribbons of arcade lights hung in rusted ropes along the boardwalk. As recreational venues, the city's amusement piers were fit for only working-class rowdies and North End ghetto kids who knew how to "throw down": us and the breakneck surfer crowd, East Coast danger junkies who carved the brown waves that churned below the shambled piers.

Behind the oceanfront, Atlantic City had the nation's third-highest percentage of residents living in public housing, a 40 percent wintertime unemployment rate, and a permanent population of about forty thousand captive poor, one-third of them senior citizens. Half the shops on the boardwalk were permanently boarded, deep in tax default. *The Washington Star* dubbed it "strictly Endsville." To the locals, it was Frantic City. To a posse of skateboarding juvenile delinquent "independents," it was paradise—Gomorrah with an ocean view. There were carnival freak shows, boxing dwarfs, clam-eating contests, transvestite revues, and weekend-long dance marathons. Every September brought a festival of legs, boobs, and teeth known as the Miss America Pageant. Yes, life was good, but God help you if you needed a square job. In the week I dropped out of Atlantic City High School, during the annual fall race riots in 1973, I filled out applications at seventeen gas stations but got no offers. By April, I was gone, one step ahead of the local constabulary, a ward of the U.S. Navy.

Filmmaker George Lucas would eventually give mythic form to the disappeared dad in the character of Darth Vader—the black-helmeted and gurgling *Ubervater* who abandoned his son, Luke Skywalker, on a desert moonscape menaced by trolls and hooded "sand people." Not for nothing did *Star Wars* become a box-office smash during a time when more than 12 million marriages dissolved.

Fractured families and the uncertain times were mirrored on television. The sitcoms of the 1970s pictured a panoply of kids living in unconventional domestic settings. "Divorce" was still an ugly word, so producers often avoided difficult discussions about single-parent families by simply killing one of them off. There were abandoned kids living in new homes (*Diff'rent Strokes*), single parents comically getting by (*The Courtship of Eddie's Father, One Day at a Time*), and widowers on the rebound (*The Brady Bunch*). When the TV sitcom writers finally caught up with the boomers a decade later in the late 1980s, the divorce rate had begun to tail. In *Roseanne*, *The Simpsons*, and *Married with Children*, couples in flawed relationships stayed together past the point at which their parents had cut and run. They bickered, then hugged, then bickered some more. Their kids were disobedient and disrespectful, but these new TV parents gutted it out.

By then, as Putnam charts in *Bowling Alone*, our loyalties had been worn to the quick. The baby boomers had given up on just about everything but family. Membership in churches, school groups, clubs, Little Leagues, labor unions, civic organizations, and political parties were all down. Traditional social organizations—the Boy Scouts, the Elks, the VFW, and the Shriners—were stagnant. Politicians shifted their message, trying to regain relevance. Strengthening "family values" and the "American family" became the rallying cry of both major political parties in the 1990s. But if the boomers were ever going to return to public life, it would have to be through some new avenue. This was particularly true where sports were concerned.

"Boomers did not exactly harbor the fondest memories of P.E.," observed Greg Critser in his slyly subversive book *Fat Land: How Americans Became the Fattest People in the World*. "Many recalled it as a time, perhaps the last, that they were unfavorably compared to other people. No, that wasn't for their child." The slide in organized youth athletics continued when the boomers became parents themselves, because they had been "physically singed," as Critser put it, and they simply weren't willing to put their own kids through the traumas they had experienced.

The new parents' protectionism was apparent almost anywhere you looked. One day it seemed as if every electrical outlet in the country had one of those little plastic safety caps on it. Meanwhile, in the nursery, Junior slept in an infant crib hung with a baby monitor that transmitted his every burp to a receiver downstairs in the kitchen, where Mom sterilized his bottle in a countertop autoclave and swabbed down his high chair with antibacterial wipes. Through successive design improvements, toddler car seats began to look more and more like survival pods. Once the precious cargo was slathered with SPF-50 sunblock and secured under the drop-down injection-molded restraint bar, the whole package could be shot from a cannon without Junior's suffering a scratch. But, just to be sure, we hung blaze-yellow signs in our car windows alerting approaching motorists to the BABY ON BOARD.

It was right about then that Americans discovered soccer in a big way. Through a coincidental vector of history, commerce, legislation, and celebrity, the game landed in the laps of the new boomer middle class around 1982. They loved everything about it. Soccer was the kinder, gentler sport—fast-paced and physical but never violent. It wasn't exclusive like the games of their youth, because it didn't offer any particular advantage to the genetically gifted. If anything, the muscle-bound lacked the agility for it, and the goons stayed away because they hated losing to girls. The dawning recognition that girls were no longer satisfied just to cheer from the sidelines worked in soccer's favor, too. Here was a sport that explicitly taught egalitarian values, a game that *everyone* could play, the antidote to Kill the Geek.

"Let there be no partiality," the Chinese philosopher Li Yü wrote in the first century A.D., describing an early form of soccer. "Determination and coolness are essential, and there must not be the slightest irritation for failure. Such is the game. Let its principles apply to life."

No irritation for failure? Clearly this was not our fathers' game. As Critser put it in *Fat Land*, it was as if 10 million boomer parents woke up one morning and decided, "This is the place for Junior."

Sam Snow remembers how abrupt that awakening was. As the director of coaching education for the U.S. Youth Soccer Association in Dallas—the largest consortium of its kind in the country, with 3.2 million members nationwide—it was his job to help manage the influx.

"The number of kids who wanted to play grew so fast that it was overwhelming," he recalls. "The demand was bigger than the number of coaches available. Then, as the number of coaches began to catch up, we didn't have enough referees. Then, as that began to catch up, we ran out of fields, which we didn't have enough of to begin with. Now we're kind of back where we started. The kids have gotten so good at the game that the coaches are having a hard time keeping up."

By 2001, Snow notes, the United States ranked first in player registrations—with more than twice the participation levels found in China, Mexico, and Brazil, and almost three times more players than there were in Germany. Of course, two important distinctions have to be made: soccer players are easier to count in the United States because they're mostly involved in organized leagues, and no other country in the world has as many young children formally registered in sports. Nonetheless, Snow told me, "our numbers are off the charts by European standards. You talk to the national team directors and soccer organizers overseas and they're just amazed that it got so big, so fast. If anything, we're overorganized, and that's been a good thing, because we never would have been able to keep up otherwise."

The numbers would be both a blessing and a curse, as I learned during my time among the Hornets. For one thing, the only way to meet the demand was through volunteerism on a huge scale. This opened the sluice gates for an outpouring of pent-up boomer altruism. Millions of Skywalker moms and dads became coaches and team managers and league commissioners. But the level of experience with organized athletics ran the gamut, and most of us had none at all. We were jocks and indies and geeks—not to mention "brainiacs," "preps," and "stoners"— finally come together. Our sensibilities of what youth athletics should be about couldn't have been more different. As we trucked our old conflicts onto the soccer sidelines, our hurt feelings and thwarted childhood ambitions and outsized protective urges made for volatile chemistry. Coaches in every sport spoke of the conflict, but none could explain it. Things got so bad that hockey and football parents made headlines.

Soccer has yet to produce any murders, but it does have peculiar cultural issues all its own. For one thing, the new egalitarian game turned out to be not quite as kind and gentle as many had been led to believe it would be. There would be a lot of fussing over that in the years ahead, as the funky, fresh flower-power sport revealed its rougher edges. The marketing bandwagon rolled on, nonetheless, and by the mid-nineties soccer had achieved critical mass and was headed toward pop culture fusion. Plundering the boomers' album collections, sporting-goods companies tapped into the latent memories of counterculture survivors with award-winning soccer ads featuring the music of Elvis Presley, Carlos Santana, Toots and the Maytals, Blondie, and the Sex Pistols, to name a few. The car companies weren't far behind in fusing the minivan, the soccer ball, and seventies classic rock. Football was Wagnerian opera. Baseball was fife and drums. The arm-waving conductor—the blustering coach, with his endless alignment shifts and two-hundred-page playbook—was center stage in both sports. But basketball was jazz and hip-hop, and soccer was rock and roll, at least in the boomer subconscious. In games with few time-outs, and no alternating offensive and defensive units, a coach could do only so much to exert his control over the players.

In his research for *Bowling Alone*, it is striking that Robert Putnam could find only two organized sports that showed sustained growth during the boomer coming-of-age: basketball and soccer, currently the number-one and the number-two youth-participation sports in the nation. The exhaustive longitudinal studies of the Sporting Goods Manufacturers Association bore out the trend. The ballmakers and shoemakers saw the whole thing coming, even if most of us didn't.

"If you fly across the state of Oregon on Saturday morning, every field is filled with kids playing soccer," Nike founder Phil Knight told *USA Today* in 2003, predicting that the sport would eventually cover the nation. "Someday, they're going to grow up." What Phil Knight and everyone else in the sporting-goods industry knew is that the twelve- to seventeen-year-old age cohort had ballooned by 20 percent in the decade from 1990 to 2000, and the eleven-and-under set had grown by 14 percent. That translates to 96.8 million sneakers per year. Whoever got to the boomers' babies first was going to make a fortune, and Knight wanted to be sure it was Nike. So he did the next logical thing. He signed the two biggest names in the two biggest sports to endorsement contracts and plastered their images all over every Nike outlet in the country. Michael Jordan and Mia Hamm—hoops and soccer—became Nike's first celebrity spokespeople. Gatorade jumped aboard in 1999 with one of the most memorable television commercials of the decade. With the Broadway ditty "Anything You Can Do, I Can Do Better" playing in the background, Hamm and Jordan squared off in everything from Ping-Pong to fencing—and the girl won every time.

While football coaches continued to invoke Lombardi and to talk about "turning boys into men" or "teaching them some discipline" or "handing down the legacy," the sports marketers were crafting a new message of empowerment for a skeptical consumer audience: "Just do it."

I knew none of this, of course, when my wife and I settled in our tidy three-bedroom white-brick colonial in the suburbs of Washington in 1994 and set about raising a family.

By then we had some pretty firm ideas about how to go about it—or, rather, how *not* to go about it. Both of us had lost our fathers when we were young. Both of our families had suffered the dislocation of divorce. We had wandered the country, refugees in the seventies diaspora. But we made it to our green tableau anyway, and we learned: life is fragile, families even more so, and children most of all. Teach kids early mastery of anything, and you increase their chances of surviving the rest. Encourage them to face their worst fears, to struggle, and they won't fold later when things really turn mean. Keep them moving, in rough physical contact with the world, because life is not kind to weaklings and fat people. Never has been, never will be. Call me insensitive, but I didn't invent the rule. The meek may inherit the earth, but they'll have trouble collecting the rent. Above all, don't let your kids get hit in the head, because that's where their brains are.

For us, soccer filled all the requirements. On the sidelines we met a lot of parents who had come to the same conclusion. We were late-thirty- and early-forty-somethings. Our life stories differed in the small details. Most of us had been through one rough passage or another. When our kids found soccer, we found our path.

Six families with twelve children between us, we loosely referred to ourselves as the "core group"—the die-hard heart and soul of the team. For almost four years we shared intimacies, broke bread, cared for one another's kids, and laughed over the eccentricities of our differing religious, racial, and ethnic backgrounds. We were Catholics, Protestants, Baptists, and Hindus, some of us "lapsed"; ages twenty-eight to fifty-two; African-American, Latino, Indian, and Anglo-German mutt. We would never have met were it not for the game.

There was K. C. Curry, who got ribbed relentlessly for being an accomplished downhill skier, because everyone knows that black men can't ski any more than white men can jump. Terry Hammond's West Virginia drawl and generous belly won him the title of resident redneck—the stereotypical backwoods sheriff of the team, our plainspoken sergeant at arms. I was subject to endless toxic-waste jokes and bad impressions of the "Joisey" accent. Rick Basdeo was an HVAC contractor who had emigrated from Guyana and knew better than to mention his fondness for cricket, for there is no game that Americans find quite so amusing. As for Nick Waring, well, the man was a walking library of endearing quirks: an inveterate poker player and eBay hustler, he had a bullet fragment in his belly from a childhood firearms mishap and an entrepreneur's tolerance for calculated risk. The only person exempt from the relentless ribbing was Rafael Guerrero, our gray eminence. The chief financial officer of Washington's largest food bank for the poor, he was the patriarch of an extended Salvadoran family and a board member of the local adult soccer Liga. If the Hornets had a center of gravity, it was the quietly dignified Rafael, with his limitless tolerance for the fiascos of the young and the witless.

Two years after I buried my old man out in the Jersey pines and carried off the cardboard box that contained his vital records, I ran into an old buddy I hadn't seen since my kids were little. It was Lou King, the USDA researcher and half-deaf bass player from the Mid-Life Crisis band. He was standing on a suburban soccer field in the standard uniform of a coach: ninety-dollar cleats, striped Adidas shorts, crisp poly jersey. Like me, he had played the delinquent gypsy rock-star circuit and come out the other side with an earring and the fashion sense of an outlaw. We greeted each other through the shock of mutual recognition.

"What the hell happened to us?" he gasped.

"You tell me"—I laughed—"'cause I ain't got a clue."

"They say soccer will do that to you," he ventured.

"Yeah? How so?"

"You start out thinking it's a game," Lou said, "then you find out it's about life."

6.

SOCCER WARS

A week after their victory over Greenbelt, the College Park Hornets faced archnemesis Upper Marlboro. In four previous outings, our kids had lost every time. Marlboro was the third-biggest club in the county, big enough to field two or three teams in some age groups—then promote and demote players between those teams as time went on until the best players were distilled into a "premier" squad. If this sounds a bit extreme at nine years old, it's not a surprising by-product of the boomer parents' impulse to overorganize, oversupervise, and overengineer everything in youth sports. It also tends to produce some very good soccer teams.

This time, however, the Hornets would prevail. They would catch the kids from Upper Marlboro at the bottom of a hill—down where the goal box was slickest and the corners were as sloppy as pudding. Swarming them in the muck, the blue-and-white jerseys would break over Marlboro's red ranks in waves to avenge more than three years of serial losses. It was to be our most significant win, a turning point from which there could be no retreat. The Marlboro Seven never knew what hit them, undoubtedly because they'd never faced a coherent defense before.

It had taken me forever to figure out the obvious. But by the spring of 2003, Rafael Guerrero had convinced me that I had been overthinking the game.

Lesson One: The coach who overemphasizes offense is doomed in soccer, because the essence of the game is defense. One strong kid like Malachi Alexander could beat a better team if its coach failed to protect his rear—and even an overwhelming squad like Upper Marlboro could be stopped cold by a well-laid backfield.

As Rafael put it, "To win in soccer, you must first be sure not to lose."

The point may seem obvious, but not for your average American youth coach—certainly not for me. It is a truism in soccer that no other sport so keenly reflects the cultural values of the place in which it is played, and the American mind is inextricably hardwired for the forward rush: the bayonet charge of Washington's ragged colonials at Trenton, the cavalry stabs of Grant and Lee, the alacrity of Patton and Halsey, distilled for the ages by Admiral David G. Farragut in his proclamation at Mobile Bay in 1864: "Damn the torpedoes, full speed ahead!" It is this American vanity that we celebrate every Sunday in the National Football League, which is the only game on earth that is so blatantly rigged in favor of the offense and so often revised to appeal to the dopiest conquest fantasies of its fan base.

Americans, we are taught from the earliest age, have cured more "incurable" diseases, won more "unwinnable" wars, fed more famished peoples, and done more to promote the common good than any other nation since Rome; and we did it by never admitting our limitations, or even acknowledging that we might have any. Our blind faith in offensive muscle is bred into us: we believe we can break down any problem, no matter how gnarled, and bash it into capitulation by force of will, ingenuity, or arms.

Why, then, we ask sheepishly, does soccer remain the one thing that we cannot do better than everyone else? How is it that we could subdue the greatest tyrants of the twentieth century but we cannot beat Brazil at soccer? The reason is that soccer is a defensive sport, and defense requires patience, and patience is not a virtue that the rest of the world would ever ascribe to us. We are, everywhere and always, on the offensive. In a nation that rarely questions its most cherished presumptions, soccer is an exercise in moral education precisely because it so good-naturedly defies us. Like a friend who tells us when we're wrong, it reveals the dark downside of every quality that ever made us great as a people, and this is what makes coaching the game such exquisite torture.

American youth coaches have been so thoroughly brainwashed by football that we barely know how to function in a sport that requires subtlety. Our first and only instinct, especially when the chips are down, is to charge.

For three years, I had stationed the most athletic kids on the team up front on offense in a static three-man line at midfield, with a fourth man immediately behind them in roughly the same spot in which a quarterback would stand. Thus there would be one big bruiser at the center-midfielder position who could disrupt an oncoming team and dislodge the ball; two fast wings to move it down the sidelines and fire crossing passes in front of the other team's net; and one very fast forward who would race ahead and finish the play.

Fully deployed, they took on the shape of a diamond that would expand and contract across an opponent's half of the field for forty or fifty minutes a game, coiling and lunging, conditioned to slash to the attack at every opportunity. Yes, they were just kids, but by this age boys have a killer instinct that makes piranhas seem sluggish. Take Braulio, for example. He wasn't taught to recklessly jam his stocky little frame into the tight cracks of daylight in front of the net; pure instinct drove him to do it. Teeth gritted, elbows out, forehead cranked down to protect his eyes, the kid usually got creamed, sandwiched between defenders, or chopped off at the ankles by a falling goalie, but it never discouraged him. Little Bee had more competitive piss and vinegar than any ten kids I ever met in rec-league soccer, and his appetite for destruction appeared bottomless. Whether or not he got a foot on the ball, he made opposing defenders quake every trip upfield, and he kept on coming until he got one goal per game. "Money in the bank," we called him, in addition to all his other nicknames.

Even when he missed completely, Braulio so badly distracted defenders that Ben and Kevin could usually converge from the wings and get off a flank shot on the loose ball before their opponents could react. By the age of nine, they loaded plenty of mustard on the ball, and they weren't the least concerned with whether or where it hit you. If the ball ricocheted off a goalpost or a defender's shins, Thomas Waring or Matt Shade could close in from midfield and take a crack at it, and they were pure power shooters. They weren't going to finesse their way inside. They simply lined up and teed off, and their mechanics were so rudimentary that the ball almost always rose in flight. By the time it reached the net, it was usually head-high.

Bryan Basdeo and a newcomer named Alex Corboy—a gangly stork of a kid who covered ground in four-foot increments and headed balls like a trained seal—served as our ready reserves at all four points of the diamond. They had the speed and shooting prowess to break the back of a weary adversary if we put them on the field at the right time.

Collectively, these seven kids called themselves the Cheetahs, and they developed a singular reputation as the spoilers of the division, the one group that could score on the biggest and best teams in the county. Kids from similarly sized towns like Lewisdale, Riverdale, Hyattsville, Clinton, Kettering, and Cheverly cringed at the sight of them. But here's what I couldn't fathom: for all their might, the Hornets had a mysterious habit of spluttering from time to time and losing by huge margins, for no apparent reason, against the big-dog teams.

I couldn't begin to decipher this anomaly, but in hindsight the math couldn't have been more straightforward. With two-thirds of our strength up front, our long-ignored defense was prone to crumble under pressure. In the backfield we had stationed Shelby and Linus, the brains of the operation, supported by a revolving cast of subs and scrubs: the newcomers and late bloomers; the halt and lame; the slowpokes and space cadets. As the roster continued to grow, and as the coaches continued to hide the less athletic kids in the backfield, the Hornets' defensive trio—Shelby, Linus, and Edward in the goal—were coming apart under the strain. As good as they were after more than two years of symbiotic partnership, they had trouble functioning whenever we substituted one of them with a less-skilled fill-in player. What's more, Shelby was starting to buckle from too many hard knocks.

In just one season, the boys had gotten so big and strong that she was getting beaten up in the backfield. It didn't stop her; no matter how outsized she was, she never quit, but she was spending a lot more time picking herself up off the ground during games. As her reputation grew in the county, Shelby had been turning down recruitment overtures from girls' teams for more than a year, choosing to stay with the gang she referred to as "my boys." Now she was the last female still playing in the league. Opposing teams often took her for a weak link and attacked her defensive position twice as hard, until she stripped them three or four times and planted their best players in the dirt. But the pressure was beginning to take its toll.

"We have to start watching her close, because she'll lie to stay on that field," Terry warned me. "You'd have to tear her legs off to keep her out of the game."

"What's going on?" I asked him.

"I don't know, but she's coming home black-and-blue lately, and she doesn't say anything until she takes a shower and comes out all bruised up like a banana. Her mom isn't too happy about it, I can tell you that."

Thanks to my infatuation with the offensive, the Mosquito was hitting a windshield every weekend. Worse, the Cheetahs had come to see the space in front of their own net as a backwater, an unworthy place for a star to tread. No matter how desperate the moment or how overwhelming an opposing team might be, the Hornets' front four refused to help the back three on defense. No matter how loudly we implored them from the sideline, it seemed that there was an invisible fence at midfield, and they piled up against it whenever the ball passed over. In effect, I had glamorized the front line at the expense of the rear, and Shelby was paying for it.

The alignment had also become an engine of perpetual parental grievances. Since there were only three defensive positions through which to rotate the rest of the substitutes standing on the sideline, there was no way to adequately apportion game minutes with so small a denominator—and no mother ever wanted to see her child wearing goalkeeper's gloves. "When does my kid get to score a goal?" was the constant refrain, as if I could snap my fingers and make anyone a Cheetah. By my own naive design, the only kids good enough to play up front were the superstars.

All of this may seem fairly obvious, even to a total bonehead, but spend enough time around the game and eventually you'll recognize that the stacked offensive formation is the dominant profile among U.S. youth soccer teams for the simple reason that most American coaches were weaned on football—a bastardized variant of British rugby based on archaic Franco-Germanic military principles. Unlike soccer, football is weighted in favor of the offense: there are five different ways to score; the quarterback has a personal bodyguard of between four and six blockers; it is a crime for a defender to touch him in most instances (or his receivers, or his kicker) unless he has the ball firmly in his grasp; and the field is patrolled by six or seven referees whose main job is to make sure none of the game's prima donnas are improperly molested. Whenever defensive players figure out ways to compensate for their disadvantages, whenever scores shrink or total yardage drops off, the NFL's Competition Committee changes the rules to grant new protections to the offensive players.

As a consequence, you can count the great defensive squads in the history of the NFL on one hand, and most American males of a certain age can name them all—because, unlike offensive units, heroic defenders in the NFL are so rare that we usually bestow upon them Olympian honorifics: the Minnesota Vikings' Purple People Eaters of the 1960s; Pittsburgh's Steel Curtain of a decade later; and the most famous of them all, the Chicago Bears' Monsters of the Midway, who lost only one game in 1985 before crushing three pretenders in the playoffs to take the Lombardi Trophy.

A European soccer fan could be forgiven, then, for questioning the sanity of NFL owners in continuing to shovel their largest salaries and promotional blazonry at the offensive stars of their game, especially after the Baltimore Ravens terrorized the league and won the 2000 Super Bowl with hardly any offense at all. But what Europeans fail to consider is that Americans are just as irrational about sports as we are about everything else. We can't stand to wait for anything, and the defensive game requires us to defer our gratification (often until the last minute). We're much more inclined toward the fling-and-gamble, the go-for-broke frontal assault that pays no mind to possible wreckage, because unlike real life, another chance to score comes along every few minutes in the NFL. In this tendency, however, lie the seeds of disaster for a soccer team.

The Marlboro Seven would learn this the hard way, for I now had a foreign adviser, someone who actually knew the game. Rafael Guerrero's influence would set the Hornets on a new course. Soccer, he told me after the Greenbelt match, was a "vertical game, not horizontal! Not like American football. You are teaching the kids to play it like football, and this is not how soccer works!" Defense, he explained, is the heart of the sport. "You must have the strong defense first! Every kid must play the defense all the time, up and down the field—not in lines! Not like football! And you most wait for your chance to strike!"

If soccer is war (and, trust me, it is), then the object of the sport is to trap and dismember the other guy's team before he traps and dismembers yours, and a stiff defense will get you there faster than anything else. The fact is, with the possible exception of chess, soccer is the one game that most precisely emulates the furious thrust and parry of armed forces in the field—and the tactics of warfare are the best model for understanding the game.

Lesson Two of Rafael's tutorial had to do with the environment—the weather, the terrain, the occasional presence of slop and standing water in front of the goal. Mud, as I would soon learn, is but one more legacy of soccer's longtime status as our national "orphaned" game. But the Hornets had been laboring in it for two years, on one field after another, so I failed to give it much thought. Washington, D.C., as every child learns in history class, was built on swampland. The place is well known for its drenching rains, and the region is crisscrossed by greater and lesser tributaries of the Chesapeake Bay. Mud, it seemed to me, was as much a feature of the place as cherry blossoms in spring. That it might have deeper significance never occurred to me.

"You *must* start seeing the field!" Rafael told me, leaning on a rain-dampened park bench after practice one evening two days before the Marlboro game. He put one hand on my shoulder and held his other hand level in front of his wire-frame glasses to form a parallel plane with the ground. "See the curves?"

"Yeah, you're right," I said. "It slopes all over the place, with maybe a five-degree grade from end to end."

"Like a *hill*!" he said. "The ball will run faster down this hill, and so will the rain, and at the bottom is where you will catch the other team—on the wet ground here."

"Raf," I said, "we've never beaten Upper Marlboro before."

"Ah, yes, but you will this time."

We would wear them down with defense, then attack them in the mud and roll them up like a cheap carpet. So said the oracle.

The conversation that night stirred something from the murk of my memory. The field, I thought, as I towed away my younger son's red wagon after practice. The wagon was laden with balls, flags, water bottles, and the usual pile of left-behind jackets, sweatshirts, and headbands. The ground . . . the field . . . where have I heard that before? After dinner that night, I pawed through my library at home. Shelby Foote's Civil War masterpiece, *Shiloh*. Hal Moore's Vietnam diary, *We Were Soldiers Once . . . and Young*. Barbara Tuchman's soaring World War I history, *The Guns of August*. It occurred to me, of course, that I might be losing it, that my obsession finally had reached the nanolevel. Then, there it was, in Sun Tzu's *The Art of War:* "Be before the enemy in occupying the raised and sunny spots. He who is prudent and lies in wait for an enemy who is not, will be victorious. . . . The fish which covets bait is caught."

The oldest military treatise in existence, *The Art of War* perfectly described the game of soccer. Everything Rafael had told me was reflected in the Chinese manual of arms written in 500 B.C. A slim and finely honed volume, it is antiquity's *Warfare for Dummies*, offering step-by-step instructions on how to strangle an adversary without getting yourself strangled in the process. Preaching careful planning, patience in action, and the wisdom of orderly retreat, it influenced Asian generals for two thousand years before it was translated by a Jesuit missionary and published in the West for the first time in the late eighteenth century. Among other things, *The Art of War* describes nine different types of battlegrounds and observes that troops—like water, boulders, and balls—move quickest on a downhill slope. But in the rush to heed gravity they are easily dispersed, entrapped, or depleted by a well-laid defense. Above all, Sun Tzu noted for the ages, "invincibility lies in the defense," without which any attack becomes an all-or-nothing proposition that stands to waste the lives and wealth of victor and vanquished alike. For he who fights naked fights desperately.

Thanks to Sun Tzu, as one commentator has observed, no people were ever better at "running away" and laying a defensive ambush than the Chinese. Later, a peasant army would borrow heavily from these treacherous designs to defeat the greatest military power in history. The U.S. Army and Marine Corps spent a decade chasing guerrillas from one hilltop and mountainside to the next in Vietnam, defying every edict of *The Art of War* and sacrificing fifty-eight thousand American lives and more than 3 million Vietnamese in futile prosecution of a seemingly feeble opponent whose only hope of victory lay in deception and planned retreat.

Reading over my collected war chronicles, I was tempted to

wonder whether we would have blundered so badly in Southeast Asia had soccer, instead of football, been our national sport. But then I had to face the fact that, long before football was invented, Western military thought had already been captivated by the teachings of Clausewitz and Napoleon, the megalomaniacal nineteenth-century German and French military leaders responsible for the slaughters on the Russian frontier. Their rapturous accounts of daring offensive aplomb and the tenfold destruction of their enemies were cited for more than 150 years as the principal support for the doctrine of massed frontal assault—the defining schematic of NFL football, without which the game would not exist.

To borrow a term from the soccer elders, football is "episodic," a game played as a series of skirmishes between two horizontally arrayed forces under the immediate control of a sideline general, while soccer is much more like modern warfare—a rapidly and continually unfolding "situational" conflict with no true front or rear. The soldiers on the field make most of the decisions; attack and counterattack, feint and strike are blended together; and the outcome is determined largely through individual contests on the periphery. The team that runs the most, the team that plays with a thin defense, the team that depends on its commanding officer for tactical directions—rather than on its sergeants in the field— will usually lose.

The U.S. military came away from Vietnam with a new appreciation for "indirect" warfare and defensive maneuver, culminating in the 1991 rout of the entrenched Iraqi Army in the Persian Gulf War. H. Norman Schwarzkopf was not the first American general to study Sun Tzu, but he was the first Western military leader to win a major land campaign without getting half his boys killed—and that singular accomplishment has made *The Art of War* one of the most widely quoted texts in U.S. military circles ever since. For whatever technological advantages

Schwarzkopf enjoyed over his Iraqi counterparts, he won the main battle through defense, deceit, and envelopment before he ever fired a shot. In other words, he played soccer instead of football.

For Rafael Guerrero, these lessons were more than mere abstractions. They were the very gears of his native game, if not a matter of life and death. In one of the most terrible episodes of his younger years—the disastrous 1969 border clash between El Salvador and Honduras—two of the most impoverished nations in Central America lunged into a bloody, destabilizing frontal war that played no small part in his eventual decision to emigrate to the United States. History records the event as the Soccer War.

In the summer of that year, an overly rough series of World Cup qualifying games between the neighboring countries led to violence in the grandstands and rioting in the streets, which quickly ignited decades of pent-up nationalistic paranoia on both sides. Within a week of the Cup qualifier, Honduras began to forcibly expel more than a hundred thousand Salvadoran farmworkers from its plantations. In retaliation, U.S.-trained Salvadoran generals—who had drunk a bit too deeply of Clausewitz's theorems on military diplomacy at the Pentagon's School of the Americas—launched a headlong frontal assault into Honduras that bogged down in the muddy jungle five miles inside the border. Honduras counterattacked with its poorly trained and outnumbered army, supported by a crude collection of World War II surplus artillery and a handful of Piper Cherokees jerry-rigged as bombers. To save its troops from annihilation, El Salvador launched its own meager flock of cast-off U.S.-made P-52 Mustangs. Leaking oil and trailing smoke, the ragged air forces shot each other to pieces in less than three days of dogfights over each other's capital.

"I woke up to hear buppa-buppa-bup!" Rafael told me one night. "And when I go outside they are shooting at each other in the sky—yes, right over my house. This is how soccer is in my country. You watch soccer, your emotions run away, like a fever. You cannot think straight. You are jumping up and down and yelling. You cannot catch your breath."

As in war, the offensive aspects of soccer require tremendous exertions of energy that deplete the attacking team. No matter how superior a squad may be, sustaining the offensive requires it to run more and to run farther. Once its energy fades late in the game, it begins to bog down and become vulnerable. An inferior opponent with vigor on its side can then overrun and destroy it. As the great Dutch master Johan Cruyff put it, nothing worried him so much after he became a coach than to see his players running too much.

The Central American Soccer War lasted four days, killed four thousand people, left uncounted more homeless and destitute, damaged the main airports and oil refineries of both countries, plunged their economies into ruin, shattered a trade pact that bound five poor Central American nations together, and drove tens of thousands of Latino émigrés north. More than 4 million Salvadoran, Guatemalan, and Honduran immigrants now live in the United States, most of them concentrated in four major urban centers, including Washington, D.C.—which is how Kevin Guerrero and Braulio Linares wound up playing soccer with the College Park Hornets, and how I was befriended by an accountant from San Salvador who set out to save me from my worst instincts.

"Few things happen in Latin America that do not have some relation with soccer," Eduardo Galeano, the Uruguayan poet and soccer commentator, once wrote. Military units, miners' unions, factory workers, even drug lords all have their own teams. Class tensions are built into the game, and teams with government or corporate backing enjoy certain undeniable advantages. Defense is the great leveler. Unlike American football, in which the number of defensive players is prescribed by the rules, soccer allows the players on the field to occupy any combination of positions that a situation might require. So an eleven-man team of campesinos might conceivably forgo the offensive altogether and play every man back on defense to stifle a muscular military squad, for example.

Thus do the passions unleashed by the game far exceed what meets the eye of the untrained observer. In some places—like Guyana, the tiny coastal nation on Brazil's northern border where Bryan Basdeo's father grew up—kids might also play a little cricket. But soccer is the only true mass sport south of Texas, which is why the world's largest arenas are in Latin America. The biggest of them all, the biggest on earth, is Maracana Stadium in Rio. It is said to contain enough steel to circle the globe twice, girding a bowl big enough to hold two hundred thousand spectators and a field surrounded by a defensive moat to keep them away from the players and the referees. Every spectator in any two of the largest football stadiums in the United States would fit inside it, with enough room left over for all the fans in a sold-out Major League Baseball game. The cheapest seats in the place are a quarter mile from the field, so vast is the vessel and so deep are the emotions conjured by the game.

American soccerheads have become so desperate for decent playing surfaces that the U.S. Soccer Foundation has forged partnerships with the Army Corps of Engineers and the Environmental Protection Agency to turn abandoned "brownfield" industrial sites into usable soccer venues—and a subsector of the U.S. construction industry has retooled itself to shape the existing swampscape into something less resembling a hog wallow. Cannon Designs of Washington, D.C., which now concentrates 30 percent of its architectural work on sports facilities, has gone so far as to perfect a drainage system that allows the construction of soccer fields on rooftops and parking decks at land-starved schools. But muck remains the defining feature of youth soccer in America.

It is the seldom-noticed variable that so often dooms the best-laid plans of a youth coach hell-bent on Napoleonic attack. The ground is often terrible; marginal land marked off for decades on county and municipal planning maps as unsuitable for anything but draining storm water, walking dogs, or grazing sheep. It is the land that remained after the public-works building boom of President Franklin D. Roosevelt's New Deal, the rocky soils and sloping riverside floodplains that the football and baseball people didn't want.

"That's what soccer fields in this country traditionally have been," explains Ray Rudolph, a civil engineer for Clough Harbour and Associates in Albany, New York, who now makes his living rescuing the sport from the mud. "It was all this leftover land that no other sport wanted, where people threw down some stripes and put up some goals and declared it a field. But every time it rains the kids are out there in a bog with mosquitoes buzzing around their heads, and the town fathers never seem to notice until it becomes a political issue. We go into some places and there's almost seven feet of elevation difference from one end of the field to the other, or four feet from sideline to sideline, and a lot of the fields are oriented east and west, so the kids are practically going blind running into the sun. I've been to some places where the conditions are so bad it's amazing they don't just quit the sport."

In three hours with Rudolph, whose engineering feats across

four states include two artificial fields at the U.S. Military Academy in West Point, my head throbs as I listen to the technical descriptions of his work: integrated sand and soil "root zones" to keep grass from rotting; "pea-stone" drainage beds to hold migrating dirt in place; underground piping systems and grading designs to coax water from its natural resting places; crossbred grasses that can survive the blights and pests that congregate in spongy places. A basic rehabilitation package can be had for as little as eight thousand dollars, depending on the size of the field, but the work seldom gets done without a fight, Rudolph noted, because few municipalities want to spend money improving something that they've thought of as wasteland for a hundred years—and entrenched boosters of other sports tend to wield much more influence in local government than the soccerheads.

"Football was king in this country for a great many years, so those fields, all across the country, pretty consistently have a crown [a raised ridge] running right down the middle from end zone to end zone," Rudolph says. "They drain beautifully. They're all one elevation. They're well maintained—fertilized, mowed, watered, and so on—and all of that costs money to keep up. So you get this built-in tension at the local level because, obviously, the dollars available are finite. Where you usually see decent soccer fields, it's either in new subdivisions or places where the soccer people have gotten the critical mass to raise a political stink. You can get these things done a lot better and a lot cheaper, because of the economies of scale, when the various constituencies get together and lobby for a multiuse facility. But that's not how these things usually go for some reason."

Case in point: the Maryland SoccerPlex outside Washington, D.C. Opposed by local Little League baseball advocates who charged that the $22 million project would gobble up future construction funds, the soccerheads packed government board meetings and public hearings in a county where they outnumber the baseballers by a two to one margin. They also enlisted business sponsors who stood to gain from the project. Today, most hotels within a ten-mile radius tout their proximity to the "Plex" in hopes of drawing in tournament visitors, who are responsible for about eighty-five cents of every dollar generated at the facility—or $1.9 million of the SoccerPlex's annual revenue take.

It didn't hurt backers of the Maryland project that their efforts came during an election year. A Democratic state governor running for reelection in a Democratically controlled county with 50,000 registered soccer parents was quick to pledge $4 million in state funds toward the soccerheads' plan to build 23 soccer fields, a 66,000-square-foot indoor soccer arena, and a 3,200-seat soccer stadium on 162 acres of exhausted farmland—which only made the baseball fanatics howl all the louder. "I've talked to people all over the country who are building similar complexes— dozens of them—and I tell them everything we learned here, and one of those things is to expect resistance," said Trish Heffelfinger, who heads the facility. "You've got to plan on things getting ugly."

A former public relations agent turned soccer mom, then team manager, Heffelfinger's congenial advocacy won her the nickname the Ninety-Pound Neutron Bomb among the baseball protesters. For behind the smiling, open face and beneath the blond flip hairdo churned the mind of a Chinese field marshal. "We were so naive at the beginning," Heffelfinger told me. "We all thought, Who could possibly have any objection to this? There was exactly one dedicated soccer field in the entire county, probably in the entire Maryland suburbs, that had lights. Baseball had plenty of dedicated fields. Nicely lit fields, right? Football goes without saying, right? You can't drive five miles around here without seeing a football field. But as soon as we unveiled our plan they came out of the woodwork. We had to fight every inch of the way."

After a brief tactical retreat, backers of the project—including five youth soccer clubs and John Hendricks, founder and CEO of the Discovery Channel—agreed to a "peace tax": they would plant a thousand trees on the site, make room for four new baseball diamonds, install drop-down basketball rims in the arena, encircle the complex with a walking trail, and add a public water park. These and other unforeseen costs, not least of which was the need to truck in tons of topsoil when the fallow farmland proved too depleted to grow grass, put the SoccerPlex about $1 million in debt before the facility ever opened. Those overages are now being paid down through increased user fees to youth soccer teams.

To behold the SoccerPlex for the first time is to appreciate the breadth and permanence of the gains won in the revolution. The complex is carved into a hilltop, with the arena and the stadium at its peak and trellised fields gently cascading down all sides, each occupying its own sculpted plateau. It is so huge that it is impossible to photograph except by helicopter. Upon first sight, I thought of illustrations I had seen of ancient Mayan gardens. Such are the lengths that the soccerheads are willing to go to secure their civilization. The generation of parents that turned child-safety doohickeys and baby fashions and educational toys into an industry worth more than $5 billion is now using earthmovers to carve out play space for its children, because other boomer parents don't want to share theirs.

Still, Heffelfinger points out, "We've barely put a dent in the overall demand. If you look at the District and at the rest of the suburban counties, the inventory of available fields is way below the level of demand, because there's no land left. Good luck getting a decent field on the weekends around here, and what fields we do have are being ruined by overuse. In some places, it's nothing but mud."

Consider Calvert Hills Park, the Hornets' home field—a former creek bed that had been filled in for a schoolyard that doubled as a dog park before it was fashioned into a makeshift soccer field. It is the morning of Saturday, March 22, 2003, and the annual spring rains in the mid-Atlantic have been soaking the ground for a couple of weeks, reducing it to twenty-seven hundred square yards of mush. On the downhill side, where the drainage grate sits just behind the goal box, the mud has the consistency of peanut butter. In Sun Tzu's system of classification, it is "difficult ground."

"Coach!" Braulio yells as the kids are warming up shortly before game time against Upper Marlboro. "Bryan just fell in doggy doo!"

"Tell him to wipe it off and get back in the game," I say.

"Yeah, man, it's fertilizer," Terry adds. "It'll help him grow."

As Rafael Guerrero had foreseen, the conditions were ideal for an ambush.

Taking my guru's advice, I had restructured the team over the course of two practices. I appointed Bryan our new defensive captain. Shelby and Braulio were to split time at forward. Ben and Alex would share goalie duties with Edward, and the Rhino would play a new position that we liked to call destroyer-mid.

The new-look Hornets were set to "go on the defensive" for the first time. Upper Marlboro was about to meet its Waterloo, and nothing would be the same after that.

7.

TEXTILE DAYS

WE ALWAYS HAD A GAME

I'm sitting in a corner bar on a blustery October night, drinking a frothing black pint of Guinness stout at the tail end of a three-day road trip—one more leg of my apostolic journey into the Soccerhead Way. I am by now hopelessly obsessed, touring the seaboard with a duffel bag full of clothes, a shaving kit, and balled-up sandwich wrappers on the floor of my car, sleeping in roadside motels with names like the Valu-Inn. My wife isn't threatening divorce, but she is concerned about my mental state: "Do you realize that all you ever talk about anymore is soccer?"

I've been out Route 88 in southeastern New York to the National Soccer Hall of Fame, then north to Albany to check out a new youth soccer complex (because New York is building them almost as fast as Virginia and California), back down Route 87, then south on Route 17 where the state line crosses into New Jersey at the town of Mahwah. I've been searching the postindustrial ruins of North Jersey for the remains of a fabled lost civilization, the ancient homeland of the soccerheads.

Past Ramsey, Paterson, Paramus, and Passaic; Teaneck, Hasbrouck Heights, and Lodi. Past the boarded shells of countless redbrick factories and tumbledown warehouses, the skeletal frames of abandoned cranes and burned-out trucks and unidentifiable, vine-covered machinery. I've been thumping over the rusted tracks of long-silent rail lines, Springsteen droning "My Hometown" on the tape deck:

> They're closing down the textile mill across the railroad tracks
> Foreman says these jobs are going, boys, and they ain't coming
> back.

Down and down, to a scruffy little town of forty thousand where the Passaic and Hackensack Rivers empty into the Hudson—to Kearny, New Jersey. This town is a legend in the unwritten annals of American soccer; so is this bar. They call it the Scots-American Club. It's a narrow little room, with a dirty linoleum floor underfoot, a nicotine-stained ceiling overhead, and fading photos of soccer players lining the walls. Billy Gonsalves, "the Babe Ruth of soccer," tended bar here in the last days of his life, working these very taps until he passed away.

In the far corner, guys from the loading docks at Port Newark are engaged in a noisy game of darts, while along the front some old-timers play shuffleboard on a table that's almost as long as the bar, sliding metal pucks down the polished pine and trading good-natured oaths in thick Scottish brogues. Next to an autographed picture of Sean Connery, above the table, is a poster inscribed with the legend "There are two kinds of people in the world—Scotsmen and those who wish they were Scotsmen." Bolted to the ceiling at either end of the room, two televisions wired to satellite dishes on the roof are showing soccer games— live, from Scotland.

This is probably the oldest continuously operated soccer club in the United States, and it's here because Kearny once boasted one of the greatest teams of all—the ONT, whose acronym stood for Our New Thread. The team dominated American soccer from 1885 to 1909. It was sponsored by Clark Thread Mills, a Scottish textile company that set up shop in Kearny in the 1860s, hiring immigrant men, women, and children by the thousands to tend its rows of looms and spindles in backbreaking twelve-hour shifts. Built with the solidity of a prison and laid out around a central courtyard, the mill complex now stands nearly empty, but it still takes up two city blocks. Within its weathered walls are one million square feet of workspace, forty outlying structures, and a rail depot. At sunset, the aging hulk casts a shadow over three blocks of working-class row house neighborhoods in south Kearny that have housed immigrant newcomers for more than a century. Today, they are Latino. A hundred years ago, they were Irish and Scots.

It was the Scots and Irish who brought soccer to these parts of New Jersey. "Aye," says Eddie Reid, white-haired and rail-thin in a spotless white shirt and a green tartan tie. "If you came looking for soccer, you came to the right place."

They still call the town parks "ovals" here, a term brought over from the Old Country and engrained into popular usage over ten generations. They were called ovals because of the shape the soccer fields took, and because any open park space in the congested city centers of London or Glasgow or Dublin was turned into a soccer field before long. So it was, too, in North Jersey at the turn of the twentieth century.

"If you were here on a Sunday back then, you would have seen the lads playing football—what you call soccer today—on every open field," recounts Jake Bradley, president of the Scots-American Club. "Soccer and maybe a little baseball, because that's all there was. The games started at sunup, and they ran all day, until long after dark. You might not always have enough to eat, aye, but you always had a game. You always had a ball. And sometimes not much of a ball."

To understand the history of soccer in America, you have to know a little about the history of the American textile industry, because soccer followed textiles the way a wagon follows a horse, and if the horse's ass walked off a cliff, as my Irish grandfather liked to say, the wagon couldn't be far behind.

For most of the nineteenth century, and into the twentieth, the East Coast was dependent upon this one industry, textiles. From New Hampshire, down to Lowell, Massachusetts, and Pawtucket, Rhode Island, on down the coast through Newark, Philadelphia, and Baltimore, big textile reigned supreme. The work was brutal and conditions were medieval: if you weren't maimed in the looms, brown lung, TB, or other respiratory diseases were bound to get you eventually. But if your feet were fine and disease didn't knock you down you could advance on the mill floor, because almost every textile company in the United States sponsored its own soccer team, or, at least, supplied local teams with a recruitment pool and a fan base.

These teams were paragons of the game. The richer of them played on company-built fields, traveled on company expense accounts, contended in international matches, and recruited prime players from top European clubs like Manchester United. They were the public face and ambassadorial emblem of the profit-grubbing mill barons. But they also managed to spawn dozens of regional professional leagues, and to foster an appreciation for the game that would survive the rough decades ahead when soccer all but vaporized across most of the country.

The mill teams became internationally known, and then disappeared without a trace. The first wave of disappearances came in the second half of the nineteenth century, when labor disputes drove some companies south into the Carolinas and Georgia, where a destitute rural workforce would do anything for a dollar. Then came the Depression, which was a massive blow to the textile industry from north to south. In relatively short order, redbrick mills from New Hampshire to Kearny, New Jersey, and beyond were shut down. The workers were strewn along the coast, forced to take jobs wherever they could find them. And their soccer teams dissolved. The Fall River Marksmen, who hailed from a tiny shirt-making town on the south coast of Massachusetts, had won the national title three times between 1924 and 1930 when the Crash unraveled them. As they went, so, too, did the JandP Coates thread team of Rhode Island and a host of perennial contenders from New Jersey's West Hudson textile region, including the Paterson Silk Sox and Paterson True Blues. And their fields closed with them.

Among the last to go was an acre of stony, hard-packed earth in Union, New Jersey. The scene of raucous matches between visiting European clubs and local teams made up of immigrant factory hands, it was dug up in 1998 for the foundation of a tool company. By then, it had been a weed lot for years. Known as Farcher's Grove, after the farmer who once owned it, the oval was visited over the years by the Glasgow Rangers and by Germany's famed Eintracht Frankfurt team, among others.

"Even in its best days, the field was horrible," recalls Joe Letters, who is now sixty-eight, an immigrant from Scotland who played for Rutgers University some fifty years ago. "It was strewn with rocks and had very little grass. You had to be tough to play there, but it was the best-known soccer venue in this part of the country for decades. It says a lot about the quality of those early working-class teams that some of the top clubs in the world came here to play—not that many people today remember any of it."

"You never left a match at Farcher's without a souvenir," says Jake Bradley, seventy-six. "A knot on your head or a few stitches, or a nail in your leg." He rolls up his pant cuff to reveal scars raking down his calf. "You didn't have these fancy plastic cleats back then," he continues. "You played with nails in the soles of your shoes. Like upholstery tacks, right? And sometimes they came out. So there was a fair bit of that mixed in the dirt at Farcher's. Aye, it was brutal. And glorious."

With the loss of their sponsors, players from these early teams were set adrift in the Depression era to ply their trade where they could. And the only place in America where a man could still earn a dollar playing soccer was in social clubs. Formed entirely along ethnic lines, these clubs dotted the landscape throughout the Northeast and the Midwest. In major cities there might be a half dozen or more, one for every sizable immigrant community—and each club sponsored soccer teams. Chicago, Boston, New York, and Philadelphia all had a German-American Club, a Polish-American Club, an Italian-American Club, and a Ukrainian-American Club. Jewish Hakoah organizations, part of a nineteenth-century Viennese fitness movement dedicated to building a "muscular Jewry," sprang up in New York and beyond. Meanwhile, Pittsburgh, home to Bethlehem Steel, saw a flourishing of German fraternal clubs formed along class lines. And the Ancient Order of Hibernians, an Irish-Catholic defense league born amid the Protestant persecutions of fifteenth-century England and transplanted to America in the 1830s to protect Irish workers, was everywhere. By the Depression, there were hundreds of Hibernian clubs in more than forty states.

Hubs of immigrant economic life, the ethnic clubs acted as banks, job-placement offices, day-care centers, and ad hoc schools. But their principle function was social. They typically featured a tavern, beer garden, or banquet hall; a park or grove; at least one soccer field; and two or three teams of graduating skill that played in professional and amateur leagues as far west as St. Louis and as far north as Chicago.

"The club was where they held your christening and your wedding reception—and where they laid you out for your wake," recounts George Brown, the Hall of Fame forward from Connecticut who played for ethnic clubs across New England before rising to prominence in the 1950s as a standout striker with the Polish-American Falcons of Elizabeth, New Jersey. "And the club was where you went on Sundays after the games. Soccer was the glue that held everything else together."

What the clubs did not usually have was a youth division—not, that is, until the abolition of child labor. By 1896, one-quarter of the textile workers of North Carolina were younger than sixteen. In 1903, Irish labor activist Mother Jones counted ten thousand children working in the carpet factories of Philadelphia, "some with their hands off, some with the thumb missing, some with their fingers off at the knuckle," she later wrote in her memoirs. "Philadelphia's mansions were built on the broken bones, the quivering hearts and drooping heads of these children," she declared. Nine years later, when workers in Lawrence, Massachusetts, rose up in protest against brutal working conditions, one account noted that half the city's population between the ages of fourteen and eighteen worked in the mills, usually in twelve-hour shifts.

H. L. Mencken, a columnist for *The Baltimore Sun* and perhaps the most influential commentator of his day, described these young workers as "a people broken to the yoke" and remarked on the duplicity of the government in launching public schools while doing little or nothing to free kids from their labors. "Baltimore city, though it is growing poorer every day, continues to erect gaudy palaces for the education of its future factory hands," Mencken acidly observed in 1932. "[And] to teach them soccer."

It wasn't until 1938 that the federal Fair Labor Standards Act finally outlawed child labor nationwide, putting an end to what the historian David M. Kennedy called "the human wreckage of a century of pell-mell, buccaneering, no-holds-barred free market industrial and agricultural capitalism."

"It probably wouldn't occur to most people today, but the child-labor laws had a huge impact on the growth of sports in this country, particularly soccer and baseball," Len Oliver had told me in his attic belfry in Washington, D.C. As states, and ultimately the federal government, began to ban the exploitation of kids in the mills, children poured onto neighborhood streets. Christian charitable organizations like the Salvation Army and the YMCA began offering athletic programs for newly idled youngsters to keep them from a life of delinquency—or, in the words of one Police Athletic League brochure, "to positively vent their aggressions and energy through sports." The ethnic clubs kicked into action, too, and started to form youth teams.

Baseball, firmly established by then as the only true mass sport in America, was the immediate beneficiary of the youth athletics movement. Football was still largely a college game; inconceivable as it sounds today, more fans clamored for tickets to major soccer meets at such venues as the Polo Grounds in New York City than they did for games of the fledgling National Football League. Crowds of up to twenty-five thousand were not uncommon at bigger soccer matches, particularly when powerhouse clubs like Bayern, Glasgow, and Manchester United were in town. But baseball was still the only sport that was sufficiently established to tout itself as an American game for American kids, and it exploded in popularity in the years after the Great Depression.

"There was so much hostility toward immigrants that ethnic parents started steering their kids away from the old traditions of their homeland—and that included soccer," said Oliver, who has written extensively about the labor movement and the early years of U.S. soccer. "Baseball was seen as the more American sport, and soccer was part of the old cultural baggage that got thrown overboard on the way to Ellis Island. Immigrants continued to play the game within their ethnic enclaves, but they encouraged their kids to play baseball to become more Americanized."

In the decrepit textile districts of the Northeast, however, soccer was cemented in place, nearly as permanent as the bricks and mortar of the mill houses themselves. "They couldn't even spell 'soccer' in most of Philadelphia," laughs Walter Bahr, the son of an immigrant German family. "But in Kensington you barely knew there was any other game. We played baseball, sure, everybody played baseball—and some basketball, which was just coming into vogue back then. And some of the tougher kids took up boxing. But soccer was the main thing."

Here, where Mother Jones scandalized the textile industry by parading amputee children before the press, the wife of a prominent attorney established a youth athletics hall called the Lighthouse Boys Club in an abandoned hospital. Set down amid the mill blocks and congested row house neighborhoods of North Philadelphia, the club served up to five hundred meals a day. It featured a three-story clubhouse and a seventeen-acre tract of woodland, out of which eventually was carved three regulation soccer fields that would become famous across four states for having actual grass growing on them.

"Let me tell you, it was a heady experience to be playing for Lighthouse back then," recalled Oliver, who followed Bahr into the club. "You really knew you were something—or you thought you were, anyway—and that was a pretty big deal for a kid growing up in a place like that."

By 1950, thirteen thousand Irish, German, and Scottish boys had passed through the Lighthouse, a virtual army of soccer players, catapulting Philadelphia to national fame by winning no fewer than sixteen league titles from 1935 to 1964.

Up the road in Kearny, the Scots-American Club was performing a similar service for displaced workers from the moribund Clark Thread plant. Uncounted thousands of kids who were saved from their parents' fate in the mills played soccer for the club and enjoyed a cross-border rivalry with the Lighthouse gang from Philly that lasted thirty years. Teams emanating from the two-story stone-front tavern on Highland Avenue won five consecutive national titles between 1937 and 1941. To this day, the club still fields squads that contend for national amateur crowns.

It's easy to see the influence of big textile on American soccer. All you have to do is study the list of national youth soccer championships, from 1935 to today. Now known as the James P. McGuire Cup (for one of the game's early benefactors), the title was won by the Lighthouse Boys Club five times between 1938 and 1967. Teams from New Jersey have won six times. Church teams from the predominantly Irish-Catholic parishes of St. Louis have won seven times. Not until 1961 did a West Coast club secure the crown, and it was the San Francisco Hakoah team. Likewise, half the teams that have ever competed for the U.S. Open Cup—the national championship game inaugurated in 1914—have come from a handful of eastern states that are former textile hubs.

Study the rosters of players representing the United States on Olympic and World Cup soccer teams: most of the players hailed from the old mill towns of Pawtucket, Fall River, West Hudson, and Kensington, or from Pittsburgh and Baltimore, which boasted the old steel league, or from the parishes of St. Louis. Only in recent decades have players from elsewhere in the United States begun to qualify.

"If you just look up the names of the Lighthouse kids alone, there's probably twenty of them in the Soccer Hall of Fame," says Oliver. "And you could probably say the same thing for the clubs from Kearny and Fall River and St. Louis. It's pretty amazing when you think about it all these years later, that these urban philanthropic organizations for wayward ethnic boys could have such a profound impact. But if you weren't from one of those incubator cities you could pretty much forget about making those early World Cup and Olympic teams. Because those are the places where the traditions of the game never died. Years after the early industry leagues and textile teams broke up—for decades after the Great Depression—you still had the old-timers hanging around in those places. So that's where the expertise was. It got handed down, from one generation to the next, and it never went away."

Nearly a century after the Clark Thread Mill closed down in Kearny, kids are still playing soccer on Gunnell Oval, down by the auto-salvage yard, across the Jersey meadowlands from Manhattan. When I drove by the old field that October afternoon, coach Marcus Dagna was preparing to put his nine-year-old girls' team through its regular Wednesday practice. A couple of hundred kids in shin guards formed sides on eight adjoining fields. A computer technician and former semiprofessional goalkeeper from Brazil, Dagna moved to New York in 1994, then migrated across the Hudson River a year later.

"When I got here from Brazil, I already knew that Kearny was the place to be," he told me. "I read about Kearny in a newspaper in Brazil, about everything that happened here. There is a lot of history. And I believe before the year 2020, the U.S. is going to be the world champions because of everything you see here—the organization, these fields, the history. Soccer has been here forever." He recites the names of famous U.S. players who have run on this oval—such modern heroes of the National Team as midfielders Tab Ramos and Johnny Harkes and goalkeeper Tony Meola, and, of course, the Portuguese Bomber, Gonsalves. All of them put down roots in this hardscrabble textile town.

"The soccer history here goes back just as far as it does in Brazil or Spain," Dagna says. "So I hear some people say soccer is not an American game, and I think to myself, What is this? They don't know about this place? Kearny, the Soccer City, in New Jersey, the Soccer State? People in Brazil know about this place. So I think it is good that people in the U.S. are starting to remember."

What the people of Brazil are most likely to remember is the Shot—the shot that came on June 29, 1950, in the Brazilian mining town of Belo Horizonte, five hundred rock-strewn miles from Rio de Janeiro. Belo Horizonte was host city to the impending World Cup Games, and it was the first time the English had agreed to participate in the international soccer championship. As the Uruguayan writer Eduardo Galeano says in his book *Soccer in Sun and Shadow*, "The English had considered such skirmishes beneath them." Not without justification. England's National Team had never lost a game on its home soil; they had recently beaten Italy 4–0 and pulverized Portugal 10–0. Its defense was thought to be impenetrable, and it had no fewer than five players on its roster who were universally regarded as among the best in the world.

Still, the team had agreed to play, and this was a preliminary match between a poorly trained, hastily formed U.S. National Team and the haughty English. Led by Tom Finney and Alf Ramsey, both of whom would later be knighted for their soccer conquests on behalf of the Union Jack, the English expected to brush the Americans off on their way to the Cup finals in Rio's spectacular new Maracana Stadium. So confident were they that they left their fearsome forward, Stanley Matthews, back at the hotel to rest up for the anticipated championship rounds to come. Thirty-seven minutes into the game, they wished they hadn't.

The Shot came from slightly right of center, off the foot of a gym teacher from Philadelphia, rocketed some twenty-six yards, then skipped off the head of a dishwasher from New York City, ricocheted past the goalkeeper, and waxed the upper-right corner of the net. For the next fifty-three minutes, the English team—lionized pros who made relatively handsome salaries in the game back home—threw themselves at the Americans, only to be stuffed by a U.S. defense anchored by a mailman and a funeral chauffeur, both from St. Louis. Among others on the team were a cannery line worker, a brickyard laborer, an office clerk, a carpenter, a truck driver, and a loom mechanic from Fall River, Massachusetts.

Two of the better-known U.S. soccer standouts who might have played for the team that day—dribbling wizard Benny McLaughlin from Philly and the bruising goalkeeper Gene Olaff of Bayonne, New Jersey—missed the plane because they couldn't get off from work. McLaughlin was employed by a water-meter company. Olaff had been sworn in as a New Jersey state trooper after his discharge from the Navy four years earlier. Both had worn out their bosses with pleas for time off to play soccer. "Times were different then," Walter Bahr told me. "The country was just coming out of a war, the Depression, jobs were hard to find, so you didn't take that lightly. It wasn't an option to just quit and go play soccer, especially for the guys who had families, because there wasn't any money in U.S. soccer then—not enough, anyway."

It was Bahr, the former Lighthouse Boys Club wunderkind, who took the Shot. It came on a throw-in from out-of-bounds. As he moved up from midfield to receive the ball, he saw a small gap opening in the English defense to his left. Bahr dribbled a few more yards, stalling for two or three heartbeats, then fired a cross-field tracer that appeared to be headed for the far post. Just as the English goalie started moving that way, however, New York dishwasher Joe Gaetjens dove and got enough of his head on the ball to deflect it into the net.

Ecstatic Brazilians mobbed the Americans. They had done the

impossible. They had pulled off the greatest upset in World Cup history, if not in the entire history of the game, sweeping away the single greatest threat to the host country's chances of winning the Cup.

"There was a big, high fence separating the audience from the field, and they went up and over it like it was nothing," midfielder and retired loom mechanic John "Clarkie" Souza told me, the light of that moment still glimmering in his eighty-three-year-old eyes. "They grabbed us like they were going to kill us, then started kissing us and carrying on, and it didn't stop there. They carried us to the clubhouse and threw us a big banquet that night, like we were national heroes."

England's fall registered in four-column headlines from Rio to Newcastle, where it was considered nothing less than a national catastrophe. *The Daily Herald* of London printed a black-bordered funeral announcement on the front page that read, "In affectionate remembrance of English football, which died at Rio." But in America the event was barely noticed. *The New York Times* covered it in a brief at the back of the sports section, wedged between a tennis match and an amateur golf tournament.

The English had committed soccer's cardinal sin in underestimating an inferior opponent. Five decades later, they were still making excuses. Bahr's unchallenged shot was a "fluke," said English fullback Laurie Hughes. Joe Gaetjens's diving header was either luck or the work of the devil. The field was rutted. The dressing rooms were shabby. The referees let the St. Louis boys commit mayhem in the box. Nonetheless, English halfback and team captain Billy Wright acknowledged to the London *Daily Mail* in 1993, "We lost, history was made and they will never let us forget it." Neither team survived its subsequent qualifying games, and both were knocked out of Cup contention early. But while the English squad was greeted by sobbing well-wishers upon their return to London, the Americans were met at the airport by their wives and drove home to get some shut-eye before going back to work in the morning. "It was just like any other day," Bahr recalls.

Walter Bahr, now seventy-seven, looks back on the early days, when the first generation of homegrown soccerheads came surging out of the old ethnic clubs. "We used to joke that we might be famous in fifty years for what we did back then," he says, riffling through a dented filing cabinet stuffed full of mementos in the garage of a converted stone farmhouse in upstate Pennsylvania. With a head like a Howitzer shell, he is still powerfully built. He has shoulders a yard wide and forearms thick as bowling pins, and he still walks like a soccer player: erect, slightly forward on the balls of his feet, the barrel of his torso rotating at the hips like a tank turret. He pulls out piles of crumbling, yellowed clippings from newspapers worldwide, and lines up the front-page banner headlines. Half a century later, the game is still recalled as one of the greatest upsets in World Cup history.

A grin works its way through the creases of his gnomic face. "We were already famous around the world," he says. "They say grown men are still crying in their beer in England over what we did to them in 1950. But here, nobody noticed." Soccer in America was very nearly dead, its heartbeat reduced to a murmur in the row house neighborhoods of the old textile wards and steel towns.

8.

THE GAME GOES BLACK

NOT READY FOR PRIME TIME

When Walter Bahr agreed to meet with me, I dropped everything, threw an armload of clothes and a tape recorder into the trunk of my car, and drove five hours through an ice storm for my audience in Boalsburg, Pennsylvania. It was Bahr's single, goal-scoring, odds-defying shot that marked the apex of U.S. soccer just before it sank into near-oblivion. If anyone could tell me how and why soccer declined so quickly, surely it was Bahr.

Traveling up through the dirty, dynamited foothills of the Pennsylvania coal country, I was apprehensive. Shale outcroppings hung overhead in frozen slabs. Passenger cars spun off the glazed two-lane road, swatted by Appalachian winds and the backdraft of tractor-trailers. But death by falling rocks or rolling steel wasn't among the things that preoccupied me.

Hard to believe, I thought to myself, but long before Penn State Coach Joe Paterno turned these hard mountains into a wellspring of college football talent, this was soccer country, the home grounds of immigrant miners and mill workers who knew nothing but the rounder ball. For weeks I had been asking experts the same question over and over: How do you reconcile the vibrant early history of soccer in America with its sudden decline? The game, it seemed, had all but gone extinct in a camera frame of time. Sure, the Depression had taken a toll. So had the anti-immigrant convulsions of the early twentieth century and the conniving of professional baseball's would-be monopolists. But we're talking about the retreat of an entire subculture here. How did the game just disappear? How did America go from embracing soccer as its second most popular pastime to "a country that usually yawns at the game," as *Time* magazine put it in 1950?

The old-timers pointed out that soccer still held its own on college campuses and in ethnic social clubs during this time, but in the age of electronic reality a thing that didn't exist on TV may as well not exist at all, and that was a good description of soccer. Reading the meager accounts of the legendary game in Belo Horizonte, Brazil, in the U.S. press, I could only imagine the bitter disappointment the players must have felt. How it must have rankled them to be so ignored in their finest hour. In the debate over the top ten goals of all time (an inexhaustible staple of pub arguments from Montevideo to Moscow), Walter Bahr's shot is almost always included for its sheer hard-hat workmanship. But it remains little known to his countrymen.

To be fair, there was nothing superlative about the Shot itself—nothing quirky, grand, or artful to demand its place in history. Still, it was the only shot ever taken by an American that the rest of the world considers worth remembering. Plus, it was made against the English, and everybody in soccer loves to hate the English—whenever they're not busy loving them, that is.

All the same, the Shot did not begin to compare with the 1938 World Cup, when Brazilian forward Leonidas da Silva floated downfield into the teeth of a monsoon rain, lost his shoe in transit, and still managed to grease a point-blank goal against Poland, barefoot. Nor was the Shot revolutionary, like the zero-gravity "bicycle kick" invented by Ramón Unzaga in the 1920s. In this maneuver, the Chilean striker executed a superhuman backflip on the run, meeting flighted balls in midair with his scissoring legs. Hammocked in space, Unzaga squared the momentum of man and sphere to the sum of gunshot velocity. It would prove to be one of the pivotal breakthroughs in the aerial game, and a sad day for goalkeepers the world over. Nor did Bahr's shot in 1950 have the frenetic grace of a Stanley Matthews's strike, in which the English typhoon stutter-stepped downfield, paddling the ball inside and out with his right foot, juking and feinting and scattering defenders until he simply walked into the net. "Defenders would grab his shirt or his shorts, they'd get him in wrestling holds or tackle him with kicks worthy of a police blotter," wrote Eduardo Galeano in his lyrical commentaries *Soccer in Sun and Shadow*. "But nothing stopped him. When he was 50 years old, Stanley Matthews still caused serious outbreaks of hysteria in British soccer."

But Matthews didn't play that fateful day in Belo Horizonte, and Walter Bahr did. And the English paid for their cockiness, embarrassed for all eternity by a team of American working stiffs who barely had time to practice before boarding the plane for South America.

St. Louis mailman and future Hall of Famer Harry Keough conceded, "If Stanley Matthews had been there, the English would have murdered us. Even if he wasn't, we couldn't have beaten them again if we played them a hundred more times. But soccer is like that. It was our day, and things just wouldn't go their way. Hell, we figured we'd be lucky to hold them to six or seven goals." Instead, the U.S. defenders "clobbered them"—Keough laughed—"and boy did they ever complain about that. Of course, they were probably right. We definitely got away with a few things in the backfield," including an illegal tackle at about the eighty-minute mark that leveled Stan Mortensen of the English team as he closed in on the U.S. goalkeeper. "Charlie Colombo, one of our midfielders, bulldozed him from behind and just wiped him out." Though neither team made it to the Cup round, the game is no less indelibly marked in the annals of soccer.

When I first spoke to Walter Bahr, I hardly knew what to say. I was familiar with his life story by then. But who was I—a hammertoed suburban youth coach—to ask this man anything? If Billy Gonsalves was the Babe Ruth of soccer, then Bahr surely was its Johnny Unitas, the analog and equal of the broken-nosed Baltimore Colts quarterback who willed his underdog team to an overtime victory against the New York Giants in the greatest pro-football matchup of all time, the 1958 national championship. Like Unitas, Bahr was the everyman Jack the Giant Killer—born of humble German stock, up from the carpet-mill wards of Philadelphia. In addition to spearheading the 1950 win over England, he played in the 1948 Olympics and on three U.S. World Cup teams. He had six league titles to his credit as a member of various Philadelphia club teams. His induction into the National Soccer Hall of Fame in 1976 was a foregone conclusion.

Pictures of him from his glory days show a buff, burr-headed battering ram with the game face of a prizefighter. But the man I met in Boalsburg had mellowed beyond recognition. Or maybe he had always been this way. We like to think of our heroes as eternally young and handsome and larger than life, and Bahr was no exception in the world of U.S. soccer. "If you're asking me if I'm glad I got to live this long," Bahr says, smiling, "it's great to see what the kids are doing with the game now—and I can finally watch the sport on TV."

I asked him the fundamental question that had brought me to Boalsburg: How could soccer have faded from the American scene so quickly, just as the sport was beginning to yield such smashing results? Bahr, reared in hard times and reluctant to brag or complain, failed me. He simply shrugged and answered, as people of that era so often do, with quiet deflection. "We got to travel to Brazil, and we were paid a hundred dollars a game," he said. "Whatever else came of it, that was a pretty good deal back then."

It was a veteran soccer coach and trainer from Maryland who snapped some of the pieces together for me. "To hear parents today standing on the sidelines and screaming *foul* at every incidental contact, you tend to forget that this was once a very hard game," said Mike Sidlak, a former University of Maryland player. "It was brutal, just brutal."

Sidlak—the microbiologist who first explained pediatric neurology to me—grew up in the old ethnic wards surrounding Baltimore's Patterson Park. A great, green oasis on the city's gritty East Side, it was shared by kids from five densely packed row house neighborhoods. Now famous as one of the deadliest, most drug-ravaged square miles in the nation, the jumbled maze of narrow streets and abandoned tenement blocks had been the arrival point for destitute immigrants for more than a century. Irish fleeing the potato famine were followed by Italians and Greeks fleeing Fascist regimes, then by Jews fleeing pogroms and Russians fleeing Stalin. All were swallowed into their respective enclaves, bound together only by the park and the game they shared. Within sight of a landmark gazebo, Italian, Greek, and Ukrainian club teams played pitched matches on weekends that Sidlak described as "barely organized gang warfare." He recalled: "There's no way a kid my size could go on the field without getting killed. It was a lot more dangerous than football. Parents today would faint if they only knew. The rules, the tactics, everything about the game was different—and the level of violence was, *whew!* People today have no idea what these guys went through to keep the sport alive, and it wasn't for money."

Like Len Oliver, Walter Bahr, and Gene Olaff before him, George Brown barnstormed through the Northeast on the weekends from his home in Connecticut, playing where he could and bouncing through several ethnic-club teams before finding some measure of fame with the Polish Falcons of Elizabeth, New Jersey. In 1957, he aced thirteen goals to become the top scorer in the loosely amalgamated American Soccer League (ASL), receiving the striker's trophy—the highest honor of the largest soccer league left in America—in a two-minute ceremony in a parking lot in the Bronx. It came wrapped in newspaper.

The man who put it in his hands was Erno Schwarz, a quietly dignified Hungarian Jew who had immigrated to the United States after touring the country in 1926 as a player with the famed Vienna Hakoah team, probably the greatest Jewish soccer squad of all time. If American youth soccer has a spiritual patriarch, it's Erno Schwarz. He was known to sell admission tickets at the gate before games, then drive off in a cloud of black smoke to buy hot dogs, potatoes, and beer to sell at halftime—"Anything to keep the game from going under," Brown said. "You're talking about a guy in a little corrugated metal shed, cooking up French fries at halftime, running the whole show by himself.

"Erno was one of those great characters you read about in the history books from that period," Brown went on. "He was a hustler—what we might call an entrepreneur today. He was forever coming up with promotions and little stunts to get the old ethnic fans to the games—fifty-fifty lotteries, raffles, I'm not even sure it was all legal. If anyone could have figured out a way to make money on soccer in those days, it was Erno. But I never saw any sign that he was in danger of getting rich. He basically ran the league out of the trunk of his car." I had to laugh. As the owner of a '91 Volvo station wagon stuffed to the dome light with soccer gear, I lovingly called my Swedish wreck the world headquarters of the College Park Hornets.

His feet up on a table in a side office at the Soccer Hall of Fame in Oneonta, where he serves as a board member, Brown howled at his memory of those times. The sport was an endless procession of cold showers, dank locker rooms, major and minor injuries, and occasional on-field brawls that cleared the bleachers. Presiding over it all was the man he habitually calls "our friend Erno."

In modern revisionist histories, Schwarz is often portrayed as a titan whose European connections enabled him to organize dozens of elaborately staged exhibition matches between American all-star squads and visiting club teams—some of which drew crowds of thirty-five thousand or more well into the 1950s—and celebrated for his role in recruiting players for U.S. Pan-American, World Cup, and Olympic teams. There was hardly a player in the country who hadn't shaken his hand at some point, and hardly anyone of note in northeastern soccer who hadn't cut his teeth in the hundreds of ASL matches that Schwarz booked from Boston to Baltimore between 1930 and the 1960s. The reality, Brown said, was slightly different: Schwarz was the benign ruler of a shrinking realm. "He kept the thing rolling until the wheels fell off," as Brown put it.

During the worst of times in American soccer, Erno was the Wizard of Oz. The archival vault at the Hall of Fame is wall to wall with outlandishly spangled jerseys of the league's later years, game-day favors, and garish posters that recall the paraphernalia of a traveling circus. Always impeccably groomed, Schwarz drove a well-worn circuit of municipal parks and bald backwater soccer ovals in a black sedan stuffed with "bags upon bags of junk." His bases of operations were the cinder fields of North Jersey, Brooklyn, the Bronx. Woefully short on hygienic conveniences, the league's premier venue, Zerega Oval, is remembered by those who played there as much for the vapors emanating from beneath the grandstands as for the ferocity of the games.

"You could not hear yourself think in there," Brown said. "You'd have these crowds of rowdy 'ethnics,' as we called them back then, paying twenty-five cents to get in, stomping their feet and banging on the metal siding," which was all that separated the arena from a surrounding junkyard in the Bronx. "I think the NYPD sent cops to every game. But you could never have enough cops at one of those things."

In one near-riot in 1956 or '57, George Brown's Polish club team from Elizabeth, New Jersey, visited the Philadelphia Ukrainian Nationals—the eventual four-time ASL champions of the 1960s. Fans of the two teams were bitter "geographic enemies," Brown explained. "Pure ethnic and national rivals, the animosity between them went back generations in Europe." After a hard foul by one of the Polish players, three thousand enraged Ukrainians breached the spectator barricades and stormed the field in the rain. A lone Philadelphia police officer thought better of getting involved, and only the intervention of the Ukrainian team captain kept the mob from killing the Polish player. Finally, three Ukrainian priests stepped down from the grandstands to restore order. The crowd parted, and the trio of holy men commenced to flog the offender with their umbrellas.

"That was the ASL." Brown laughed. "If you look at the team names from those days, you'll see the Kearny Scots, the Kearny Irish, the Philadelphia Germans, the German-Hungarians, the Lithuanians, the New York Hungarians, the New York Hakoah, the Brooklyn Hispano and Brooklyn Italian, the Baltimore Pompeii, and on and on—all with pure ethnic followings. Anytime something went wrong in Europe, it would wash up on these shores and roll through the ASL. . . . There were always teams folding and being re-created. Some came and went in a year. Owners appeared and disappeared. There was no economic reason to invest in American soccer, because the fans were running in a hundred different directions. The power, the politics, the money were all a mess."

With the advent of sports broadcasting, Brown noted, soccer's continued fragmentation and reliance on its ethnic fan base proved to be its undoing. Baseball as we know it today was built on radio dollars, and the success of professional football and basketball hinged on their ease of translation as television spectacles. But soccer was so decentralized—with more than fifty competing national professional leagues and uncounted semipro ventures—that even newspapers had a hard time covering the game.

As rival U.S. sports leagues grew into transnational behemoths on television revenue, and as athletics increasingly became an armchair pastime, soccer's dependence on local ticket sales and old tribal loyalties left it at a fatal competitive disadvantage. The game was so malnourished, in fact, that it was eventually muscled out of the electronic marketplace altogether by an arcane and truly foreign sport called ice hockey that would otherwise have been hard to sell in the temperate United States.

"The total chaos and cacophony besetting this world could not have been in starker contrast to the monopolistic organization and pyramidal structure of soccer . . . in most countries," note the authors of *Offside: Soccer and American Exceptionalism* in their exhaustive analysis of the rise of U.S. pro sports in the twentieth century.

"The whole picture changed after World War II," George Brown told me forlornly. "You had a major shift in the U.S. immigration laws as time went on. The walls came up; immigration was cut to a trickle by the '60s. So the fan base started to shrink, and kids weren't really playing the game anymore. That's a little-known fact, I think. The immigration laws really hurt soccer. Over the long run, they also killed the ethnic clubs, for the simple fact that they weren't getting any new members. As the fans died off, you had to find another way to sell the game, and soccer failed to do that—failed miserably."

The chance for a revival would not come again for another fifty years—until the Latino population boom and the spread of cable and satellite television, whose operators are now major stakeholders in U.S. professional soccer.

Compared with the riotous ASL in the Northeast, soccer in the Midwest had fewer ethnic flashpoints, Harry Keough told me. Predominantly Irish- and Italian-Catholic St. Louis teams were usually owned or sponsored by small-business operators who calculated that it was "cheaper to get their company name mentioned in the headlines of the sports section than it was to buy advertising in the paper." Playing in a loose belt of leagues that ran north to Chicago and east to Pittsburgh, these teams had few pretenses of ever being moneymaking ventures. So there was little motive for owners to centralize their assets, invest in permanent venues, or recruit outside their rich local talent pools.

As revenues and salaries dried up, the hazards of the game took a heavy toll on the players. The ball back then was made of cowhide, and on the frozen tundra of a cinder oval in November it took on the force of a nine-pound cannonball. Players had to wear steel-toed boots just to move the thing when it got wet. Even minor miscalculation could lead to major injury. Broken noses, broken legs, broken fingers, compound fractures, concussions, and back injuries were all common. A player who struck a "header" for his team was likely to receive a tattoo of the ball's laces on his forehead and a crashing migraine for a day or two afterward. New York writer Pete Hamill, in his celebrated memoir *A Drinking Life*, described how his immigrant Irish father was injured in a game: "He was kicked very hard and his leg was broken and they left him on the sideline while they waited for an ambulance. But there were no doctors to treat him and by the next day gangrene had set in and they had to cut off his leg."

"How did they do that?" Hamill asked his mother.

"With a saw," she said.

On the way home from Oneonta, I stopped off in south-central New Jersey to see a man named Gene Olaff—whom George Brown had told me was, "without question, the premier American goalkeeper of the 1940s."

"He was a lion in the box, an oak of a man," Brown said, a goalkeeper so big, ornery, and fast that he intimidated two generations of professional players and sent more than a few of them home packed in ice during the barnstorming, knuckle-busting, bar-brawling days of American soccer at mid-century.

"Nicest guy you'd ever want to meet," vouched Len Oliver. "But goalies are all a bit loony. Seriously, they're different from other people. You have to have a cast-iron stomach to play that position. And back in those days they were a bloodthirsty bunch. Gene has mellowed over the years, but don't let him fool you. He was one tough S.O.B. in 1945."

If I wanted to know the story of how soccer declined in America, Brown and Oliver told me, then Gene Olaff was somebody I had to see. He is a well-known figure in the rural working-class town of Florence, a pancake-flat agricultural and trucking hub carved into the piney landscape off Exit 6 of the New Jersey Turnpike. The retired chief of the state police, he is an elder at his local church and a daily presence at the youth athletic field that rolls for several thick green acres across the street from his home. But few people in Florence know who he really is—the legend, that is, a man of prodigious dimensions in a time long ago.

His dog could care less.

For more than three hours, dog and man jostled each other

from room to room, vying for the same space in Olaff's little white bungalow—the aged stork and his excitable companion— knocking into the furniture, tipping the lamps, rattling the bric- a-brac. Wherever the man went, the dog followed. There was never enough room for both of them. And neither was inclined to give the other an inch. "Damn dog!" Olaff snapped. "Go lay down!"

Olaff eventually excused himself to whip us up some tuna salad sandwiches in his corner galley kitchen. At seventy-seven years old, he is white-haired and slightly stoop-shouldered. The dog is in the prime of his life. His name is Donovan. He's a ginger- colored anvil-headed pit bull with darting eyes and a set of gnashing chops that are the hallmark of his breed. Donovan was quick. Donovan was strong. Donovan was looking for an open lane to the countertop. I sat at the kitchen table, biting my lip to keep from laughing.

Donovan lunged for the loaf of bread next to the sink, but Olaff had anticipated the move. Never looking up, he side- stepped into Donovan's path and delivered a crunching hip check that sent the animal sailing across the kitchen. Donovan looped into the far wall, tail over head, no doubt wondering how the old man did it.

"Not this time, dog!" Olaff sneered. "You lose!"

He was cradling a slice of toasted white bread in a gnarled left hand. His fingers were crooked, bent at odd angles, with knobs of scar tissue that marked the spots where the many bones were broken many years ago. His spine has been surgically fused in a couple of places, so his movements are a little stiff. But the old quickness was still very much in evidence.

The bread disappeared from view inside Olaff's immense mitt, as Donovan collected himself off the floor and made another run for the counter, aiming to duck under his elbow. Again the dog miscalculated the man's reach. Olaff has the wingspan of a California condor and the homing instincts of a bat. He sensed his opponent's movement, pinned him to the oven door with a splayed right knee, and rapped him neatly on the skull. "Not fast enough!" Olaff scoffed. "You'll never be fast enough!"

Such is the life of a dog, sharing a house with a Hall of Fame goalie.

Olaff scratched his way through the Depression in a succession of club teams after learning to play keeper with the Bayonne Rinky-Dinks in a factory lot on the banks of Newark Bay. By the 1940s, he was the starting goalie with the Brooklyn Hispano team, playing behind the great Billy Gonsalves against dynastic wrecking crews like Inter Milan, Manchester United, and Liverpool. He was a minor celebrity on the soccer ovals of Ebbets Field, the Polo Grounds, Randalls Island, Yankee Stadium, and Starlight Park in Brooklyn—back when forty-five thousand fans still occasionally showed for a major game if Erno Schwarz priced the tickets right. With Olaff in goal and the incomparable Gonsalves running the offense, the Hispano won Sir Thomas Dewar's U.S. Open Cup twice, in 1943 and 1944.

"It was all very exciting and romantic, you might say," Olaff told me. "Most of us were street waifs really, tough kids who got into soccer as an easy way to make a few bucks. But it got harder to stay in the game as the years went by. If you blew up your knee or ruined your back, well, that was your problem."

After misjudging an oncoming shot during a rainy game in Brooklyn, Olaff told me, he once took a ball "right between the eyes." He was immediately bowled over, trampled by opposing players, and gang-kicked into his own net, along with the ball, in a stunt known as "bundling." (Goalies enjoyed few of the protections they do today.) Only after both black eyes swelled shut and his nose became too clogged with dried blood to breathe did his manager finally yank him from the game and give him some coins for the subway ride home. "There I was, bouncing along on the train, almost blind, covered with mud," he said. "I must have looked pretty bad, because nobody would sit anywhere near me."

By the end of his career, he said with a grin, "I had been kicked and punched everywhere a person could be kicked or punched. The referees back in those days didn't call a lot of fouls, so the goal box was where everything got settled. If one of your guys did one of my guys dirty on the field, then one of your guys was going to pay for it the next time a crowd formed in the box. All sorts of stuff happened in there."

This is what American soccer at mid-century was like. It was a relic of a by-gone time, willed forward by a dwindling generation of players, managers, and coaches who had nothing left to lose. At the height of his powers, Olaff was playing for one of the most famous teams in the history of American soccer and earning just nine dollars a game. The awesome Hispano team was already on the verge of bankruptcy, owned by a man who made his living running a waterfront cathouse in lower Manhattan called the El Mundo Hotel. "I stayed there once and never went back again," Olaff recalled. "There were murders in the bar and everything else."

With the coming of postwar prosperity in the 1950s, players of that generation bailed out of the game at the first tug of an available rip cord. G.I. vouchers in hand, they left for college or took jobs in the newly burgeoning economy, looking to put as much distance as they could between themselves and their immigrant pasts. "There was just no way you could raise a family on a soccer salary, and the potential for serious injury was just terrific," Len Oliver told me. "If you read about the old NFL players from that time, their stories are very similar—cracked vertebrae, herniated disks, knee surgeries, all of that. But once TV money started flowing into football, a player could justify the risk. You might end up disabled or arthritic or something in your later years, but if you could last awhile in that game you'd be set for life. That was never the case in soccer, not here anyway."

"The thing that kept it moving forward was pride," Walter Bahr said. "Pride in your club, pride in your city, pride in your nationality . . . but you can't feed a family on pride." Or on obsession.

In the hardest of times, the adrenal surge and hypnotic effect induced by soccer was a powerful soporific that could blot out the problems of the world. As Oliver described it: "I can still remember what it felt like to step on that field when I was young. No matter what else was going wrong in your life, it all ceased to exist the minute you crossed that touchline. The game never stopped, so there was no time to think about anything else. It was just tremendously liberating. You would do anything for that feeling."

As the last of his bankable stars departed, Erno Schwarz's American Soccer League died a wasting death. The old man sought to link up with rival leagues in the Northeast, and he mounted a last-ditch expansion effort to find a wider fan base as far west as California and south to Virginia, but both plans flopped and by the 1960s the ASL had gone into a terminal spiral. The arrival of the dazzling North American Soccer League— with its roster of international stars led by the incomparable Pelé—sucked the fan base out from underneath the old immigrant league and introduced the game to a new generation of Americans who had never heard of Belo Horizonte, ONT, St. Leo's Parrish, or Mother Jones.

The coup de grâce came with the advent of the fast-paced and furious Indoor Soccer League. Student loans had transported the children of the blue-collar "ethnics" onto university campuses, triggering a soccer craze that would ultimately echo through collegiate athletic programs nationwide. The first crop of these players to graduate—well-muscled, photogenic heartthrobs like Harvard University goalie Shep Messing—brought young fans to the new indoor "box soccer" league. It offered nonstop, hard-hitting action similar to hockey, and the ten-city circuit ran through the heart of what might be called the immigrant Soccer Belt. Dowdy by comparison, Erno Schwarz's Old World product couldn't begin to compete with the sexier arena version of the game, much less with Pelé's flying circus. American soccer's gentleman envoy died in Queens in 1974, and the league collapsed within a decade.

"The ASL closed up shop in 1983," reads the league's epitaph in the indispensable *Encyclopedia of American Soccer History*. "But it had lasted nearly three times as long as any other professional or semipro soccer league in the United States ever has." It kept the American game alive, it pushed the sport into rural provinces where it had never been seen before, and it did much to advance an American style of play—a stubbornly physical, headlong approach to the sport that defied the pretentiousness of European soccer. Most important, it provided a home for a generation of men who would father the youth boom of the 1980s.

Unknown to most parents sitting on the sidelines at kids' soccer games today, the steady hands of the old-timers are largely responsible for the modern soccer renaissance that now occupies some 20 million Americans. Standing in his garage that cold, rainy day in Boalsburg, flipping through the yellow clippings commemorating the U.S. triumph over England, Walter Bahr rattled off a long list of former Lighthouse Boys Club players, members of the soccer army who emerged from the Kensington mill ward and left Philadelphia to coach, referee, and set up youth leagues across the country.

"You won't see their names in any books or magazine write-ups," he told me. "But those are the guys who carried it all forward. There's probably two hundred Lighthouse guys I could tell you about, guys from St. Louis, too, and up in Kearny, guys from the old ASL. They had to leave the game to make a living, but they all came back to it later and kept it moving forward."

George Brown went on to help establish one of the earliest youth leagues in Texas during his career as a personnel manager in the oil and gas industry. Gene Olaff brought soccer across the Pine Barrens to southern New Jersey upon retiring as chief of the state police. After a career as a program director for the National Endowment for the Humanities, Len Oliver became the best-known coaching instructor in Maryland, Virginia, and Washington, D.C. Harry Keough, the mailman-defender who stifled the English in 1950, went on to coach the St. Louis University team to five national collegiate titles during a fourteen-year career there. And Walter Bahr coached at Temple University and Penn State, amassing a lifetime record of 448-137-70.

"He was tough as nails," recalled Ashley Halsey, a former Temple defenseman who now works as an editor at *The Washington Post.* "We hardly played a game that didn't end up in a fight at some point, because Walter always had these badasses from Kensington on the team, guys who probably never would have gone to college if not for him. A lot of them went on to become coaches, too."

They all were to be trustees-in-waiting for the day when, in Bahr's words, "the next wave hit." That day came in 1972, the year 0001 A.G. In the world of U.S. soccer, the resurrection of the American game began with the Arrival of the Girls.

9.

PRETTY IN PINK, FEROCIOUS IN UNIFORM

ALL MY FRIENDS WERE SOCCER PLAYERS

It's a sound like no other in the world of sports—a rising soprano peal that travels through the frequency range from somewhere around high C to high E, like the whine of a jet engine revving for takeoff. At its peak, the shriek rests for two or three beats, until the fillings in your molars start to ache, before spending itself in a final expulsion of glee.

"MeeeeeeeEEEEEEEEEE-YAH!!!"

Not since the Beatles' arrival at Shea Stadium in 1965 has America heard anything quite like it. But the hysteria then was all about lust. Now the cause is love, and maybe something more, something vaguely unsettling to the male ear. There's an edge to the sound now. It is the full-throated sound of feminine aggression, the banshee ululation of the warrior maidens.

The first time it hit me was on a breezy evening in spring, 2003, in the lower deck of the cavernous Robert F. Kennedy Memorial Stadium in Washington, D.C.—the former home of the Washington Redskins, one of the oldest and most celebrated teams in the National Football League. Like every other red-blooded Washington male, I have many a fond memory of chilly Sundays in this place, shoulder to shoulder with my buddies, adding our hoarse voices to the multitudinous roar that made RFK's concrete bowl legendary as one of the loudest and most inhospitable venues in the NFL for visiting teams, most especially for the hated Dallas Cowboys.

But that was then and this was now. The Redskins were gone, moved to newer quarters, and RFK had been ceded to the Women's United Soccer Association (WUSA).

In attendance for the season-opening home game between the Washington Freedom and the New York Power that April night were half the College Park Hornets, there to see what we had been told was some of the best team-oriented professional soccer to be found anywhere in the world. The WUSA was clustered with marquee stars—including most of the players from the 1999 World Cup campaign—but the women's game is rightly more famous for its choreography: crisp passing, instinctual tactical movement, and that ineffable quality known as "flow." On that long-ago day over lunch at his home in New Jersey, Hall of Fame goalkeeper Gene Olaff called it "some of the most beautiful soccer I have ever seen." Where men's teams might rely on brilliant individual performances, brute strength, and spectacular diving plays, women tend to prevail with their heads, exploiting soccer's geometric junctions and their superior predictive powers to "get where the ball will be three seconds from now," as Olaff described it, "instead of where it is right now."

Most of the Hornets were by then overcoming the last of their childhood motor disorders. The fumbling squad that Bryan Basdeo's mother called "our precious little maul-ballers" were no longer colliding into one another and tripping over the ball. They were beginning to show signs of intelligence and poise, and the coaches thought a dose of pro soccer might help move things along. But nothing we had read or heard about the WUSA prepared us for the sound in the grandstands, and it would change everything for the Mosquito. Seated front and center, with the boys gathered around her, Shelby Hammond was about to have her small world rocked.

From two rows back—so close to the action that we could actually see beads of sweat fly from the players' ponytails—I watched the transformation come over Shelby. Her freckled face was flushed. The cockeyed grin turned horizontal and spread nearly to reach her ears. Her head swiveled, soaking up every detail of her first experience among her own kind.

There, swarming around us, 7,238 screaming soccer fans, most of them girls in their team uniforms, leaped and slapped high fives as forward Jacqui Little pounded in a pair of goals to give Washington a 2–1 lead. A disorienting blur of bouncing yellow, green, blue, and red jerseys greeted every move on the field, until their goddess took center stage. It happened in the second half, after an illegal tackle by a New York defender sent one of the Freedom women cartwheeling in front of the goal. The referee issued a penalty kick to Washington, and the stadium fell silent as Mia Hamm approached the ball, settled herself, then charged and fired a rocket past New York's goalkeeper, ballooning the back of the net and pulling the pin on the release valve in the grandstands. The cheer rolled up the bleachers from the 100-level sideline seats to the 200-section, then the 300, then washed over the concessions deck, pinging off the forty-two-year-old concrete walls and steel I-beams of RFK.

"MeeeeeeeeeEEEEEE-YAH!" Flying their club flags, the girls from Netforce and the Bethesda Blitz, the Montgomery Mustangs and the Calverton Tornadoes, the Bowie Lightning and the Burke Fuerz Azul went berserk in unison. The few who weren't wearing jerseys had their sentiments silk-screened on the backs of their T-shirts: "Girls Rock!" and "Girls Rule" and "If you want it done right, pass to a girl"—and, my personal favorite: "Pretty in Pink . . . Ferocious in Uniform."

The person responsible for the hair-raising wail in the stands that night—the woman who put the colors on most of the kids in the stadium—lives alone in a modest rancher in the distant Virginia suburbs of Washington, out beyond the Colonial-themed subdivisions, on the westernmost fringe of the D.C. sprawl where the roads begin to rise toward the distant Shenandoahs. Her name is Adele Dolansky.

By most accounts, she is the grandmother of American girls' soccer, the iron-willed Mrs. D. who took on government and league officials in two southern states, dragged them from their primordial ponds, and clubbed them over their heads with her now famous appeal to common sense, fairness, and decency: "What kind of bullshit is this?" Cofounder and chief executor of one of the oldest and largest girls' leagues in the nation, Dolansky designed the template of confrontational community activism that would be duplicated for decades by girls' league organizers from Sussex County, New Jersey, to San Diego, California.

A native Floridian whose father hauled block ice for a living, Adele Dolansky was elected president in 1977 of a start-up organization called Washington Area Girls Soccer—known nationwide by the acronym WAGS. Founded three years earlier with just four teams and roughly fifty girls from Maryland and Virginia, it was administered from a Ping-Pong table in Dolansky's basement for more than two decades. By the mid-1990s it had grown into the largest girls' soccer league in the country, a grassroots bellwether of gender equity in sports, with more than four hundred elite "travel" teams in two states and the District of Columbia and around six thousand juvenile players on its rosters.

"When we first got started, it was the old-school way of thinking," Dolansky told me, fielding phone calls at her home office in Fairfax, Virginia, between sips of spring water. "'Adele,' the old boys would say, 'we've always done it this way,' and 'Adele, please just be patient.' So we went into it knowing we would have to knock on the door and keep on knocking—and sometimes we got tired of knocking and just kicked it down. Sometimes we just had to tell them, 'Whatever you do for the boys in this state, you're damn well going to do for the girls.'"

Red-haired, blue-eyed, gravel-voiced, and sixty-three years old, Dolansky is the recently widowed mother of two grown kids, the grandmother of five, and a walking institution in Washington soccer. She comes off as a slightly cranky elf; impatient, at times brusque, and sweetly profane, her persona far exceeds her physical dimensions. Over the years she has fought local county councils, commissions, and parks departments for equal field time, referee services, uniforms, and trophies. When she discovered, in the early 1980s, that Maryland had a State Cup soccer championship series for boys, but none for girls, Dolansky barged into an annual meeting of league officials in Baltimore and demanded a statewide tournament within one year, "or we'll pack the lobby with three thousand pissed-off little girls in shin guards tomorrow morning." The Maryland State Youth Soccer Association quickly obliged.

"Everyone was scared to death of her—especially the politicians—because her reputation preceded her," recalls Kathie Diapoulis, who succeeded Dolansky as WAGS's president when she stepped down in 1997. "Everyone knew that . . . all she had to do was pick up the phone and twenty thousand parents and little girls would be on your back the next day."

"It was all pretty ridiculous," Dolansky says today. "But it wasn't all that long ago that girls had to borrow uniforms from the boys' teams, then wash and fold them and give them back at night—and nobody saw anything wrong with that. Like our girls had nothing better to do than wash the boys' laundry. There aren't many people dumb enough to think they could get away with that today."

That's because two things happened during those years that enlightened the small-town burghers and provincial rec-board overseers to the fact that a new age had dawned. First, court opinions and equal-opportunity rulings finally caught up with Dolansky's personal law, ratifying most of what she had fought for and extinguishing any knuckle dragger's dream that unequal treatment of girls could possibly stand up to legal challenge. Second, WAGS became a crackling success story. In 1975 the league launched the first major national tournament for girls, drawing teams first from twelve states, then twenty, then thirty—teams from as far away as Texas and California, Florida and Louisiana, Michigan and Illinois. Today, the WAGS combine is considered a "can't miss" event, with more than three hundred top-tier teams participating and recruiters from more than two hundred colleges and universities prowling the sidelines every October. The scouts come because they all know that there's hardly an American woman playing at the World Cup or Olympic level today who didn't appear in the WAGS tournament as a kid.

Dolansky barely started talking about those girls before she was reaching for a Kleenex. "I have the entire 1999 Women's World Cup on videotape, and every time I watch it I cry," she told me. "I can't even talk about it without crying, because I knew most of them when they were coming up. I used to tell people way back then that these little girls will win the World Cup someday. Way before the U.S. Men ever win the Cup, I told everyone, these girls will do it. And they did, twice, in '91 and again in '99."

They did it with WAGS's most famous alumna in the mix, a puny girl from Wichita Falls, Texas, who, at fifteen, became the youngest member of the U.S. Women's National Team. She was a military brat who liked to dance and play the guitar and knock soccer balls around with her big brother; a "cute, goofy kid," as her coach described her. When her father was transferred overseas by the Air Force in 1987, the soft-spoken teen moved in with relatives in northern Virginia in order to finish high school. She had spent most of her childhood on boys' teams because girls' squads were few and far between back then. When she got to Burke, Virginia, she joined the Braddock Road Shooting Stars and went on a tear through WAGS that ended with the Virginia State Cup in 1988. Soon enough, the entire world would know the name Mia Hamm.

"She was already this recognized phenom by then, and she always had that speed, that first step, the great touch on the ball," says Denise Mishalow, the Braddock coach. "Believe me, you noticed her on a field. But to say she was this amazing athlete who was far superior to her teammates? That wasn't Mia. I remember saying once, 'When do I get to see the real you? When do I get to meet this kid I've heard so much about?' Then I realized all of that was embarrassing to her. When you think about the pressure she has had to bear, the burden of all those expectations, the critics who said women don't belong in sports? All of that was stacked on the shoulders of this sweet fifteen-year-old girl."

Almost two decades later, Hamm was still in her cleats. After pounding home the insurance goal at RFK that night in April, she acknowledged her little sisters in the gallery with her head down. Eyes on the turf, left hand on hip, she waved her right arm at the stands, her signature number 9 jersey billowing in the warm breeze like a flag. The eruption in the stands couldn't help but put a lump in my throat. For these kids, in this sport, she *is* Michael Jordan.

I had no women heroes while I was growing up, except maybe my mother, but the Hornets' boys clamored for Mia Hamm

T-shirts after the game and lined up along the rails above the Freedom bench to vie for her autograph. Ice bags wrapped around her knees, the most recognizable woman athlete in the world stood on the field signing balls and arms and the toes of sneakers as a nimbus of kids wearing replicas of her jersey hovered above her. Traditionally worn by forwards in the game of soccer, "9" has achieved international fame as the on-field marker of Brazilian "Fenomeno" Ronaldo; goal-scoring machine Juan Pablo Angel of the British pro team Aston Villa; and dribbling prodigy Marco van Basten of the Amsterdam club Ajax, among many other luminaries. But American girls—and more than a few American boys— wear it because it is Mia's number. No other is more sought after on youth-league uniform handout nights. Shelby would show up an hour early and dig through boxes of jerseys to be sure no one got Mia's number before she did.

For U.S. soccer organizers, it has even larger meaning: "9" is the emblem, proximate cause, and guarantor of the late-twentieth-century soccer resurgence. A squib of congressional revision to the U.S. Education Amendments Act of 1972 required all federally subsidized schools to offer athletic programs and scholarships for female students on an equal footing with males. *The New York Times* called the law, known as Title IX, a "Bill of Rights for female athletes," and its impact on soccer was huge: over the next two decades, 7.4 million women and girls would strap on shin guards and tug on cleats to double the number of registered players nationwide and transform a dying sport into the native game of suburbia.

"It was the great immigration numbers that drove the first soccer boom in this country up through the nineteen-twenties and into the forties and fifties," WUSA commissioner Tony DiCicco told me when I called him at his office in Connecticut. "As long as the immigrants kept coming, soccer survived on the constant infusion of new blood. Once that dried up, the question became 'Who's next? Where is the next wave going to come from?' The answer, starting about three decades ago, was the girls."

DiCicco was a former collegiate and professional goalkeeper running a modest chain of New England soccer camps at the time. He had made his reputation as a hard-charger who turned skinny chowderheads into alpha males. But his registration numbers suddenly spiked in the early eighties as the first generation of Title IX girls started arriving at his camps by the busload.

"It was like trying to learn a foreign language," he said. "And I had to learn it fast. We went from something like 98.9 percent boys to twenty percent girls, then thirty percent, then forty percent, then forty-five," he recalled. "I had to start adding staff, and the girls just kept on coming. Every summer there were more and more of them. People all over the country started to ask themselves, 'What's really going on here?' All of a sudden, soccer was everywhere—thousands upon thousands of kids, tens of thousands—and they just kept on coming. It was this demographic tidal wave."

In time, it became clear that Title IX was the immediate cause, because it "provided the moral and legal imperative that got them out on the field," DiCicco said. "Soccer wasn't a gender-exclusive sport, so we were the immediate beneficiaries of that onrush of interest, us and basketball." But the story is a bit more complicated than it first seems.

Three years after Title IX passed in Congress, number 10 arrived. That is to say, Pelé appeared in New York. Just as college regents, school boards, and local recreation departments were looking for sports for girls, Pelé and the New York Cosmos took off, lending drama and glamour to the game, and phys-ed directors discovered what mill foremen, factory owners, plantation bosses, and English missionaries had learned a century earlier: "Soccer not only was cheap, it accommodated a large number of people—more players than any other team sport," as Donna Lopiano, director of the influential Women's Sports Foundation, explains it. "If you're looking to build up big participation numbers fast, with minimal staff and low budgets, without spending a dime on new facilities, soccer is the obvious place to look. And that's what a lot of major institutions did to buy themselves some time, while they dragged Title IX through the courts."

More than fifteen hundred colleges, universities, school boards, and fraternal groups contested Title IX—denying that they had unequal facilities, uneven funding, or unfair scholarship allocations for women's sports. Soccer programs served as a good defense against lawsuits, because "that's twenty to twenty-five players, two or three times the numbers you could generate with, say, a women's basketball or lacrosse program," as soccer historian Len Oliver points out. Such diverse institutions as Auburn, UCLA, Iowa State, Louisiana State, and Texas Tech, among many others, added fully funded women's teams by the mid-1990s. In fact, from 1981 to 2001, the number of women's collegiate soccer teams grew more than tenfold, until they eventually exceeded the number of men's programs by more than a hundred varsity squads.

Soccer, then, became a useful counterweight against plaintiffs' complaints about bloated men's football programs. But instead of trimming football budgets university trustees often funded women's soccer by cutting less popular men's sports. The backlash wasn't far behind.

No less a champion of American Tory conservatism than commentator George Will—whose romantic musings on the ecstasies of baseball have distinguished him as a latter-day Byron of the stick-and-pebble game—has called Title IX a "feminist's fetish" and a "train wreck," chafing that four hundred collegiate men's teams have been eliminated to pay for women's teams. "Many schools have had to achieve equality partly by reducing the number of male athletes by killing men's wrestling, swimming, baseball, gymnastics and other teams," Will wrote in 2004, complaining that this was especially unfair considering that "more young men than young women care about playing sports."

This argument epitomizes the hardest line of the anti–Title IX faction. The fact is, however, that it is contradicted by reams of analysis from a broad spectrum of sources. More than that, it is utterly destroyed every weekend on the soccer fields of America. There are now nearly three times more female soccer players in the United States than there are Girl Scouts, for example. From virtual "base-zero" in 1972, women and girls now constitute 41 percent of registered players nationwide and half or more of youth-club master rosters. In the year that Title IX was signed into law—the year Mia Hamm was born—a piddling 28 high schools in the entire country had girls' soccer teams. Today, there are more than 8,000. The number of elite girl players at this level rose from just 700 to more than 290,000 today. That's five times more than for field hockey, ten times more than for lacrosse, twelve times more than for gymnastics, and nearly as many as for softball.

Thus did the game seem to burst so suddenly into national consciousness. With the election-year signing of Title IX by President Richard M. Nixon, the population of youth soccer players doubled nearly overnight. Little more than a decade later, U.S. women mounted their assault on the world's game with a teenager named Mia in the front line and swept virtually all rivals from the field. They would own the sport for the next fifteen years.

After "a century of forbidden participation," as the author Jere Longman later wrote in *The Girls of Summer*, his book about the 1999 World Cup campaign, so many women and girls flooded U.S. soccer leagues that their ranks eventually swelled to eight times the number in any other industrialized country. As soccer became a rallying point for frustrations over the lack of athletic opportunities for young girls, the parents of soccer-playing boys, incensed over their treatment by local football and baseball boosters, joined the cause. That, says Sylvia McPherson, was when soccer began to turn into a power base in local suburban politics. "When you put the parents of the girls and the boys together, that's when soccer got the irresistible numbers."

Now seventy-one and silver-haired, McPherson took leave of her job as an elementary-school teacher in Montgomery County, Maryland, when she and her husband decided to have children. By 1975 her three kids were on their feet and McPherson was getting ready to go back to the classroom when a neighbor asked her if she would be interested in heading up a nonprofit corporation called MSI. Montgomery Soccer Inc. had been launched only recently by a group of parents who were fed up with the county-run recreation department's long-deferred promises to start a league. The Washington Diplomats of the North American Soccer League had popularized the game as a spectator sport. Pelé had been a frequent visitor at local dinner parties and charitable events, and soccer was sweeping such venerable southern campuses as George Mason, the University of Virginia, UNC, and South Carolina. But on the playgrounds of suburban Washington the sport hardly existed. For girls, sports were mostly limited to softball in the spring, swimming in the summer, and cheerleading in the fall. Title IX no longer allowed league officials to keep them out of boys' sports, but neither were girls particularly keen on getting trampled. Farther to the south and west, Len Oliver's Stoddert Soccer League and Adele Dolansky's WAGS were moving aggressively to fill the niche.

"People would see girls quitting boys' teams and say, 'See, girls don't like sports!'" McPherson recalls. "What really was going on is that girls didn't like playing with boys, particularly after about age nine or ten, when the boys started putting on upper-body mass. That's when the girls would say, 'Enough of this.'"

Into this void stepped MSI—reaping an unforeseen boon. A decade after the club was founded in her neighbor's garage, McPherson told me, the board of directors decided to launch an experimental girls' league, over the objection of some parents who insisted that the sport was too physically demanding for young ladies. "If you offer it, they will come, that was our guiding thought, and boy did they come," she says. "Once the word got out that we had a girls' league, my God, the numbers just took off." By the mid-1990s, the organization had grown into one of the largest privately run recreational sports leagues in the nation—an eighteen-thousand-member soccer stronghold. Girls not only doubled the size of the club but brought financial stability in the form of a durable, dues-paying membership base. While boys' rosters fluctuated over time as some were recruited away from their MSI teams to play other sports, girls' squads that formed in the first grade often held together until their members graduated from high school.

"It just turned into this powerful machine," McPherson marvels. "By pooling the resources of boys and girls soccer and pulling in such huge numbers, MSI became this major political force—by accident, you might say."

With more than thirty thousand parents in its database, the organization constitutes one of the most potent constituent groups in the county. Lobbying by MSI over the years has stopped two proposals to institute field-usage fees in Maryland's biggest suburb; won the support of local school principals to open playgrounds and gymnasiums to youth athletic leagues; and helped to push through the controversial plan to build what is arguably the most elaborate youth-soccer complex in the nation. Today, the Maryland SoccerPlex and Discovery Sports Center, off Route 270 outside Washington, D.C., stands as a crown jewel of U.S. youth soccer, and MSI is one of its biggest sponsors.

"In hindsight, our success, in large part, was because of the girls," McPherson says today. "In my opinion, we would not be what we are today were it not for the board's decision in 1985 to start a girls' league. We would not have gotten the numbers we have, or the attention from government, and soccer would not be what it is today: the biggest sport in this county, by far and away."

Talk to anyone in American soccer, from the directors of the largest camp programs to the head of the smallest hometown rec club, and you will hear about "the numbers." For girls are what gave soccer its defiant demographic gravity, the elemental force that beat back the football and baseball factions that didn't want to share their fields or budgets. Even in mostly rural southern counties, where the tradition of Friday Night Football meant everything, soccer eventually intruded and prevailed.

"The girls gave soccer critical mass, no question about it," says Renee Milligan, the Hornets' club president. "Before we offered girls' soccer, frankly, this sport was a pain. We had constant problems getting field time. Soccer players were seen as this bunch of weirdos who didn't recognize the traditional seasons. They played year-round, and they weren't even paying their own way."

A native of basketball-crazy Indiana and a onetime distance runner, this mother of two athletic girls had moved to the Washington suburbs because of her husband's new job with the U.S. Information Agency. The couple eventually bought a house in this tiny college town in predominantly African-American Prince George's County—one of the most affluent black suburbs in the nation, a place where youth football and basketball leagues have a drawing power surpassed only by churches.

"Boys' soccer barely paid for itself," Milligan recalls. "And it didn't draw big enough crowds to turn a profit at the snack bar on Friday nights, which is a big revenue source for the clubs in this county. With baseball, you could sell a hundred hot dogs at a buck apiece in a couple of hours, and the football people will eat hamburgers as fast as you can grill them. So there was a good bit of resentment over soccer, as you can imagine, because it seemed to be pulling kids away from other sports that were, let's face it, more profitable."

Today, however, soccer dues are the club's leading source of revenue—money that began to flow only after Milligan and a group of interested mothers decided, one winter in 1997, to hold a girls-only soccer clinic in the gym of a neighborhood recreation center. They drew about fifteen kids that first weekend, twenty the following weekend; then the girls came in waves. The biggest contingent had been getting up at the crack of dawn on Sundays for a forty-mile drive to play in a girls' league at Andrews Air Force Base in southern Maryland. All piled into Milligan's clinic.

"We were all looking at each other, saying, 'Well, isn't this cool!' Looking back now, it's pretty obvious that there was this pent-up demand that didn't have anywhere to go. To think that all you had to do to have a successful program was open the gym door and hand out some T-shirts! Girls' soccer, girls' sports in general, was at a tipping point in the county. We pushed it a little, and it went right over the edge. We knew it was big when the cheerleaders starting signing up" to play soccer.

Twenty-five years after the passage of Title IX, girls' athletics finally achieved parity in one small southern town, Milligan says, for reasons that had almost nothing to do with gender equity, the law, or any sort of feminist organizing urge. It was more a function of economics. "Once the girls came in, soccer became a moneymaker. In this very conservative and traditional place, people also had some pretty narrow ideas about what was appropriate for girls. No one ever expected them to come out the way they did, or for soccer to bring in the kind of money it did, or for girls to stick with a game that was supposedly too demanding for them."

Ray Fetterer, a friend of Milligan's who had been pushing the county to start a girls' league for years, told me his favorite story from that time. "I remember this one guy who said it would never work because 'girls don't like to sweat,' if you can believe that. . . . Remember, this was only six or seven years ago, not exactly the Dark Ages, but it was like no one around here had ever heard of Mia Hamm."

At Milligan's suggestion, I called Mark Weiss, an early supporter of girls' soccer who managed youth athletics programs for the county Sports and Permits Office, to ask him what sort of ripple effect the girls' soccer movement might have had in the intervening years. Basketball, he told me, is still the undisputed king in the county, where formerly segregated play space left African-American kids to make do for decades with asphalt courts and run-down gyms. But the influx of girls into the tottering soccer program "made the sport viable."

"It was only a matter of a few years, I guess, before soccer surpassed baseball and softball," Weiss said. "And in terms of sheer numbers it's starting to inch up on football. The interesting trend we're all watching now is the influx of Latino and African immigrants into the county from big soccer-playing countries. How that might affect youth soccer is a big unknown variable. But we're already seeing a jump in the number of field applications for adult soccer, which is a fairly new phenomenon."

The Washington, D.C., region now hosts so many leagues—African, Latino, International, youth rec, travel, peewee, over-forty, collegiate, high school, developmental, intermediate, and advanced—that some clubs are now building all-weather, year-round composite plastic-and-rubber fields. Because the grass, everywhere, is getting trampled to death, owing largely to Title IX.

"Because of the girls, soccer got the numbers," DiCicco says. "And once we had the numbers everything else just naturally followed from there. There was this domino effect, and it hit everywhere at the same time."

Ask the old hands about girls' soccer and the next thing you're likely to hear is how profoundly females have affected the American game. Not only are girls more loyal, they are more willful, more democratic, more inclined to demand explanations of their coaches about the direction and makeup of the roster. Boys will do almost anything they're told, ten times harder than they're asked to do it. Girls want to know why, and they'll sour on a coach they think is abusing his or her authority within the group.

I had seen this phenomenon more than once on youth squads—I watched one team of "prohibitive favorites" disintegrate in a tournament after their coach chided a popular defender in public—and it made me leery of ever coaching girls. With boys, I figured you could correct an unruly kid or get a scatterbrained team focused with a stern voice or a corrective lap and the event would be forgotten five minutes later. Girls had longer memories. Neither was I sufficiently indifferent to the concept of winning, which tends to be far down on the list of priorities for young female athletes.

Heather Schou was one of the first people to try to explain the psyche of the girl player to me. Now a police officer in Annapolis, Maryland, she was working as a trainer at a soccer camp when we first met. A "space brat" whose father was a NASA physicist, she grew up living wherever his job took the family and she played for a succession of boys' teams before finally arriving in Alta Loma, California, and her first girls' squad, the Bumblebees. From there, her résumé includes stints on two powerhouse club teams, her high school squad, and the Cal State Northridge women's team by 1996. She has a jagged scar on her ankle where the surgeon's knife went in, a marker of those times. She "played hurt" for years—in spite of warnings from her doctor that she risked crippling herself—because the thought of leaving her friends was unbearable. "And all my friends were soccer players," she says.

"As a kid, it seemed like I was always playing with the boys," she goes on. "We had a basketball team, and I was the only girl on the team. That's just the way it was. There weren't enough girls involved in sports back then to make a team, so you were always playing with boys. It was always me and maybe a couple other hardheaded girls in this gang of boys—and boys, after they're seven, they just want to fight each other. Really, it's all they ever do. Coaches would yell at them, and they really seemed to respond to that. When they messed up on the field, a coach would yell and the boys would just go out and say, you know, 'I'll show him what I can do.'"

Later, at Cal State, she watched teammates cry and disappear from the game when coaches used similar methods with women. "I had played with boys and I was used to being yelled at"—she laughs—"but I knew a lot of women who couldn't handle it. The coach would think he was waking them up and getting them motivated, but it would just totally take them out of their game. They'd be a wreck afterward. With women, you need to be softer, less critical. They have to feel good about the team and the coach and their position in order to play well. With guys, that kind of stuff makes a little less difference. But with girls there's more reliance on skill than power, and more reliance on the team. You can't mess with their chemistry and expect them to do well." Women "have a 'relationship' with the team that is hard for a guy to get," she says. "It's complicated."

Another major difference is that girls place much greater emphasis on performing well as a team than they do on winning. "I still have friends I've known since elementary school, and we played together for years—different teams, different coaches, but always the same group of girls," Schou says. "We just loved it, and we couldn't imagine not doing it, so we kind of got pretty good. We played for the State Cup, played in the San Diego Surf Classic a couple of times, which was a pretty big deal, I guess."

"You *guess?*" I interject, pointing out that the Surf is one of the biggest girls' tournaments in the country and that the California State Cup is one of the most prestigious. "You *guess?*"

"I can't remember if we ever won," she says curiously. "And I can't remember the scores, but I remember we played a bunch of times, and I can tell you the name of every girl on those teams." Off the top of her head, she recites their wedding dates, home phone numbers, college alma maters, and current employers. She cannot, however, remember the names of most of her coaches. "Wow!" she says. "That's pretty weird, huh?"

For Tony DiCicco, the father of four boys, who was propelled on a career course he had never imagined for himself—first as goalie coach to the U.S. Women's National Team, then as head coach, then as trustee of the women's game—this "team first" dynamic was the hardest adjustment to make. "It takes subtlety to coach girls, and humanity," he told me. "To girls, the coach is a member of the team, or not. They will choose their own hierarchy, their own leaders, and sometimes it's not the players a coach might expect based on his or her objective assessment. That's the first thing you have to figure out. Who have they chosen? You have to coach the team *through* the team, *through* their leaders. It's very humbling for a coach and, I think, it's been good for the game. We're now seeing that leadership style take hold everywhere—and not just in soccer.

"You look at a guy like Dick Vermeil in Kansas City and what he's been able to do with the Chiefs. He's very open with his team, emotionally honest. The guy cries at press conferences—not something we're used to seeing from head coaches in the

NFL. But his players would kill for him. People might argue the point with me, but I think that's what women's soccer has brought to the world of sports. Emotional honesty, the sense that we're all in this together, and that the coach doesn't have all the answers. He or she is still the boss, there should never be any doubt about that, but the team bears the first responsibility for its fate, and the coach is part of the team."

Because, yes, much of what happens in sports, probably most of what happens, is beyond a coach's control—and some of the things that happen are the last things you'd expect.

As the Hornets left RFK Stadium that April night wearing their new blue souvenir number 9 Mia Hamm T-shirts, I could sense that things were changing. For the first time, Shelby drew away from the group as we all meandered through the main concourse to the gates. The boys stuck together, pelting one another with peanuts, smearing cotton candy in their hair, all the usual gorilla antics of juvenile males, but the Mosquito flitted in and out of the stadium tunnels alone to steal parting looks at the emerald expanse of field below.

She would return many more times that spring and summer, her parents in tow, patiently posting herself on the sidelines before and after games, waiting, waiting, waiting for her chance. Wondering when and how and whether it would happen, until that night in June. "She did it!" Terry hollered into his cell phone on the way home from the stadium. "She got Mia's autograph! Got to talk to her, too!"

"Well, you know our girl is persistent," I told him. "It was just a matter of time."

10.

IN THESE TIMES

LA PELOTA LOCA

It was 1:10 in the afternoon and the sun was already cranking down in the west, covering the lower end of Calvert Hills Park with a white glare as the ref walked to the circle for the coin toss. Two of Upper Marlboro's biggest "horses" tested their cleats in the sponge cake at midfield, hands on hips, jutting their chins at the Hornets' bench. They had never lost a game to College Park, and they didn't plan to start now.

For the first time, I felt as if I actually knew what I was doing. But for all Rafael's lectures—for all I had learned about the game that spring and the previous fall, for all the hours of conversation with the Hall of Fame masters, all the tips and pointers—I still couldn't shake my pregame jitters. None of us could, because this was Marlboro. How many youth coaches in the entire country possessed diagrams of the Penn State defense hand-drawn by the great Walter Bahr? How many had been personally tutored by Len Oliver and George Brown and Harry Keough? How many had read *The Art of War?* As a class, youth coaches are famously obsessive, but it's doubtful that there are many who were as obsessed as I was in 2002–2003. The Upper Marlboro game, then, had become a defining moment, both for the Hornets and for their coach.

Like it or not, the whole point of sports by this age is to find a way to win. As a team comes into its own, it begins to develop a will to succeed. There are fewer opportunities for the kind of New Age social engineering that boomer parents brought to pee-wee soccer; notions of enforced equality are crowded out; the halt, lame, and weak can no longer be protected from the forces of natural selection—not in a sport this demanding. As the team seeks to satisfy its own ends, the coach faces increasing pressure to choose whose side he's on, the athletes' or the hobbyists'.

By the start of the season I had straddled the question as long as I could. The parents of the more casual players had me down as a win-at-all-cost elitist who didn't give their children anywhere near enough playing time. They charged me with showing naked favoritism to the stars, and a few had clocked the games to prove it. But the fact was that the stars actually came to practice and, therefore, could run for more than five minutes without cramping up. Meanwhile, the parents of the stars thought I was a politically correct cream puff who had cost the team countless games by playing less able kids at critical moments. This was also true, but I was duty-bound to uphold the Boys and Girls Club credo of inclusion—no matter how physically challenged a kid might be or how little his parents invested in the welfare of the team.

This infernal code of politeness is what allows hecklers like Los Angeles sportscaster Jim Rome to call soccer a sissy game, "a fourth-rate sport" that requires no skill, no guts, and none of the uniquely American virtues exhibited in football. "Like all real Americans, I hate soccer." Rome has said. "My son is not playing soccer. I will hand him ice skates and a shimmering sequined blouse before I hand him a soccer ball." Rome speaks for a substantial sector of middle-aged American men who are put off by the insistence of youth-soccer advocates that the sport should be run like a petunia garden, where the self-esteem of the most fragile flowers can flourish. Prohibitions against "inappropriate behavior" and "improper conduct" and "unsporting demeanor" are so much a part of the literature of youth soccer that the game starts to sound like a round of Duck Duck Goose, and the coach who's dumb enough to believe it is in for a shock. Struggle though he may to keep the game kind and gentle, his kids will come to understand the true nature of the sport by the time they are nine, and they will begin to play a different game from the one he is coaching.

Whatever else a youth coach may wish to achieve, he has to figure out a way to win, or dissension will rend his team.

"Bry," I told our new captain of the guard before he went out, "if we win the coin toss, make sure you pick the muddy end of the field in the first half. We want them running into the sun. We clear?"

"Yep," he said.

"We're gonna grind them down in the first half."

"And shoot out their lights in the second," he replied.

"That's right. Now go out there and win us the ball."

We had missed this kid terribly the previous fall. A whip-smart honor roll student with the prototypical Cheetah physique, Bryan had taken himself out of a preseason scrimmage on the eve of our Triple-A opener, then collapsed on the sideline clutching his stomach, ashen-faced. I tried to give him some water, but he refused. Drinking made him want to pee, he said, and it hurt to pee. It was the last time we would see him for six months. He finally returned in March 2003—just in time for the Greenbelt game—sporting a seven-inch surgical scar.

In the life of a youth soccer team, there are trials that each kid within the group undergoes that none but a trusted few know much about. As dicey as Bryan's bladder operation was, fewer than half of the Hornets had any idea why he was missing, and most of their parents knew only that he was sick, if they noted his absence at all. Other kids went through struggles of their own: the first diagnosis of a learning disability, mostly hyperactivity and "processing" disorders; speech pathologies; language barriers; ugly divorces; absentee fathers—the full menu of childhood afflictions. Most were secure in the bosom of middle-class homes, at least partially insured, but there were always a few who absorbed body blows that their parents couldn't deflect.

The saddest case was a bright blond kid I'll call Bobby. He joined the team early on, played for a season, then suddenly began cutting practices the following spring. He magically appeared on Saturdays with his uncle, eager to play in the weekly games, but it was never that easy. Even then some parents grumbled if I gave game-day minutes to anyone who missed practice. "It's hard to play him when he never shows up," I told his uncle. "If there's some kind of problem, you need to tell me about it, or else tell his mom to start getting him to practice." He hesitated for a second, staring at his paint-spattered boots, then sidled closer. "Look, Coach, I'm not really his uncle," he said. "Just a close friend of the family, you might say."

Bobby's mom had been arrested for drug possession, and his father was "nobody knows where." The kid was now living in the city, and Saturday soccer was the only time he got to see his old classmates and neighborhood buddies from the suburbs. "He needs this," his adoptive uncle whispered.

"Enough said," I replied without looking up from my clipboard. "He's in the rotation."

These are the external forces, the pressures that no coach foresees when he first hangs a whistle around his neck. These quiet intrigues and private injuries are almost always felt more intensely in soccer, because it's the first mass sport in America that isn't confined to a single season. Between the spring, fall, and winter indoor leagues, the semiannual tournaments and pre-season scrimmages, the game hardly stops. Aside from brief breaks during the coldest months of the winter and the dog days of summer, teams stick together throughout the year—one year after another—until they are so tightly bound that they start to feel like moon cults. People make friendships in this game that will last forever.

The problems faced by the kids always change, but for the coach the hardest part is always the same: keeping the grown-ups happy. You can read the coaching manuals for a thousand hours and never find a word about this, but a youth soccer coach spends more time tending to the needs of the adults than to those of the children. If a team has twelve kids, the head coach has to manage up to twenty-four adult egos, and that's before you start counting the grandparents. Overburden your roster—say, take on six more players—and you add eighteen beating hearts, and that's before you figure in the "grands." Take a head count and that's as many as a hundred and twenty-six people following the team around. There are hamlets in New England smaller than that.

Over the years, I had been asked by divorcé fathers to transmit messages to their ex-wives. I had written letters to school boards on behalf of foreign-born kids whose parents hadn't mastered English well enough to do it themselves, and I had presented myself to principals as a surrogate guardian to bust kids out of after-school programs so they could come to practice. I had forged more league applications and medical waivers than I could count when parents were too busy to make it to sign-ups. Some days, Terry and I ran an informal bus service to get kids to the field on time, and we often wound up bringing them home with us afterward until their parents got out of work.

All of this is to say that, a youth soccer coach is much more than a coach. He's more like the besieged mayor of a small town.

Every resident wields a vote over the team's destiny no matter how tenuous or transient his or her involvement, and no faction wields its votes more fiercely than the uncommitted—the agnostic parents who are here one season and gone the next, and back again one year later to assert their claim to an even share of all the good that flows from membership. Most of them are oblivious to the sacrifices and tribulations the team has endured to stay together in the meantime, but they are acutely attuned to any word or gesture that conveys their child's less-than-equal status within the group. Loosely quoting Winston Churchill's definition of socialism, soccer commissioner Dave Olfky once described coaching to me as the "art of making everyone miserable, equally," particularly when it comes to apportioning playing time and even if it means the team may lose. But Dave also knew well that such a state of studied indifference takes years of dermal toughening, and that most recreation league coaches never achieve it.

"The harder you work, the harder it is to surrender," Vince Lombardi once said, and the Hornets had worked awfully hard in their quest for a perfect season. The cast of secondary characters, meanwhile, changed constantly—the two dozen kids and their respective entourages who came and went from the team over the years, drifting through games and questioning referees and earnestly seeking explanations for every coaching decision, most of which had no rhyme or reason because we were usually too busy trying to police the mob scene on our bench to give anything else much thought. Coaches seldom acknowledge it, but the constant kvetching is part of the charm, because every new class of klutzes brings the possibility of one or two who might have the ember of desire glowing in them. Once that has been determined, tolerance for parental eccentricities tends to rise proportionally. It is the talent of the kid that determines whether a difficult parent is regarded as a pain in the ass or as merely weird, and the merely weird are treated differently. Coaching them to enlightened detachment is what allows the kid to flourish.

In the meantime, a coach must steel himself or herself for "Drama Mondays," as my wife called the weekly postgame grievance sessions. Particularly after a tough match, like the Greenbelt game, the phones started ringing around dinnertime and by midnight my e-mail had clogged.

Kid X complained that I took away his Cheese Doodles on the sideline, which "hurt his feelings." Kid Y alerted his mom that I told him to pee in the bushes instead of walking three hundred yards to the men's room at the snack bar, and this was deemed "inappropriate." Kid Z was upset that his grandfather, who was visiting from out of town, got lost on the Beltway, missed most of the game, and didn't get to see him play, which meant that I was "insensitive"—even though I had no idea Gramps was in town. And, while she was at it, Kid Z's mother also wanted to know, for the hundredth time, why her son never got to play offense, a question for which there was no polite reply. "Don't answer it and maybe it'll go away," became my wife's automatic counsel when the phone rang.

Thank the soccer gods, then, for the handful of Hornets who had older brothers or sisters who were already involved in the game. Their folks knew the pitfalls, paid less attention to the minor intrigues, granted their kids more autonomy, weren't so easily ruffled. The second son of Walter and Deysis Linares was our sterling example. Braulio had come out of nowhere, a walk-on, the runt of the group. There was every reason to believe that he wouldn't be able to hold his own among the bigger kids. In his first few months with the team, he got boxed around at practice so badly that he became famous for his free-flowing nasal hemorrhages—gruesome debouchments that left us both bloody to the elbows. One night his mother arrived to pick him up and found her baby boy generously smeared. "Not for you to worry," Deysis told me offhandedly. "Braulio, he is a bleeder."

"In life, you must be strong, and soccer is good for teaching this," Rafael Guerrero, my soccer counselor, said afterward. "Hispanic people want the coach to be strong, too, but you are still learning. You still worry too much and listen too much to the parents." Yes, the man called me a wimp, as only he could. "Braulio is becoming a better player because of you," he added. "And you are becoming a better coach because of Braulio."

On the morning of the Marlboro game, we all woke up more nervous than usual. The kids never slept well before a big match, and Terry called by 6:00 a.m. to tell me that Shelby had been dressed for an hour, clomping outside his bedroom door in her cleats. No slouch himself, Ben was out in the yard at sunrise pounding practice shots against the fence and knocking a few more pickets into the street. Resetting the slats every spring had become a postseason ritual.

"Hey, man, while I'm thinking of it, where's the cards?" I asked Terry.

"I gave them to you," he said.

"No, *you* had them last," I said.

"Yeah, and I gave them back to *you* at practice on Tuesday," he insisted.

"No, you didn't."

"Yeah, I did."

"You sure?"

"Hell, yes," he said. "I hate those things."

We had lost the team's ID cards so many times that neither of us wanted to be responsible for them anymore. But not having them in hand was to risk forfeiture if an opposing coach decided to challenge the age of one of our kids, and goalie Edward Curry was so huge that he invited challenges the moment he walked onto the field. "Did you check the equipment bag?" Terry snickered, knowing full well that the Hornets' blue nylon duffel was so full of junk—a dozen balls, three dozen cones, assorted water bottles, chemical ice packs, T-shirts, wads of dirty gauze, a clipboard, three or four gummed-up whistles, and crushed first-aid kits—that you could lose a watermelon inside it.

"Dude," I said, "if you know where they are, please spare me digging through that bag."

For all the sedition among the Hornets' camp followers, few had any idea how much labor went into fielding a team and keeping it intact from one season to the next. There were always five or six hours of work to be done for every hour of playing time. "You won't believe what the club needs us to do now," I would tell the Hornets' dads. Their reply, the standard inside joke, was always "Who's buying?"

There is no end of communal exertion in soccer, because the sport does not enjoy a legacy of government subsidies—the permanent mounds, dugouts, uprights, and rims of America's traditional games. Our goals come in clattering hundred-pound vinyl sacks and are thrown up and hammered down minutes before kickoff. You are not a soccer coach until you can perform this feat in predawn darkness without herniating a lumbar disk and smashing both thumbs. When county public-works crews failed to appear on their tractors in time for big games, we loaded push mowers into our cars and cut acres of grass by hand. If an overnight storm erased the field lines, we hauled out hundred-yard surveyor tapes, spray-painted fresh boundaries on our hands and knees, and spread fifty-pound sacks of kitty litter to soak up the slop at midfield. Our cars became rolling locker rooms. Our cell-phone bills soared with calls for rides, calls for volunteer ground crews, calls for last-minute items like water and ice and shin guards when any of the kids forgot to bring theirs.

My cell bill for 2003 ran to $1,149.95, which is to say nothing of the $279 I spent on beer that year to coax my compatriots from their paying jobs.

The normal game-day state of mind for the average youth soccer coach is exhaustion. The poor grunt with the bandaged fingers often has been up since dawn, yacking on his cell, packing up his gear, downloading directions to some swamp of a field twenty miles from home, and trying to make sure a minimum number of his kids get there on time so the team doesn't have to forfeit. If he has "home-field advantage," it only adds to the logistical chaos. By 6:30 on the morning of the Marlboro game Terry and I were skidding around in the mud, wrestling aluminum poles and tangled orange netting into place, and scrounging for tent stakes in my toolshed to pin down the goal.

"You got a mallet or a hammer or something?" he asked.

"Yeah," I said. "In the back of the Volvo." Which is how we found the Hornets' cards. They were in the wheel well, jammed between the spare tire and the jack. How they got there was anyone's guess.

Bryan came running back to the sideline. "We won the toss! They're running into the sun, just like you said."

"Good man," I told him, turning to the rest of the team. "Okay, guys, you know what to do."

"Stop them at midfield," Edward said.

"Double-team their wings," Bryan echoed.

"Kick their butts for once!" Shelby said, stirred at the thought of what her backfield was about to do now that they were no longer second-class citizens.

"On three. HORNETS!"

The kids swept onto the field and took up their new positions—a 180-degree departure from every previous match. The

familiar "compressed diamond" was now in the backfield, a classic four-man defense. If it was good enough to beat the English at
Belo Horizonte, good enough for Rafael and Sun Tzu, I was willing to try it, even though it defied everything I thought I knew
about sports. Bryan was the rear guard, the last sentry at the gate,
a position known in soccer as the "sweeper." His main job was to
reinforce the flank defenders when they came under attack from
Marlboro, to rush out and set up a double-team trap. His speed
gave him license to roam the entire backfield. Posted to his left
was Shelby, out along the touchline as the strong-side defender.
Between them, at the top of the diamond in the midfield circle,
stood the indomitable Rhino, 110 pounds of immovable object
called a "stopper." Edward Curry was the rock who would split
Marlboro's initial downhill rush—Sun Tzu's "strong point"—and
force their strikers outside to be cut up by the rest of the defense.

Up front, we started the game with just two forwards, unas-
sisted "scouts" running uphill. Any goals we got in the first half
would have to come from Kevin Guerrero and Braulio, but we
weren't counting on them to score. "Guys, just make them run,"
I told them. "Make them run until their tongues are hanging out.
Make them fight you for every ball. *La pelota loca,* eh?" Crazy
ball. My Spanish was so bad that it never failed to crack them up.
Far in the rear, their ace wingman was tending the goal for the
first time. The kid with the blond bowl haircut wasn't at all
happy to be grounded in the box, but at that point the Hornets
needed his hands more than his magic left foot.

What few people knew that day was that Ben's small, well-ordered
universe had been pitched upside down. He and his little brother,
Sam, hadn't seen their mother in days, and the phone rang every
night with more terrible news from Chicago. Their grandmother—who flew to Maryland two or three times a year to ad-

mire and lavish them with gifts, who had spent every summer vacation with us at the beach in North Carolina for as long as our kids could remember—was dying. The day-to-day regularity and domestic symmetry that Donna insisted upon quickly came unbolted. Dirty dishes piled up in the sink. Laundry collected at the bottom of the basement stairs. As she spent longer stretches of time away from home, heaps of unopened mail and unread newspapers accumulated on the dining-room table. We lived on pizza and take-out spaghetti dinners from the nearby Plato's Diner.

Donna had been gone for a week when I slumped through the Warings' side door one night without knocking to pick up our kids after work. Thomas, our big midfielder, and Ben were in the family room, thoroughly engrossed in a video game, and their little brothers were busy tearing through the house. I was played out, way past exhausted. I fell into a chair without an invitation. Nick and Cindy were eating dinner, spicy Thai beef and green beans. It was raining outside, and I was thoroughly doused. Nick put a plate of food in front of me without asking.

"Everybody comes into soccer thinking it's just this weird little sport," Cindy said a few minutes later, after I thanked her again for all she had done for us in Donna's absence—laundry, fresh flowers, picking up the kids after school. "But underneath it I think we're all looking for something bigger, not sure what that 'thing' is and probably not believing we'll ever find it. You start looking for some kind of *community*. That probably sounds a little corny or whatever, but that's what soccer's been for us. It's way more than just a game."

"Yeah." Nick laughed. "It'll take over your life if you let it!" And we had, for larger reasons that we seldom considered. Cindy described a few of them that night far more eloquently than anything I had heard or read before. She had been an Outward Bound girl, later majored in horticulture, and worked with handicapped kids. She was one of the Hornets' philosophers in residence, a small group that included Rafael and K. C. Curry. K.C.'s father had been one of the Tuskegee Airmen in World War II, the highly decorated African-American fighter squadron, and he made sure his son never lost his sense of history or social responsibility. At various times that season they each had mentioned the same idea, that soccer had become an anchor in their lives. "The world's a scary place these days," K.C. told me one night. "You have to give people a really good reason to leave the house."

In these times and in this place, you needed soccer or religion or something like it to get you through. All the adults in the Hornets' orbit now seemed ever on the alert for the next flash bulletin on CNN, their basements stocked with bottled water and canned beans and flashlight batteries. Since the team first formed, the World Trade Center had collapsed and the Pentagon stood agape; anthrax spores were found three miles outside College Park in a postal depot in Brentwood, Maryland; concrete dragons' teeth were installed on Pennsylvania Avenue to keep truck bombers away from the White House. Patrolling F-16 fighters carved contrails over our practice fields. To live anywhere near the nation's capital was to be constantly reminded that the essence of life is jeopardy, and routine its only veil. Whether it was church or school or team, people clung more tightly to the nearest rock.

On my way home from the Warings' house that night, the boys fell asleep in the backseat and I thought about September 11. I had covered the Pentagon and the World Trade Center crash sites for *The Baltimore Sun*, staring into both pits in the first seventy-two hours. By the time I got off I-95 in College Park after two days in lower Manhattan, I was an emotional wreck, convinced that life as I knew it had ended. Then there they were, charging down the bald little field across the street from my house, flying across Guilford Avenue, crashing through my front gate, waving sweatshirts, crowding into the yard, shrieking "Welcome home!" and

"Go Hornets!" Braulio helpfully confirmed that after five days of living out of my car I didn't look so hot. "Coach," he said, "you *stink*!" Nick called it "fairly ripe." Terry ordered, "Go to bed—we can talk later." Ben yelled, "Mom says call her at work as soon as you get in." Everything and nothing had changed. I went upstairs and fell asleep in less than five minutes, lulled by the sound of Hornets and whistles under my bedroom window.

The game began and Upper Marlboro came out in a standard 2-2-2 formation—two defenders, two midfielders, and two forwards standing in parallel vertical ranks—looking to flatten us for the fifth time. At the kickoff they spread out into a 2-4 as soon as they got the ball. All four strikers charged away from their defenders in an excited downhill rush, a horizontal line of cavalry, straight into the teeth of the entrenched blue-and-white backfield.

"Well, let's see how this goes," Terry said sarcastically.

"Just hold up a second," I told him. "Everything's gonna work out fine."

"You hope," he said.

"That's true." I laughed.

With their backs to the drainage sluice and their feet firmly planted in the mud, the Hornets hardly had to move to present Marlboro's strikers with an insoluble problem. There were too many blue jerseys for the red attackers to move in straight lines, and the ground broke away under their feet whenever they tried to dodge us. At the first challenge from Shelby on the left side, Marlboro's star forward went down in a pile of knees and elbows, coughing up the ball and sending it piddling away over the middle. Ben broke from the box and pounded it so far upfield that it landed fifteen yards in front of Marlboro's startled goalkeeper. Both defenders tried to beat him to it, but Kevin got there first. Pushing the ball outside toward the right corner, he made a pair of sharp, ninety-degree cuts that took him back to where he started, back toward the goal, as the keeper retreated deeper into his net. A more experienced goalie might have attacked, capitalizing on his strength of numbers and his own advantage in being able to use his hands. But competent keepers are rare at this age.

At the last second, Kevin popped up his head, found his man sprinting for the goal, and pooched a soft pass behind the defenders that came to a stop fifteen feet from the right post, setting up a point-blank, dead-ball "golf shot." The goalie never had a chance. "WHOA!" the ref said. "Now that's something you don't see every day." Braulio threw himself into the shot so hard that he ended up in the back of the net with the ball, hung like a fly in a spider's web.

"Let's start the rotation," I told Terry, gesturing at the platoon of subs gawking on the sideline.

"Don't you think we ought to wait until we get another goal at least?"

"We aren't gonna get another goal," I said. "Marlboro is going to have no choice now but to pack their A squad onto the field to get that one back, and I want them to run into a wall of big bodies. Just leave Bryan and Ben back there and fill the space in front of them with monsters. We got plenty of them."

"You sure 'bout this?"

"Yeah, yeah, yeah, I'm sure, man. You'll see. We're gonna bust this thing open in the second half."

As if only too happy to endorse the decision, Marlboro's coach yanked out both of his defenders and one midfielder, then shuttled in all of his stars and switched to a 3-3 line for the next kickoff. Up front, Marlboro now featured two Gigantors at the wings and a fidgety kid at forward who looked as if he were about to leap out of his shoes. There, revealed for the first time, was the cream of his roster, squinting into the sun and itching for a payback.

"Okay, I think I get where you're going with this. Shelby, Linus, OUT!" Terry called, grabbing two of the biggest substitutes from the sideline mob and thrusting them onto the field. "Go on, get! Just don't let anybody come down the sidelines, especially not those big kids."

"Nobody gets through," I echoed. "Don't worry about foul calls at midfield. Go in on them hard, but not near the box. Let Bryan and Ben handle the box. Stay *out* of the box!" In this most sensitive part of the field, I wanted our deftest players doing the dirty work.

Law XIII of the soccer rule book, and its evil stepsister Law XIV, are at their most unforgiving in and around the box, the painted white rectangle in front of the goal. In its most basic reading, Law XIII says that the referee can stop the game anytime a player commits a foul and can give the other team a "free kick." Law XIV says that if the foul happens inside the box the opposing team gets a penalty kick (PK), essentially a free chop from a spot immediately in front of the net. Under either law, an unopposed shot at a stationary ball anywhere near the goal is a nerve-racking event for the keeper, who must defend a vault up to eight yards wide and eight feet high. The net in kids' soccer is usually about two-thirds of these dimensions, but still far too large for one person to consistently protect.

The goalkeeper's disadvantage is compounded by the fact that, unlike other sports, the player who is fouled does not have to take the foul shot. Rather, a coach is free to send whomever he or she pleases to make the penalty kick, and it's usually the hardest shooter on the field. At every age and echelon of the game, there is no charity or politeness in a PK. Like a field-goal kick in football, all action stops. Eyeball to eyeball, two players stand alone awaiting the signal from the referee. Then the shooter strikes the ball as hard as he or she can, endeavoring to drive it over, under, or through the goalie.

Stripped of all correctness, the principle is precisely the inverse at midfield. With Edward and two jumbo-size kids on his flanks, the Hornets now had a bruising 350-pound triangle flung across Marlboro's path, and we expected those kids to commit fouls, if not deliberately then certainly incidentally. Since a foul call at midfield does not yield a close-range free kick—and since it is far from certain that a referee will call one anyway—physical play near the line is the essence of the midfielder's First Commandment: "The man *or* the ball, but never the man *and* the ball." Translation: it's okay to let one or the other get by you, but the two together are a threat to score. The striker must be separated from the ball before he or she reaches the box. Hence the increasing roughness at midfield as the players get older and bigger.

Most of the Hornets' "veterans" understood all of this at nine years old. But for the rest of the team the distinction between hard defense at midfield and elegance in the backfield could be learned only by coaching and practice, and our practice schedule had been in tatters for more than a year. The previous fall season had been interrupted by the Beltway snipers, a pair of wandering psychopaths who circled the Washington suburbs shooting people at random from a peeling blue Chevy Caprice. In the first seventy-two hours of October 2002, they picked off six victims.

The police issued a Code Red lockdown within hours. Sports fields and playgrounds were closed; games were postponed indefinitely; armed guards were posted in the parking lots of schools at pickup and drop-off times. Weeks went by, and kids barely saw sunlight. "I don't know about your guys, but mine are bouncing off the walls," a fellow coach told me on the phone one night shortly after the snipers shot a thirteen-year-old kid outside a local middle school. "I'll be damned if I'm going to have my kids completely traumatized by this. I mean, what are we going to do? Keep them locked up inside until Christmas?" Soccer, he proposed, was the obvious antidote.

By the following Friday we had eight or nine kids running outside again at a place they called the Train Park. Hidden deep inside a residential neighborhood and effectively walled off by an elevated commuter-rail trestle, it was a natural haven for the duration of the manhunt. Word of mouth quickly spread. By the following week there were fifteen kids, then twenty, then twenty-five—ages six to thirteen—from a half dozen teams in the area. One of the moms eventually thought to bring a cooler of drinks. Then another showed up a week later with a box of chicken wings. Nick formed a beer brigade. The gatherings turned into ad hoc picnics. After dark, we lined up our cars, lit the field with headlights, and watched the kids chase glowing balls through the shadows. Sentimentality may be the worst crutch of sportswriters. But there are times when a game is, in fact, much more than a game.

Between the mud and the sun in their faces and all the heavyweights stacked in our backfield, Marlboro couldn't budge the ball without getting smacked. Against a steady rotation of wide-bodies, their strikers and flankers were pinballing into the muck. Edward set the tone, and the rest of our big boys followed his lead. If there was any doubt in the minds of Marlboro's parents that soccer was a contact sport, the Rhino was performing the same service for them that Bowie's fullbacks had performed for us in the Snow Bowl five months earlier. There was hardly a Hornet who wasn't black-and-blue that day, but they walked away better for it. Edward later won the club's Rookie Sportsman of the Year award for his goalkeeping heroics that day, which included playing the entire second half with his outer jersey frozen on his back.

If this was Marlboro's induction into hardihood, there were worse places to earn it, because Edward didn't have a mean bone in his body. He was, however, built like a tractor, and he had learned to turn this disadvantage to good use.

With our strikers all but irrelevant in the first half, we were free to stick almost anyone up front. Rafael's defensive scheme was working so well that Terry and I flooded the field with scrubs, comfortable that Bryan and Ben could hold up the rear alone if they had to and thoroughly pleased that Edward was destroying every offensive thrust before it ever reached them. Long before halftime, Marlboro was beginning to disintegrate, bickering and blaming one another. Everything was against them—the back-field arithmetic, the terrain, the angle of the sun—but their coach persisted in attacking until his squad was dappled with contusions and fondued in mud.

Every Hornet got to play the star positions on offense. Every parent was smiling. At long last I felt that I was finally coaching the kids to a win instead of just screaming and hoping and pray-ing for our studs to gut it out for us. As the clock ran down on the first half of play, the deck was stacked so high in our favor that the outcome felt certain.

Under the rules of soccer the two teams switched sides of the field at halftime, so the downhill advantage would be ours for the rest of the game, and all of our starters were rested. At the kickoff, as Rafael had predicted, Marlboro's coach made no concessions for the mire around his net. Desperate for a goal, he sent his four strikers charging uphill and left a pair of lonely defenders to cover the slop against a hive of Hornets. What we had so easily de-fended with a nearly stationary four-man defense was impossible for the two Marlboro kids to cover alone on the run. "Would you look at that!" Terry said as the Hornets tore into them. Shelby scored first, then Ben, then Kevin. The prettiest goal of the day came about twelve minutes into the half, when tiny Michael

Thomas—a shrimp of a kid who somehow kept his courage for the game despite getting buffeted around every time he stepped onto the field—charged into the box, dove into the mud, and slid three feet on his back to spear the ball past the keeper.

Flailing in the pudding, the red-and-white backfield fell victim to Laws XIII and XIV no fewer than six times before the ref finally informed me that he was suspending the rule against hand balls. "We'll be here all day if I call a foul every time they touch the ball," he confided. Instead of having our strikers take the freebies, we had wheeled up our midfielders to do it. Edward, Matt, and Thomas all scored on thundering PKs. Meanwhile, with Braulio and Bryan anchoring the defense and the lanky Alex Corboy in at keeper, Marlboro managed three shots on goal in the second half. Only one found the mark, a lucky squib that bounced just past Alex's outstretched fingers as he leaped sideways in the goal.

After three years of toil and setbacks, it was a measure of the day that the most valiant play—a display of guts that would be celebrated for weeks—was a failed attempt to stop the other team from scoring. At the final whistle, the tally was 8–1, a landslide win that youth soccer coaches generally try to avoid because it demoralizes the opposing team, who are, after all, just kids. But Marlboro had never shown us such courtesy in four prior meetings, and once our strikers were loose it was impossible to get them back on a leash. No Hornet ever expected kindness on a soccer field from anyone in a red jersey, and they showed none when their chance came to settle overdue accounts.

The bigger victory, however, appeared nowhere on the official game report to the county league office. Our kids were finally playing as a team, and their coach was finally over his lingering misconceptions about soccer. It was a sport, all right, and sometimes it could be more, once you learned to do less.

11.

ENDGAME

PLAYING INTO SPACE

The first sign of trouble was a profusion of green mucus and a hacking miner's cough that gave way within forty-eight hours to consumptive fevers, earaches, and all-night vomiting. "Patient Zero" was Kevin Guerrero, but fallen Hornets soon piled up two-deep in the hurt locker. On the heels of the biggest win in the team's history—the precisely calculated slaughter of Upper Marlboro—a virus cut down half the roster within a matter of days.

Just as my newly retooled team seemed poised to rampage through the league, just as the crowning payoff was within reach, it crumbled like a stale cracker. By the Wednesday night after the Marlboro game, I, too, was among the casualties. The demons of spring were finally upon us. The annual Easter tempests hit the same week, interspersed with brief periods of sunshine that turned our practice field into an overgrown frog pond. When the grass got ankle-high, the city sent a squadron of rider-mowers to churn the muck some more until it was perfect for a monster truck rally. Over the next month, we managed three workouts, much less than half our usual regimen.

It is said that there are five stages of dying. So, too, are there stages to the soccer life. In the terminal phase—after a coach has been through naive enthusiasm, obsession, and disillusion—he or she approaches an evolutionary fork: resignation or possession. Flee or surrender. He can either shuck all the aggravation and quit or suck it up and move to the next plateau of the game. If a coach has begun to feel a sense of responsibility for the integrity of the sport itself, it is probably too late to save him. The best you can hope for then is that he achieves the final stage, enlightenment, before alcohol and insomnia kill him.

Coaching is really three separate and distinct skills: you have to know your sport, you have to know kids, and you have to keep advancing your knowledge of both to avoid making everyone around you miserable. Most youth coaches fail at one or more of these things, and incompetence eventually does them in. The education of the average youth coach is normally measured by the number of accidental encounters he has with people who actually know what they're doing, and whether he's awake enough to notice those moments when they happen. If not, he'll become obsolete. At age nine, the gentle developmental curve of the child athlete spikes sharply. The game accelerates. And the unprepared coach becomes a bystander to his own undoing. In this very public theater, this can be a lonely and embarrassing period in a person's life.

No sooner did the flu subside than the spring-break cycle began. The members of the Hornets went to six different schools, so their vacations came at different times and their parents seldom consulted the soccer calendar when making plans for family getaways. Between rainouts and the stomach bug, we hadn't seen a third of them in weeks, and few had bothered to call. I couldn't fault them for wanting to get out of the viral boglands for a while—it was opening day of trout season in Pennsylvania, and I knew where I'd rather be—but absconding with my players without so much as a moment's notice bordered on treason. It was the principle of the thing: a commitment was a commitment. I hadn't seen the Juniata River, or the Outer Banks of North Carolina for the autumn striped-bass run, in three *years*. I knew other coaches whose golf handicaps had gone to hell, a life's work down the drain. We had given up nights out, movies, the glorious indolence of a wasted Sunday watching NFL football—all for this. Did these parents not feel our pain? Did they not care that we were within range of our first county championship?

The team began a long slog through the month of April with an average of nine kids on the roster—the usual seven, plus two or three others who changed from week to week. Even so, the loyal Hornets managed to pound out a 5-5 goal ratio over the second half of the season, delivering us to a 2-0-3 record, undefeated for the first time, alone at the top of the division. We could have taken the title outright with just one more win, but we were always one pair of legs short, one five-minute spurt shy. I would have given almost anything for that one extra goal, but it was not to be.

The consolation was that we got to witness the emergence of two natural leaders on the team: in a rematch against Greenbelt, Ben and Bryan took over the Hornets. The secrets of the game had opened up for them. They were talking on the field now, shouting instructions, signaling to each other from their opposite positions on the left and the right, moving the ball from backfield to front, usually with Braulio or Alex between them as their pivot man. At kickoffs, the threesome ganged together at the circle, barking and pointing, bouncing on the balls of their feet, anything to fluster the opposition.

Greenbelt's coach, assuming that we would "mark" his biggest star again if he tried to play him as a striker, shifted Malachi Alexander to center-midfielder. Thomas Waring and Matt Shade took turns bumping and banging Malachi, but he still managed to torch us for a goal with an arcing shot that had just enough English on it to slip through Edward's hands.

This is often your best chance of beating a four-man defensive formation—pull up and shoot long before the defenders organize themselves and compress down into the box—but there aren't that many nine-year-olds who can mortar a ball thirty yards, and there weren't that many Hornets who could maintain their composure once it happened. This time, however, they took their cues from Ben and Bryan, neither of whom seemed the least bit concerned.

The change in attitude came not a moment too soon, because with so many holes in the lineup I was out of plans, hope, and energy. The familiar late-season malaise had set in. At a certain point in the schedule, all I wanted was a lazy weekend at home and more than five or six hours' sleep. Both Terry and I worked hard at our regular jobs, and the only way we made it through a season was by not doing much of anything else. He installed cabinets and dealt with customers and laid out kitchen plans sixty hours a week, while I spent my time reporting from the slums of Baltimore. Where neighborhood beefs were once settled on a soccer field in Patterson Park, guns now do most of the talking, and murder was part of my beat. It was one of those jobs where you saw things you wish you hadn't.

Part of the allure of coaching was that it kept me reasonably sane, but soccer is much like a drug. The approach of every new season brings a rush of excitement, but the end of it finds you weak at the knees. As the novelty fades, you sustain yourself on the buzz of game day—the rush of caffeine and adrenaline. The frequency and pitch of the sideline needling between opposing coaches invariably subsides as the games wear on, and so do the parental lamentations, because the long campaigns just wear people out. Terry and I called it "going around the bend"—that point in the season when the adults are too far gone to argue anymore. This, coincidentally, was when the kids seemed to start playing at their very best, when the coaches and parents finally shut up.

By this point in any season, my house was a shambles. The spring of 2003 was no different from the rest. Portable goals were stacked in my side yard. Half the picket fence was down. A mound of gear appeared on my front porch every Sunday and dwindled as the week went on, picked over by coaches who came and went at all hours, helping themselves to whatever they needed. Our refrigerator door disappeared behind a flurry of league schedules, sign-up notices, and club newsletters. No matter how often my wife and I cleaned, the floors were perpetually coated with a film of tracked-in grime. On weekends, cleats and shinnies piled up by the front door as kids in sweaty jerseys stormed in after games for PlayStation World Cup tournaments and all-you-can-eat PBJ buffets.

When you're in this deep, when soccer becomes the unifying force of your life, your perspective on everything begins to change. Your kids live in warm-ups and want to wear Adidas flip-flops to school in December. Your house fills with tournament memorabilia. Your wife gives you a replica jersey from the Brazilian National Team for Christmas. You hear about a terrorist bombing overseas and you say a small prayer that none of the players from Real Madrid or Manchester United or Inter Milan were hurt. You start to *care* about all kinds of things you never cared about before. The dull *whap!* of size-one mini-balls against the wall of the basement rec room echoed through our house year-round now. Ben couldn't walk past a ball, any ball—tennis ball, golf ball, Super Ball—without stopping to futz with it. Kevin and Braulio lived on fields, an endless circuit of Latino *liga* games, Hornets practices, festivals, and tournaments. Bryan had killed the grass on the north side of the Basdeos' house, cranking hundreds of shots into the side of their redbrick rancher. Shelby hardly went anywhere without her gym bag, which usually contained her "game ball" and her "practice ball." For more than a year, she and Ben had a regular date, meeting on Sundays to hammer shots into the wall of the school across the street. All of them played other sports, baseball and basketball to be sure, but they put away their stuff at the end of every season. Soccer was their constant.

"You know, they're getting to where it's all they want to do," Terry had said as we sat at the picnic table one Sunday, watching our kids rip away at the wall. "And once that happens this isn't going to be enough for them."

Not only were Ben and Bryan leading the team now, they were redesigning it on the fly. Alex Corboy had always played with some hesitancy, but he now came alive on the right wing—one minute charging the goal, the next holding back to help Bryan on defense. We also had a newcomer, a quiet sub named Cody Young who had never played soccer before. The youngest son of a venerated local baseball coach, he was naturally athletic, built more for contact sports than his wiry older brothers. But he lacked confidence in this new game until Bryan started telling him what to do and how to do it.

The four of them were moving together now in a diamond in the middle of the field, as if leashed together by invisible bungees. Bryan played in back with his arms spread wide, pointing at undefended spots, chattering at his flankers, while Ben hunted for the ball at the top of the diamond. Braulio and Shelby orbited around them. They were playing Rafael's "vertical game" on instinct, usually moving together but breaking into separate triangles as conditions required. No matter where he went, Malachi found himself surrounded.

As the end of the first half approached, Bryan suddenly decided to revolutionize the Hornets' game. It was another one of those moments that coaches live for, when a flash of innovation by a single player ripples through the team and alerts them to some new possibility, a fresh approach. Stripping the ball from a Greenbelt striker near our goal, Bryan dribbled down the right sideline, then looked up and saw an open lane through the middle. At the point at which he would normally have launched a "clearing kick" to our forwards, he cut left and spontaneously combusted through the opposing defenders and midfielders in a tango of spins, stutter steps, and feints. No one was more shocked than he when he arrived at the line with the ball still at his feet and four would-be challengers trailing after him.

"Ouch!" said Mike Fleming, Greenbelt's head coach. "How did he do that?"

"I have no idea," I replied. "And he probably doesn't, either."

I was lying, of course, and Mike probably knew it because soccer is a liar's game, like poker. No kid uncorks a series of perfect moves unless something is going on. Not at nine years old, not in America, where amateur coaches are so enthralled with the British wallop-punt-cross-and-shoot style of play. Kid defenders are usually taught to clear the ball as fast as they can, lest they be overcome by enemy strikers in front of their own net. "Don't diddle with it!" is the nearly universal coaching directive. "Get rid of it!" The occasional Latino kid may try the fancy scrollwork his father taught him, the small foot movements designed to fake out a challenger, but even he usually gives it up after being called "ball hog" or "hot dog" enough times. So when a defender suddenly pulls a stunt the way Bryan did, dribbling like a Brazilian or a Dutchman, an opposing coach is very likely to recognize that he's been had. If nothing else, he'll at least know that his team is in serious trouble, because the last thing his players will expect is for a fullback to go on the offensive.

Arriving at the circle still unchallenged, Bryan blinked over at us with a "What next?" look on his face. There was nowhere to dump a pass because Ben and Braulio were already gone, tearing for Greenbelt's net. "Go!" I yelled. "Make a run!" Still unopposed and moving like a miniature Franz Beckenbauer—the German defender of the 1960s and '70s who invented the "attacking sweeper" position for the famed Bayern Munich team—Bryan crossed over to striker. The result was an "overload," three Hornets versus two defenders (otherwise known as a 3-v-2). When one of the Greenbelt kids rushed out to meet Bryan, he left Braulio unguarded in front of the goal in the middle of an open swath of grass as wide as a barn door.

"Kick to space!" Terry shouted.

This was a new wrinkle for most of the kids. After years of coaching them to pass to each other, as they might in basketball, Terry and I had been trying to correct our mistake by getting them to use the field. In soccer you don't pass *to* a teammate, because it forces him to stop or slow down to collect the ball, which makes him a sitting duck for a fullback. Rather, you pass to the nearest piece of undefended turf, so your buddy can "run onto the ball" at speed. Bryan needed no prompting. The pass was away before Terry drew his next breath, moving on a diagonal through the vacant patch toward Braulio, who lit after it as the defenders wheeled to squash him. Whether by accident or by design, Bee jumped over the ball and let it pass toward the left post—the back door of the play. Ben dug his toe under the ball and popped it into the air, a perfect "can opener" that whirled past the bewildered keeper and into the roof of the net.

This time there was none of the usual crazed elation. Ben smiled. Bryan gave me a thumbs-up. Braulio scowled, as always. Mike Fleming had seen enough. The Greenbelt coach tossed Malachi a goalkeeper's jersey from the sideline, switched to a 4-2 formation, and stood back chewing his knuckle for the next twenty-five minutes. In one of the more improbable matches I ever watched, Ben and Bryan all but took over the field. Greenbelt's defenders barely slowed them down. The game turned into a two-on-one dogfight as they barraged Malachi at close range. Shots rattled the goal frame and thumped into his chest, but the big kid didn't falter. At one point he dove and pinched the ball right off the end of Shelby's toe.

"I don't know too many grown men who could handle the kind of pressure he's getting," Terry said.

"Me neither, but he has to crack sometime," I replied.

He never did. The game ended in another tie, 1–1, good enough for the undefeated Hornets to knock Greenbelt out of the running and advance to the championship round but not enough for us to win the contest and clinch the county title on points. The day belonged to Malachi Alexander.

Truth be told, the Hornets' newfound self-possession had almost nothing to do with Terry and me. We knew practically nothing at our picnic-table discussion the previous summer about the next level of the game, except that there were four privately run clubs in the county that offered something called travel soccer, and we decided to look into the particulars.

Here, for a fee, kids ran on impeccably groomed fields and wore flashy team uniforms, often underwritten by sponsorship deals with major sporting-goods companies. Here they encountered professional trainers for the first time, actual soccer players who knew the sport. Once a kid made the cut and was invited to join, usually after two or three grueling tryout sessions, he or she got to play against the best kids in their age group across a six- or seven-county area—hence the word "travel"; there's a lot of driving involved. By the start of the spring 2003 season, Bryan, Ben, and Shelby were all working out twice a week with travel teams on their days off from the Hornets. They had gotten very good, very fast.

Terry, Nick, and I would struggle to keep the Hornets together for another year, because it was painful to let go of something that had become the center of our lives, but the inevitable unraveling had begun. By then, too, I was wearying of the competing parental expectations that plague recreation-league sports. The immediate cause of my disaffection, the event that clarified all the tensions within the club and on the team, was "the Nick Waring diet." After one of the newcomers threw up on the sidelines in the heat of the Marlboro game and keeled over like a wounded elk, Nick had proposed that we send an e-mail to the Hornets' parents suggesting that they cut greasy, sugary, salty, processed foods from their children's menus during soccer season. The source of the lad's gastric distress was an all-you-can-eat seafood buffet the night before, topped off the morning of the game with some sort of bacon, egg, and cheese extravaganza from a well-known fast-food chain—washed down with what appeared to be a quart of fructose fizz. Nick inspected the leavings on bended knee and asked, "What are the parents *feeding* these kids? No wonder some of them can't last more than five minutes."

It was the simplicity of the observation and all it implied that snapped everything else into focus for me. Some parents fed their kids cereal and juice before games, while others fed them fast food and soda—and these two groups of parents were bound to see soccer in very different terms. For the former, the game had become a serious competitive sport. For everybody else, it was still a social outing, a chance to see friends and get a little exercise. Either way, a coach had to draw the line somewhere, and anti-barfing measures seemed reasonable. Our carefully worded dietary bulletin went out two days later, and was immediately taken as proof by at least one mother that the coaches had finally gone off the deep end. As her anonymous note to the Boys and Girls Club board put it, we had become "food Nazis," meddling in private domestic prerogatives. She did not mention the profusion of kids in the league who were too big to meet the weight standards for county football, too slow for basketball, and too uncoordinated for baseball. By the time these kids were nine years old, the rigors of organized sports began to press down hard, and soccer was often the last stop. As the games became more demanding, I was spending inordinate amounts of time trying to figure out ways to keep all the families happy and the team playing well at the same time.

Hell, I was spending inordinate amounts of time just trying to keep the team together. Dave Olfky, without whom I might never have come into the game, drew the lines of the dilemma: "We develop them, and just when they're starting to get good travel takes them." As we watched a couple of hundred kids run around Duvall Field at a spring season warm-up event, he continued. "I try not to take it personally, because these are just the choices some parents make, but it's hard to watch our program get pulled apart over and over again, and it defeats the whole purpose of why we all came into this in the first place."

I knew exactly how he felt. Eventually, the more athletic kids and their parents will want more than a parade of break-even seasons, marshy hometown fields, and sideline arguments over who got more minutes than whom. There is no broad middle ground in most places between "rec" and "travel"—also known as "select" or "club" soccer—so there is nowhere for them to go except into the privately run leagues. As the stars drift off to tryouts around age nine, recreational squads begin to fall apart. Peewee basketball and baseball teams lose their mainspring players at about the same time. The "pay for play" phenomenon is also growing in youth hockey. All are crowded into the same corner by football, which relies on government- and school-sponsored leagues for its existence. Played by a fraction of American kids, all of them male, football's enormous equipment, insurance, staffing, training, and facilities expenses consume the largest share of athletic budgets everywhere the game is played. At the youth level, it also tends to be the only sport that is immune to the inclusiveness policies that baby boom parents brought to kids' athletics. Seldom do the boomers examine how their tax money is spent in the realm of youth sports, or America's most vainglorious game might be voted out of existence.

The truth is, inclusiveness has its hidden costs, and this is one of them: the inarguable benefits of providing universal access to team sports for children—a three- or four-year opportunity to adopt good habits and a measure of physical conditioning—are impossible to maintain as an entitlement now that free-market forces have come to kids' athletics. "I can't just *give* this to your son anymore, because the rest of these kids have worked years for it, and if they leave the team will cease to exist," I told several mothers in the spring of 2003. "Those who miss practice simply will not play." This speech never went over well, even as the Hornets began to fall apart.

A major fallacy in recreational leagues is that travel sports are so expensive that the "cost barrier" will keep players from quitting. In soccer, this is decidedly untrue. While a kid's fees may jump from $50 per season to $500 or more, travel soccer is still cheaper at twice the price than almost any other childhood activity—far cheaper than baseball, hockey, ballet, gymnastics, or lacrosse; cheaper, even, than karate—because the equipment costs are so low. By long tradition, clubs also maintain contingency funds to pay the way for kids who can't afford it, so price seldom trumps potential. The Washington, D.C., Stoddert League, for example, keeps a $35,000 scholarship account for just this purpose. The only real requirements are stamina and desire.

What is especially unfortunate is that the talent drain hits recreational programs from all sides—not only do the teams lose their best players and their most committed volunteer parents, they tend to lose their most experienced coaches, too. "The better coaches follow their best kids into the travel leagues," says Sam Snow of the U.S. Youth Soccer Association, "just as they're starting to learn the game well enough to be good coaches." Thus do the blanket inclusiveness policies of the egalitarian boomer age wind up promoting the very thing they were designed to counteract: a caste system in youth sports. By insisting that all players be treated equally no matter what else they do, inclusion tears at team loyalties until squads collapse. Some of the kids who are left behind are the very ones who need athletics most, but many public recreation leagues have a hard time maintaining the necessary numbers to keep up their programs past a certain age. It's not in the coaching manuals or the feel-good youth-league brochures, but from the moment a peewee team forms the clock starts ticking.

Six of the Hornets whom I coached and comforted and cajoled up from the duckling leagues—five of the boys, plus Shelby—would ultimately make it onto travel teams. From the start, I felt good about their chances and proud of their accomplishments, until I walked them onto a field behind Briggs Chaney Middle School in Silver Spring, Maryland, and beheld the testosterone maelstrom of a travel-league tryout for the first time.

Swarms of boys flew by, chasing the one who had the ball, until someone knocked him down and ran off with it to begin the brawl anew. Among the forty or fifty prospects, some had already decided that this wasn't for them. Before the selection process even got under way, they were limping for the parking lot. Within three days, the group would be down to fourteen. Only two of the Hornets would be among them, and one would be gone in a month. Standing in the middle of it all was a guy my age in aviator shades with a clipboard in one hand, a pen in the other, and a strained smile on his face. Head coach Jeff Kestner hadn't expected anything quite like this when he put out the word that he was starting a travel team.

"Did anybody get the number on that truck?" he asked, motioning at a broad-shouldered Korean kid who had just squashed four other boys to get to the ball. "Is that one of the Park brothers? What are their names—Peter, Paul? You know, the twins."

"Yeah," the guy next to him said. "I can't tell them apart, but the other one is around here somewhere. If you want one, I think you have to take them both." That fast, two of the available slots were gone.

A self-made software entrepreneur and onetime football player, Jeff had been coaching his son's rec-league team for several years. Concussed six times as an undersized high school linebacker, he wasn't too inclined to romanticize youth athletics. His first assistant, Clyde DeLuca, had bailed out of rec soccer over the protectionist policies of his local club. Clyde was an old-school, blood-and-thunder type who had come up in the ancient German beer-garden leagues of Pittsburgh and had war stories to tell of snow-swept games on frozen fields where the mighty Bethlehem Steel once bested the world. At forty-two, his right knee was shot. He wore a blue, double-hinged, molded plastic brace and a lanyard around his neck that contained no fewer than fifteen whistles, talismans of his decades as a referee and a coach. He was an explosives engineer by training, thoroughly accustomed to military procedure and protocol, and he had no illusions that soccer could ever be a petunia garden. I knew him from the P. G.

County league, and we shared a certain aversion to the precious correctness that pervaded the dumpling divisions. He had no trouble convincing Jeff that an extra pair of hands would be a good thing to have around. The last thing I needed was to be coaching two teams, but I was a soccer addict by then. So I agreed to become the second assistant coach of the Calverton Soccer Club Flames.

From day one, it was clear that the Park twins were the class of the lot, a matched pair of wreckers with unnaturally developed upper bodies and no apparent pain threshold. Later, while making a diving save against a team from Frederick, Maryland, Paul would clang his head against an aluminum goalpost hard enough to move the entire frame, without registering any personal discomfort or reduction in brain function. Then, there was Jonathan Rodriguez, whose feet barely touched the ground when he dribbled. If you were the least bit insecure about your abilities as a soccer player—and at this age most kids are insecure about their rank in any social group—Jon could make you feel very small. The team had four natural lefties; six with at least one parent of foreign extraction; five who had won league championships; and one who may have been the fastest ten-year-old in the state of Maryland.

My son was the quickest kid on the Hornets' roster, one of the fastest in the P.G. league, but he could finish no closer than five lengths behind Amos Mobaidin in a fifty-yard dash. Amos of the bleached blond hair and the washboard stomach and the sutured nose (twenty-three stitches in all, an heirloom of a toddler's encounter with a window sill) weighed all of forty-two pounds. He had the metabolism and the build of a hummingbird, and his shooting mechanics were flawless. His right shoe might just as well have been filled with concrete.

In this group, my son and Kevin Guerrero exceeded the median by increments. The pride of the College Park Hornets, the kids who could do it all, the ones who were always "marked" on game day, were only slightly above average. Kevin began to fade in a matter of weeks, too young to deal with the pressure of twice-a-week practices and schoolwork in his second language on top of that. Ben's left foot and extraordinary "field vision"—the ability to keep his head up and maintain a sense of the relative positions of both teams—gained him a niche as an assist man. He could find the open spot on any field, "clean up" a wild pass, and send it on to another player as a "quality ball," well-timed and well-controlled, not too hard and not too soft, a setup pass that a forward could shoot at. But he was small and skinny and skittish about taking the ball inside himself, because at this level the box turned mean. The contact was no longer incidental. The slide tackle, which was discouraged in recreation league, was in full effect. The fullbacks usually outweighed everyone else by a good twenty pounds, and they were fast. The hardest adjustment a kid had to make was to the doubled speed of the game.

Thomas Waring and Bryan Basdeo had missed the cut by one slot. But Bryan refused to leave it at that. He worked out with the team for almost a year until he finally made it onto the roster as a substitute. His "get-to-know-you" moment came at his first practice, when he challenged Peter Park for an open ball at a full run. They were roughly the same size, so Bryan failed to perceive the danger until it was too late. Pete—a martial artist who knew a few things about leverage—beat him to the ball, shouldered him in the sternum, and blew straight through him, stepping on his arm and chest. The first ones to arrive at Bryan's side as he writhed on the ground were the twins, Peter and Paul, the Apostles as they were known. Next were the Stallions, the three Italians—midfielders Michael Fazio, Ben Fleri, and Andy DeLuca—who had taken a special interest in Bryan as the only walk-on who had lasted more than a couple of months with the team. They carried him to the sideline, where Ben tended to him until he could breathe again. Bryan's father watched, wise enough not to intervene.

What the smaller boys endured together during their first year as members of the Calverton Flames was enough to give any boomer parent second thoughts about high-level youth athletics. The coaches spent most of their time just trying to keep the kids from hurting one another, and Jeff's lad, Landon, was the smallest of them all, a casualty at nearly every practice. As rough as the practices were, the games were sometimes hard to watch. Most Sundays, Ben would moan in the back of the car on the way home, massaging his various lumps and bruises. Lying on the couch with a bag of ice on his knee or ankle, he usually fell asleep by seven o'clock. I knew travel soccer wasn't going to be kind or gentle, but I hadn't expected it to be tougher than football, and it gave me newfound empathy for the worrywarts among the Hornets' parents during that long-ago season at AAA. At the same time, I discovered, you could protect your kid for only so long before he or she started to resent it.

"Quit?" Ben said, drying his tears in the car after absorbing a thirty-minute pounding in one of the Flames' early games.

"Well, you look miserable," I said. "You're smaller than a lot of these guys, and it's not going to get any easier. You got beat up pretty bad today. There's plenty of other stuff you could be doing, and the Hornets are still together, so it's no big deal if you want to quit."

"I'm not quitting," he said. "I never think of quitting. Don't talk about quitting. You can quit if you want to, but I'm not."

Had I known what he was in for, I might not have given him the choice. But I also knew that if I pulled him out now he might go a very long time before so big a chance to prove himself came again. When your kid is braver than you are, it's probably time to reconsider a few things.

As the Hornets battled through the spring to maintain their undefeated record, the Flames took a beating. In their first game they were outmaneuvered, outhustled, and overrun by a team called the Bravehearts that played precision English-style soccer. Where the Flames were excitable, the Bravehearts were cool. They didn't panic, they didn't break formation, they never stopped pressing, and they were huge. For all their individual talents, our boys looked like lost sheep on a highway. They refused to pass to anyone who wasn't on their old rec squad. They tried to dazzle their way past the other team's fullbacks, who weren't easily dazzled; and when that failed they simply whacked the ball away. Pete and Paul turned every possession into a game of keep-away against the remaining twelve players from both teams. This might not have been so bad if they showed any interest in scoring, but it appeared to be the last thing on their minds.

"I am absolutely confident that we have the most athletically gifted group of kids in the league," Jeff Kestner said a couple of nights later over beers at a local tavern. "For the life of me, I can't figure out why they're not playing like it." Listening to him, I could hear my own voice, the spluttering of yet another coach verging on manic obsession. If misery loves company, I had found some in Jeff and Clyde. If history was any teacher, there were plenty of clues to the Flames' problems.

Over the ensuing weeks, I polled the boys' parents and discovered that almost every one of the kids had been a striker before coming to the team. The very things that had caught Jeff's eye on a tryout field—their speed, ballhandling, and shooting ability—were the result of years of pursuing the offensive. They had almost no idea how to counterattack or defend. Two-thirds of them had late birthdays, meaning they were younger overall than most of the teams they were playing against. Four of them were asthmatic. Several were obviously hyperactive, and a few others were having trouble processing what was going on in this faster-paced version of the game. Most of the universals in youth sports had followed us.

"We aren't going to be able to coach our way past these problems overnight," I told Jeff. "We can run them, scream and whistle at them until we're blue, drill them into formations. We can cut half the team at the end of every season, but the next crop will have the same issues. You're going to have to come up with a better way, maybe something that no one has thought of yet, or we're going to lose a lot of games."

"And that's not a good option," Clyde said.

"No, because the parents of your best kids will walk away," I said.

"So what do we do?" Jeff asked.

"If I knew, I probably wouldn't be here," I said.

Then Jeff let slip a disturbing idea. "Are we even qualified to coach at this level?" he asked, only half in jest. "Or are we just setting these kids up to get slaughtered?"

I looked into this question, too, and the answer was unequivocal. Hard as it would be for any father to admit, the numbers were against us—and not by a little. If we let our own egos decide the team's course, if we tried to coach our way through the gauntlet by ourselves, the years ahead would be nothing but heartbreak, if not substantial injury. The rapid increase in skills and tactics required to play at this level was more than most amateur coaches could handle.

We had entered our team into the biggest boys' travel league in the mid-Atlantic; one of the biggest in the country, in fact. It meandered over five thousand square miles of Maryland, Virginia, and the District of Columbia, encompassing a population of more than 3 million. Barely a thousand boys qualified to play at the eleven-year-old level of the National Capital Soccer League (NCSL). There were exactly sixty-one teams in our age group, divided into six divisions of graduating competitiveness. Fewer than 350 kids were good enough to play in the upper echelons. The rest toughed it out in the lower divisions, hoping to one day catch a break and win promotion. But most would stall by age thirteen, and some sooner than that. By age sixteen, almost a third of the teams would fold. By the time they reached seventeen, only thirty-six teams would remain.

What we didn't know then—but soon would learn—was that the larger clubs in the area, the "super clubs" with player rosters in the hundreds, usually enter multiple teams in the lower-age groups and reconstitute them from one season to the next until they concentrate their biggest, fastest, and strongest players onto a flagship squad for an eventual assault on the State Cup. By the time these kids were eleven years old, most of them would have paid professional coaches—former British players, mostly, with a smattering of South Americans and onetime U.S. collegiate players. Rare is the amateur coach who can match them on game day. In effect, the NCSL is a thresher that churns out the chaff, year by year, until only the strongest players remain. A very small number of them will one day represent the United States of America.

While it was possible in the bottom divisions simply to play for fun, a team had to be very good to have much fun at the top—that is, if your idea of fun included winning games, which tends to be the very definition of "fun" for adults. The Flames themselves exhibited a remarkable lack of concern about whether they won or not, which is a bad habit for a coach to let his players get into, because if their parents aren't having fun it's only a matter of time before they take their sons elsewhere. In the end, the central existential dilemma of modern youth coaching is figuring out how to make sports fun for boomer parents without making the kids miserable enough to quit. In travel soccer, this is excruciatingly hard to do.

Of the original nationwide talent pool of 8.7 million boys and girls below the age of twelve who are registered soccer players, only about 7 percent will make it as far as a high school team, and nearly all of them will come this way: brought into the sport by reluctant coaches like me, Terry, and Nick; weaned of their awkwardness and fears through sixty or seventy hometown matches and a hundred and fifty practices; acculturated by constant exposure; borne forth by a handful of "core" parents who have enough faith to trust in the good intentions of fools; then dropped here. And here the opportunities to play begin to shrink dramatically.

Of the millions who take up the sport, less than a third will win a slot on a team playing for one of 3,500 U.S. travel clubs—and most will go no farther. Of the 600,000 kids who are good enough to make it into a set of high school colors, there are only about 10,000 full-tuition college soccer scholarships available nationwide, and roughly 60 percent of those are for women's teams. For boys, there is only one college scholarship for every *seventy-eight* high school soccer hopefuls. Among those who make the collegiate cut, fewer than one in four hundred has a chance of making the U.S. National Team.

At the pro level, the numbers become crushing. The odds of a high school player making it into Major League Soccer are, at best, about a thousand to one. By comparison, the odds of a hometown football hero winding up in the NFL, according to a DePauw University study, are six times as long; and a basketball prospect faces a harrowing ten thousand to one chance of making the NBA. But those numbers are better understood among peewee football and basketball coaches than they are in soccer circles, where above-average kids are routinely referred to as "scholarship material" before they withstand their first travel tryout. Very few youth soccer coaches and even fewer parents are aware of the game's demanding pyramidal structure, so most continue to believe that they are producing future superstars, until their "studs" are trounced in a club game. From there, the reality of the situation sinks in fairly quickly. The average youth team may have one or two future high school players on the roster, but predicting that any kid is college-bound in American soccer today is like betting on roulette. A gifted soccer kid has a better chance than a football or basketball prospect, but the odds are still laughably long.

Again, the Flames' coaches knew none of this. But what we did know fairly quickly was this: we were in over our heads.

Presented with the evidence, Jeff Kestner did something that would change the fortunes of both the Flames and the Hornets in the course of two seasons, launching them on a string of championship runs that should not have been possible. What he did was to find one of the best soccer trainers in the state—a guy who had grown up playing on the textile grounds of New Jersey before being swept up in the southern collegiate soccer renaissance of the 1970s; a midfielder, no less; someone who intimately understood the American game, the game that Billy, Walter, Len, and George Brown had played; the game that beat the Brits at Belo Horizonte.

Jeff Kestner hired a professional.

12.

THE WARLORDS CONVENE

WARM-UP SUITS DON'T MAKE THE MAN

I'm still not exactly sure what I hoped to find in Charlotte. Mostly, I think, it was simple curiosity that put me on the plane for North Carolina at the crack of dawn one morning—a reporter's natural desire to witness a public spectacle and maybe rub elbows with the best minds in the coaching business, the true professionals. I was also hoping to find some solid evidence that the Soccer Nation was in good health at the dawn of the new millennium. At that moment, I had begun to have my doubts.

Unlike youth hockey, football, and hoops, soccer has yet to record any homicides, as far as I could tell. But it did have a way of inflaming certain primal passions, both on and off the field. How much longer could dumb luck hold up if a couple of days of idle Internet surfing were enough to fill a file folder on my desk marked "Bad Behavior" and "Mayhem"? Among a random sampling of incidents: A local soccer team of fourteen-year-old girls was disbanded after their parents jeered a referee to tears and scrawled obscenities on her car. A twelve-year-old boy was ejected from a game after spewing a string of verbiage that would have gotten him bounced from a waterfront saloon. And, more recently, an on-field brawl during a high school game resulted in one girl being charged with assault, another with her hand in a cast, and a third being sent to an oral surgeon to have three teeth wired back into her mouth. Yes, soccer is a tough game, but nobody signs up for youth sports these days expecting to get cussed out or punched in the face—and the thought of suburban parents vandalizing a referee's car is a bit much to contemplate.

I stuffed the file into my briefcase on my way out the door and thumbed through the printouts and accumulated newspaper clippings when I was thirty-eight thousand feet over Virginia, wondering whether anyone in Charlotte could explain why kids' sports are now so firmly associated with anger-management issues—and why so many kids are quitting over it. I got off U.S. Airways flight 293 shortly after nine o'clock on a brilliant blue-sky morning and walked under a twenty-foot-wide white vinyl banner in the main concourse of the airport: Welcome soccer coaches to the NSCAA Convention, the National Soccer Coaches Association of America, the world's largest gathering of soccer overlords, the realm of the truly absorbed.

Conventions are one of the perils of journalism, and in twenty-five years I've covered my share: law-enforcement conclaves, environmental summits, boat shows. I once attended a two-day symposium on bluegrass music and the jangling of massed banjos put my teeth on edge for a week. I've learned that all conventions have one thing in common, besides desiccated chicken banquets. Conventions bring out the rabidly obsessed freaks who keep a subculture alive, the 3.4 percent who are willing to give up a long weekend, travel hundreds of miles, and spend upward of a thousand dollars apiece in hopes of achieving ever more extreme states of devotion to a hobby, cause, or profession about which the majority of humanity knows little and could care less.

Here in Charlotte, I knew, I would find the guys with soccer balls on their boxer shorts, and soccer-ball key chains in their pockets, and little soccer balls hanging from their rearview mirrors. Guys who had lost marriages over soccer. Guys who had shut down cocktail parties babbling about soccer. Here I would come face-to-face with my own alter ego, the overextended, superhero, soccer-dad coach. Here, mercifully, I would find deliverance from my obsession.

By 11:00 a.m., I was walking into the vast main hall of the Charlotte Convention Center as the warlords convened in the thousands—a great, pulsing amoeba of soccerheads. Most of them were youth coaches, men of great power and influence in adolescent suburbia, dressed for battle in nearly identical Adidas warm-up suits and Velcro cell-phone holsters and little web backpacks plastered with soccer logos. The predominating color scheme was red, white, and black, the tritones of Manchester United and fully half of all U.S. youth club teams.

Here and there, middle-aged Attilas with potbellies and retreating hairlines paced the corridors in hundred-dollar gum-soled indoor soccer shoes. The backs of their sideline jackets bristled with the badges of their children's conquests: division championships, regional titles, state cups of every shape and size. These were the hard campaigners, the weekend generalissimos who had directed midget armies to glory over the chilly fields of late fall and thence upon the summer tournament grounds at Disney's Wide World of Sports soccer complex near Orlando.

I myself had just orchestrated my first major tournament win—leading the Hornets to a 4–0 sweep in the county's weekend Harvest Classic, outscoring the opposition by a combined goal differential of 19–2 on a steel-gray autumn day, and utterly drubbing our archrivals from neighboring Lewisdale for the seventh time in two years. I followed that resounding triumph with a five-game winning streak in winter-league indoor soccer, three by shutout, before giving up a tie, then one loss, then resuming my quest for glory with another nine wins and another championship title to stretch my record to 14-1-1 (eighteen wins if you included the Harvest tournament, twenty-six if you added in the previous fall season). Of those games, only one was really close: a 2–1, come-from-behind ass-whipping in the final ninety-seven seconds over the mega-club Bowie. In a master stroke of coaching vision—with my team down 1–0—I moved a ballistic nine-year-old defender up to the forward position as time was expiring in an indoor game in Glenn Dale, Maryland. She was a walk-on, a sturdy, fearless kid named Samantha Brayman who might have played twelve minutes of offense in her life. In my mind I had already written off the game when she grabbed a fistful of my T-shirt on the sideline.

"Put me up front, Coach!" she demanded. "I just figured it out! We can beat them!"

"Oh, what the hell," I said. "Go ahead, Sam. Go get us a goal." Less than twenty seconds later she rolled up Bowie's left side, conked their defender with a high elbow, and chopped the ball into the net. As the digital clock on the wall wound down toward zero, my son followed the same track into the goal box and netted the winning ball. The buzzer sounded, the bleachers erupted, and Bowie's normally stoic nine-year-old goalkeeper flushed into tears. We had finally avenged the Snow Bowl, that long-ago game in which Bowie's fullbacks had beaten our kids black-and-blue in the frozen muck of Marlton Park.

So, yes, I had earned my place among these great chieftains gathering in Charlotte, and the knowledge filled with me with a sense of well-being. Few positions I had held in my life were quite as rewarding as that of "winning coach." The accolades from parents, the trophies piling up in my kid's bedroom more than made up for the lost sleep and income and leisure hours. I had firmly embraced the jock ethic. I didn't even bother trying to accommodate the uncommitted any longer, and they had gradually ebbed away as a result. I was not, however, without misgivings.

No "successful" youth coach I ever met would admit it, but our patches and badges and trophies and stats are purchased with unavoidable trauma to somebody else's kids—and maybe to our own as well, because it's hard to work children into the state of competitive frenzy that produces such results without "pushing" them at least a little. How many of us, I wondered, ever considered whether that was a good or a bad thing? Or was it simply American to view competitive pressure as an essential component of child development? We did not, after all, become the last superpower on earth by teaching our children how to win at checkers. Our grandfathers did not scour the caves at Okinawa and take the beaches at Normandy with skills learned on a tennis court. As the Duke of Wellington once said of his country's most resounding military victory, "The Battle of Waterloo was won on the playing fields of Eton."

Still, the question remained: were there any lines that we wouldn't cross? Especially those of us who drew salaries from the private travel clubs for coaching? (I was not among them.) When your ego, much less your paycheck, is pegged to the win-loss record stitched to the back of your windbreaker, how hard will you drive a pack of kids to achieve outcomes that so many parents so deeply desire?

Just as I was mulling this over, Anson Dorrance ambled in, the Elvis of American soccer, the King. There was no flourish of herald horns or rolling out of crimson carpets, but the air was suddenly electrified by his presence.

Anson Dorrance—supreme commander of the seventeen-time national champion University of North Carolina women's team, Mia Hamm's college coach, trustee of UNC's preposterous 532-25-15 record—owned a winning aura that few coaches in the world could match. Every blade of his magnificent razor-cut coiffure was blow-dried and sculpted into place. His fangs were polished white, his patrician face was perfectly gaunt. Anson, who quotes Napoleon and George Bernard Shaw and King Philip II of Macedon—"A herd of deer led by a lion is more to be feared than a pride of lions led by a deer," among other proverbs—was resplendent in an unstructured mint-green suit, a crisp white collar, and a coordinated silk tie. He wore no polyester warm-up jacket, required no regimental badges on his back, for he was Anson, alone in his class.

Then came Tony DiCicco, steward of the women's pro game, the architect of the 1999 Pasadena triumph, now commissioner of the Women's United Soccer Association. DiCicco's swarthy complexion and neatly trimmed black mustache were offset by a camel-hair sports coat, a chocolate-brown turtleneck, and caramel-colored Italian slip-ons. After that came Jerry Yeagley, pale blue eyes glistening, barrel frame wrapped in a double-breasted suit the color of teak wood. The winningest coach in men's collegiate soccer, Yeagley is the retiring head of the five-time national champion Hoosiers of Indiana University. Now, there was Lauren Gregg—former all-American, team captain, and assistant coach at UNC; DiCicco's aide-de-camp in Pasadena; head coach of both the University of Virginia and the U.S. Under-21 Women's Teams. She was effortlessly elegant and assured in white linen, exuding an air of tranquillity that is the sign of true arrival in the world of sport.

Behind them came the men in the black-and-orange parachute jumpers—the Dutch ambassadorial corps, instructors from the Royal Netherlands Soccer Academy. They came to preach the bible of "Total Soccer," the precision ball-control game perfected by the great Ajax coach Rinus Michels and his star pupil, Cruyff, and to hawk their CD-ROMs to the benighted mass of youth coaches. And the English, omnipresent at American soccer gatherings, stood by in their professorial tweeds, knights-errant of the One True Faith, keepers of the Holy Triangle Formation, purveyors of training manuals and team uniforms, possessors of the lilting accent that is embedded in the primal American hindbrain. That voice continues to hold U.S. soccer in its irresistible, imperial thrall. Above the din, the limey inflections keened, "Bloody good to see you!" And "Bloody hell, it's been too long!" And "bloody" this. And "bloody" that.

Compared with the beautiful, ethereal Brazilians—with their oiled corkscrew locks and rows of silver earrings, their billowing black slacks and kid-leather sandals, their easy smiles and loose-jointed grace—the Brits looked like pensioners on holiday. The heirs of Pelé and the only ones in history to win five World Cups, the South Americans are much beloved here, and they know it.

Dorrance paused momentarily at the top of the escalator. Outthrust hands reached toward him, waving profiles of teenage players and highlight videos for his consideration. The acronyms flew. "Coach!" a muffled voice cried out from somewhere inside the blob. "My daughter is a four-time first-division MVP with a 3.8 GPA, and her heart is set on UNC. Could you take a look at her CV?" Yes, teenage soccer players in America now have résumés.

Ever magnanimous, Dorrance shook each supplicant's hand and in turn received the anxiously proffered business cards. Throughout the weekend I seldom saw him without a nylon satchel over his shoulder brimming with videocassettes and

DVDs, like a prospector with his saddlebag. "Fortunately for us," he would later say in a keynote address, "recruitment is never a problem at Carolina."

Nearby, Walter Bahr, Harry Keough, and John Souza—the ancient warriors who vanquished the English in 1950—stood with their hands in the pockets of their well-worn khakis, chatting about old times. Few people in attendance at the convention had any idea who they were.

I leaned against a far wall, drinking my fourth cup of coffee of the morning, taking in the irony of it all. Only in America, where everything old is new again within five years, where history repeats itself within half a generation, where you need a stopwatch to clock the national attention span, do we spend so much time relearning what we once knew by heart. The AM radio sports yackers continue to call soccer a foreign game, but in the age of globalization, half our baseball players are now built in the Dominican Republic, Puerto Rico, and Japan. Some of our best quarterbacks are seasoned in Canada and Germany, and one of the most imposing centers in basketball is a Chinese guy named Yao. Soccer may have been invented by Native Americans or Chinese soldiers, depending on which book you read, but in any case the English version arrived here before it ever got to Brazil. Yet here the mob throbs, eager for international instructors to teach it the subtleties of a game that captivated American spectators long before football and basketball were even conceived.

And here's an even greater irony: many of the foreign emissaries are here because they are acutely aware that the future of international soccer lies in reviving the wealthy North American market and gaining access to its vast media complex. Nowhere else are sports as profitable as in the United States, where television rights alone generate more than $7 billion annually by some estimates—or roughly equal to the rest of the world's TV revenues combined. Across much of the globe, including Brazil and most of Africa, soccer is bankrupt. Millions may play the game in underdeveloped countries, but they do it on dirt fields. What stadiums exist are crumbling, most famously Rio's magnificent Maracana, because ticket sales alone don't cover expenses. Sports are perishable products in the global bazaar and the only way to deliver them is through television, but the biggest pipeline runs through New York and Los Angeles. Even in Europe, barely a third of professional games are televised. If soccer is to generate the capital it needs, it has to grow a generation of American consumers who will demand it on their TV screens. The kids' game, then, is the proverbial golden goose. The guardians of international soccer want to make sure we treat it well.

I walked toward the escalators and happened to pass a thirty-foot-long bulletin board plastered with job postings—soccer jobs, good jobs, with nice paychecks and health-insurance benefits and tuition perks for the kids. There were youth clubs looking for trainers and small colleges seeking head coaches and prep schools in need of soccer gurus. The U.S. Merchant Marine Academy in Kings Point, New York, was in the market, among the more recent of the national service academies to field soccer teams. The U.S. Naval Academy was the first, in 1921, for if the fleet's thirteen-inch guns were to serve as America's "big stick," as Teddy Roosevelt had proposed, her officers also needed to "speak softly" in "the language of the world." Judging by the want ads, U.S. soccer appeared to be in pretty good health.

Downstairs in the main exhibition hall, it appeared to be on steroids. There, in an open concrete cavern the size of a blimp hangar, the sport had been market-segmented into hundreds of booths covering a half million square feet of floor space—an immense clearinghouse of goods, services, and information, nearly all of it featuring images of happy kids as a sales draw.

Building a soccer complex? There were trade reps in Charlotte from three artificial-turf companies, all bearing samples of their bristled product and hustling brochures graced with glossy photos of boys and girls chasing soccer balls hither upon the patented perma-sward. Want to meet the entire sales force in less than fifteen seconds? All you had to do was run your fingers through a competitor's carpet sample and you would soon be told more than you ever wanted to know about drainage rates, fire resistance, and relative shock-absorbency coefficients—along with a comparative analysis of why the other guys' plastic grass isn't as safe or durable or fun.

And how 'bout those stats, Coach? No less than six companies were selling the latest installments of their charting and graphing software for your home desktop or Palm Pilot to help you amass visuals of your players' performance on ten or twenty or thirty different graduating scales of excellence or poverty. Got a goalie who's struggling? According to one company's promotional video, which played on a constant tape loop all weekend long, "a kid has got to feel good about his gloves, or it's going to work on his head psychologically." The announcer spoke with an English accent, so you knew it had to be true. And the gloves cost seventy-five bucks, so you knew they had to be good.

Around the corner, three satellite-TV companies were booking subscribers for their twenty-four-hour soccer channels—enough soccer to obliterate your social calendar from now until the day they cremate you in your $200 kangaroo-leather Adidas Predator cleats and present your long-suffering widow with the ashes attractively enshrined in a replica of the State Cup made by one of the five trophy companies prowling the convention floor.

Over yonder, a multitude of "scouting agencies" and "player reps" hawked the latest in computer-assisted "placement services." For somewhere between $1,200 and $3,000, your child star could have his or her own Web site designed and posted on the Internet, a professionally prepared résumé generated, a game-day highlight video produced, and the entire package circulated to recruiters for the top clubs, high schools, and colleges in the country. It's "fame in a can," and many a soccer parent lined up to buy it. "Most of them, the first time we talk to them, have no idea that less than five percent of U.S. youth athletes ever qualify for some kind of scholarship in any sport," one rep gingerly told me. "Particularly in soccer, with college recruitment budgets as tight as they are, most coaches only ever know about the top one or two hundred players—the kids who get the magazine profiles and the write-ups in the big state newspapers. And that's where we come in. That's the service we provide. We make the calls and knock on the doors and bring the rest of these kids to their at-tention."

These are the same parents who might also be willing to lay out $3,000 for a telescoping, pole-mounted video camera called the Hi-Pod that will enable them to get professional-quality, "eye-in-the-sky" footage of their scampering progeny. Once you see the results, there can be no question that it has the potential to revolutionize home movies and sports photography for decades to come. So promises Rick Morales, former high school soccer player, former children's cartoon producer, former videographer, current self-described "guy who likes to tinker with things," and inventor of the world's first eighteen-foot-tall video periscope. "See, they can't keep their hands off it," Morales told me after another group of roving coaches jockeyed for a demonstration. "It's just too cool!"

As I wandered this Ponderosa of mercantile know-how—of soccer academies and summer camps, of bounce-back nets and bungee-cord resistance leashes, of sweat-wicking jerseys and fiber-composite shin guards and soccer shoes that looked as if they'd been designed by NASA—I had to quickly recalibrate my definition of "obsession." It wasn't nearly big enough.

"Soccer is a very simple game," Hall of Famer Len Oliver told me in his kitchen one sunny afternoon back home in Washington. "A ball, five of your buddies, and two trash barrels for a goal—that's all you need. That's all we had as kids growing up in Philly. I tell coaches all the time, 'The best teacher of the game is the game. Shut up and let the kids play. The game will do the rest.'

"So many of the problems we see in youth soccer today—youth sports in general—are the result of money. Once adults spend money on something, they want to control it. They expect results, and in sports that means winning. If you're a coach, that's how you're measured. So there's this real push-pull between giving the kids what they want—a game and a fun afternoon—and giving the parents what they demand. This generation of coaches is so constantly torn between the two, I don't know how some of them do it."

Later that night, after my first day of conventioneering, I walked into the Adam's Mark Hotel and folded myself into a seat at the bar to await a table in the lobby grill. Before long I struck up a conversation with the guy next to me, a "soccer dad from Oklahoma, by way of Texas." His son had just won a full scholarship to a major university—"the biggest kiss I ever got," the old man called it.

He emptied a glass of house white, then tipped his head back and laughed. "Of course, if you added up all the money I spent on his soccer career over the years, the thirty or forty thousand bucks, whatever it is, fifty thousand is probably more like it—hell, could be sixty for all I know, never actually sat down and ran the numbers, probably afraid to, might look too much like a second mortgage—anyway, if you figured in the interest on top of that, well, I might have been able to send him to Princeton by now. It nearly killed me when he quit football, not that it would have been any cheaper, but at least it would have been a sport I know. But this is what he wanted, and I'm damned fortunate it turned out the way it did. Like I said, biggest kiss I ever got!"

With that, he excused himself to use the men's room, leaving me to cipher out my suspicions on a cocktail napkin: my nine-year-old boy's annual soccer habit—$1,000 in camps every summer; close to another grand annually in club dues, league charges, and trainer fees; maybe $150 for replica jerseys, balls, two pairs of new cleats, his *Soccer Jr.* magazine subscription, tickets to pro games—was already running me close to $2,500 per year. Figure in his little brother's nominal rec-league costs, probably another $250. Then, the thirty-two hundred miles of travel expenses to their practices and games, the gallons of Gatorade, my own wardrobe requirements, coach's licensing fees, the fifteen pounds of tournament souvenirs, books, training videos, cones, gym bags, and flags—to say nothing of my nonreimbursable personal hours spent coaching this game. As Chaucer put it, "Love is a thing . . . full of busy dread."

The Adam's Mark grill was running a nice special that night in Charlotte, a twenty-four-dollar venison plate—medallions of deer meat and a generous mound of garlic mashed potatoes, with some tossed greens on the side.

"I'll have Bambi, medium rare," I told the waitress.

"Rough day?" she said.

Upstairs in my room afterward, I went through my "Mayhem" file again, reviewing the tales of parental barbarism and coaches gone haywire and happy little imps mutating into fire-breathing gargoyles on the field. In the league my kid plays in—the National Capital Soccer League (NCSL)—thirty coaches and sixty-three kids were serving suspensions for disciplinary violations. One coach from Virginia had been banned from the game for four years. In one of the premier youth leagues in the nation, the NCSL board of directors was obliged to hold about a dozen full-blown hearings, most of them involving allegations of "bad calls" by referees, as if adults didn't have anything better to do than litigate a children's game. As the novelist Jim Harrison once wrote, "There is no kind of absurdity we'll refuse to perform if the economics are tangible."

Casting back over the previous year, I had personally witnessed, among other things: the father of a six-year-old boy rush onto the field, grab another kid by the shoulders, and shake him for knocking down his son at a peewee practice; the father of a nine-year-old who was having a bad game charge the team bench and yell at his kid, "Wake the hell up, or I'll take you home"; a travel coach scream "Jackass!" at an opposing coach in front of two dozen ten-year-olds during a deadlocked tournament match. Then I came upon this hairy little factoid in a clip from *The Baltimore Sun:* a third of the soccer referees in the state of Maryland—570 trained and certified refs—quit the game in 2001 alone rather than endure any more abuse.

Ray Fetterer, a research zoologist from my hometown who moonlights as a youth soccer referee, told me that kids now go so far as to beseech refs during games to eject their belligerent parents and coaches from the field. "I'd venture to guess that if you polled twenty referees, two-thirds of them will tell you they've experienced something similar," he said. "A kid comes up to you on the field, tugs on your sleeve, and says, 'Hey, Ref, could you just toss our coach out of the game? He's embarrassing us.' And you look over on the sideline at this red-faced guy screaming his head off, and you wonder how he ever got his hands on a clipboard."

"The problems start with inexperienced youth coaches and

parents and spiral out from there to include all kinds of bad and unsportsmanlike behavior," Rob Miller of the National Association of Intercollegiate Athletics (NAIA) told me in Charlotte. "Kids are seeing atrocious conduct from adults during games that is not only tolerated, it's considered *normal*. And they internalize it, and they act out themselves—until the kid gets to college and runs up against a ref who has some administrative protection and real power, and that's how you wind up with fourteen hundred ejections a year in collegiate soccer."

It was Miller who suggested that I look into a 1991 study by the Michigan State University Institute for the Study of Youth Sports if I wanted to see the end result of all this hypertension in kids' athletics. In the most comprehensive attitude survey ever undertaken in this country, researchers polled ten thousand youngsters and found that most of them were in real distress. Of the 38 million U.S. children involved in sports—a number that has remained fairly constant for decades—the study revealed that almost a third quit every year; that 45 percent reported being verbally abused or "called names" by coaches; and that a staggering 75 percent drop out of athletics by age fifteen.

"Why?" researchers asked. "Lost interest" and "No longer fun" were the leading responses, followed closely by "Favoritism." At the moment, nearly 85 percent of coaches are fathers coaching their own kids—real-life Homer Simpsons promoting their own little Barts to quarterback—and fewer than one out of twenty has received any training or certification to work with children. Even among the nation's 750,000 scholastic coaches, fewer than 10 percent are licensed or certified in any sport.

Hence the warm-up suits. If you really don't know what you're doing, it becomes imperative that you at least *look* as if you do. In my case, it had taken four years of nearly constant study and two licensing courses before I finally felt semiconversant in child psychology and physiology. Looking back on the early years, it is frightening how little I knew about adolescent skeletal growth, for example, and how easily a kid can be disabled by growth-plate fractures. If you don't know what growth plates are, you probably should find out, because most parents have never heard of them. It's also not a good idea to teach little kids to head the ball, because it can make them stupid, but plenty of rube coaches still hand out fifteen reps to the forehead at practice.

Only after I was licensed did I become aware of these things. Only then did I begin to gain competence in coaching the game. Only then was I secure enough to stare down a fuming father or stand up to a motherly harangue without melting into a puddle of self-doubt and apologies.

"When the kid complains to the parent that they're not getting to play as much as they think they should, they always complain that the coach is screwing them," Anson Dorrance said in his keynote address in Charlotte. "All the parent knows is that the kid is unhappy, so it must be the coach's fault. Thank goodness I've never had to be a youth coach, because honestly, I don't know how you guys do it. My hat is off to you, sincerely." The ballroom chandeliers shook from the applause as a thousand coaches had their worst agony acknowledged by the King.

How did all of this come to pass, I wondered? How did the early joys of youth sports devolve as the years went by into such a trial for so many kids, and such a drain for so many coaches? Everyone I met in the game brimmed with good intentions, but I might have known five or six who actually knew what they were doing. How did any of us wind up with whistles?

On the flight to North Carolina that morning, I had begun plowing through a pile of adolescent health reports and trend stories from such essential publications as *Sports Illustrated* and *Soccer*

America, both of which devote considerable ink to the decline in youth athletics and coaching expertise in the United States. The deeper causes of most of the problems in kids' sports, it turns out, are not so much a matter of bad parents or bad coaches as they are the result of rotten circumstances that no one seems to recognize.

Over the past two decades, school budget cuts have shrunk or killed physical-education programs for nearly half of American kids, while simultaneously reducing the ranks of professional youth coaches—the fully degreed, bonded, and school board–accountable gym teachers of yore, men like Walter Bahr.

At the same time, as a 1994 study by the Centers for Disease Control and Prevention detailed, nearly half of American adults had come to consider their neighborhoods to be unsafe—even though crime rates have been declining steadily for years. What accounted for the misperception? Well, to a certain degree the danger was a media invention. While actual crime was decreasing, the appetite of television broadcasters for crime *stories* was increasing. Nothing boosts TV ratings like a hysterical "babynapper" story or the arrest of a kiddy-porn trafficker. These monsters, in fact, are few and far between, but Eyewitness-Action-Inside-Breaking-Hardball News turned them into a seemingly omnipresent menace in the 1980s and '90s. Pictures of missing kids appeared on milk cartons, suburban police departments launched fingerprint drives in elementary schools, and a raging paranoia among boomer parents led them to "bubble-wrap" all childhood activity occurring outside the home, as Greg Critser put it in his book *Fat Land*.

Thus did youth sports become a highly organized and heavily supervised enterprise. "Play" was no longer merely play. Worse, there were fewer and fewer professional coaches on the scene as the games were evicted from schools and tumbled into the hands of volunteer organizations and private clubs. So not only did most kids come to be coached by men who know next to nothing about coaching—men like me—but the rigidly enforced game-day conduct codes once imposed by school boards vanished. In the absence of mediating authorities, mothers and fathers are now fully "empowered" to act as agents and ombudsmen for their children. And the fact that parents have to pay dues and trainers' fees and equipment costs invests them with a sense of entitlement that lingers in the air around youth leagues like fumes in a mine shaft.

Money can also buy a say in how a team is trained, managed, and run on game day, whether or not a parent has any actual expertise to draw on. The American Youth Soccer Organization (AYSO), which claims 500,000 members and circulates reams of how-to papers to hundreds of recreational clubs nationwide, tries to fill the deplorable gap in fitness know-how left by the retreat of the public schools. But its founding motto, "Every child plays," has become a Gordian knot. Laudable in its intention to promote fitness and sports participation, the AYSO creed has been widely interpreted to mean that practice attendance and physical performance standards have no place in the world of youth soccer, so amateur soccer coaches have found themselves pinned between hyperachievers and underachievers. All too often, their response is to break the game down into its component parts—offense, defense, the midfield transition area, throw-ins, corner kicks, penalty shots, triangle formations—and train their most athletic kids to specialize in one position or another at the earliest possible age. Some coaches go even further, discouraging their stars from becoming involved in other sports that might distract them from the job at hand. I have seen amateur youth coaches in every sport follow this model, confining kids to set positions and drilling them into patterned "plays" until they can respond with Pavlovian predictability at the shout of a code phrase during a game. The result is the rapid development of skills in certain kids that enables a team to excel despite the presence on the field of marginal or less committed players.

Legendary Baltimore Orioles shortstop Cal Ripken, who was a soccer and basketball player in his youth, has decried the emergence of similar methods in Little League baseball, making him perhaps the most recognizable spokesman for a national "fun first" movement that opposes the systematizing of kids' sports. Advocates argue that it not only marginalizes less able kids but also pigeonholes the gifted and leads to repetition injuries previously unheard of in kids' games. Unfortunately, Ripken and his ilk are swimming against a torrent, because specialization works. By robotizing their teams within formations and assigned positions, youth coaches are able to circumvent the sense of entitlement that boomer parents now bring to sports. Sure, every kid may get on the field or the court, but if the game plan works out right the "slackers" never touch the ball. More competitive parents now pay upward of a thousand dollars per season for trainers and camps that promise to drill their kids in one school of play or another, which serves only to further widen the gap between the athletic haves and have-nots.

Leaving aside the fact that "system sports" can be about as much fun as breaking rocks on a penal chain gang, it is also an unregulated industry in which quackery and shams abound. This message was repeated over and over in Charlotte, so many times and in so many different settings that it was impossible to miss the point that the high ministers of the American game regard it as one of the greatest threats to the future of the Soccer Nation. Kids in every sport are being overcoached, overpressured, overstructured, oversupervised, and just plain worn out by it all.

"American coaches like to coach and to coach and to coach," Nico Romeijn of the Royal Netherlands Academy told me. "But it is much better to just let the kids play and discover their own solutions, because that is what will work for them in a game situation. Coaches and parents like to teach the way something is *supposed* to be done, not necessarily the way that is *possible* for the kids to do. All the time, they want for everybody to be a great player. And this is not possible in soccer. Even with the best players in the world on the field, it is not possible. So why do we think it is possible for children?"

U.S. Men's National Team coach Bruce Arena has compared it to teaching Shakespeare to first graders, saying that amateur "parent-coaches" simply don't understand "how limited kids are in what they're capable of doing on the field, mentally and physically. They have their own vision of what they want their children to be and how they're going to get there—and they don't really understand the stages of development that kids go through. They don't have the patience."

Later that weekend, after giving a seminar on the methods he uses to turn his practices at UNC into "a competitive cauldron" designed to boil off the pretenders in his ranks and temper the survivors, Dorrance was asked by one hopeful youth coach how soon he should turn up the heat on his kids back home. The King paused, looked down at the lectern and sighed, then slowly measured out his words. "I don't think junior year in *high school* is a moment too soon for a coach to *start* thinking about these things," he said, sucking the air from the room. "If you're coaching kids *younger* than that, you probably ought to just let them *play*."

This idea is so radical in American youth sports that Tony Di-Cicco, the mastermind of Pasadena, devoted a 216-page book to it. Titled *Catch Them Being Good*, it preaches humanistic coaching. Good coaching, DiCicco asserts, is the applied science of holding your own ego in check, allowing your team's natural leaders to lead, and praising your players to high heaven whenever they do something right. When I approached him in Charlotte and asked him to inscribe a copy of his book for a friend of mine, he immediately asked, "How old are your buddy's kids?"

"They're between nine and eleven," I replied.

"That's such a great age," DiCicco said. "Please tell him I said thanks, and remind him for me that the best way to coach kids that age is to just let 'em play."

So this was the great secret, the anti-venom for all the tantrums in youth athletics? Beneath all the marketing puffery and achievement-mongering by the sports academies—one of which peddled its wares in Charlotte with the slogan "Doing your best is winning!"—was the revolutionary message that playing should be fun.

"The changes have to start somewhere, and if not with our coaches, then somebody please tell me where?" Rob Miller of the NAIA implored a roomful of coaches during one seminar. "Coaches now set the tone for everything, and the kids 'vote' on how well we're doing by whether they come back for another season or not, and a lot of them are voting with their feet."

When he finished his sermon, a roiling argument broke out that lasted nearly an hour. Voices were heard from nearly every faction, from rec-league amateurs to collegiate field marshals, from soft-bellied social-welfare types propounding "zero tolerance" for all bad behavior to rock-ribbed division titleholders who thought a little cussing and fussing were natural features of the competitive environment. But no one quarreled with Miller's premise. To call yourself a coach, as one athletic director from a small Christian college put it, is to "be responsible for everything."

"We write rules for seventeen sports, and we see these problems in all of them, so it's not just soccer by any means," said Tim Flannery of the National Federation of State High School Associations, an umbrella group for secondary-school coaches and athletic directors. "We're seeing it in golf and tennis—kids dropping the 'F bomb' on line judges, parents yelling all sorts of stuff from the grandstands, and everybody is standing around waiting to see what the ref does about it, when it should be the coaches who drop the hammer."

I left this impromptu debate with my ears burning, cataloging my own sins as I wandered through the main corridor of the convention center to the main bulletin board, where the hundreds of seminars for the weekend were listed. I wanted to check on a hunch. As I suspected, 90 percent of the presentations centered on the how-to aspects of coaching: Formations and Styles of Play; High-Pressure Defending; Realistic Penalty Area Situations. But, at almost any given time of day, panels were also convening to discuss child psychology, character building, and on-field ethics. And in almost every one coaches were being confronted with their shortcomings and failures. "For the good of the game," they subjected themselves to rhetorical beatings over gender equity, racial inclusion, and their treatment of referees.

If there was any doubt left in my mind that fun was the shortest route to achievement, it evaporated the next morning after a chance encounter with a kid from Potomac, Maryland. Shepherded by a striking blond bodyguard in a severe navy pantsuit, he rounded a corner in the convention center and almost ran right into me. The cover boy on a half dozen magazines and a guest on MTV's top-rated *Total Request Live* the day before, he was the most talked-about prospect in Major League Soccer's annual draft, which would be televised live by FOX TV from the convention floor that morning. It was a foregone conclusion that he would be taken in the first round by Washington's D.C. United team. If Freddy Adu was nervous, he wasn't showing it.

I introduced myself as a coach and a writer from Washington and told him how happy I was, as a local fan, that he was going to stay in the Potomac Basin. "My kid already has your poster on his wall," I said.

"Thanks," Freddy replied, shaking my hand. "I just want to help the team any way I can. I'm still young, and these guys are my heroes, so it's really an honor." He went on for another minute in this language that he is only just learning—American celebrity "jockspeak"—before lapsing back into the earnest, forthright persona that made him a media darling in the first place. An immigrant from Ghana at the age of eight, the son of a cleaning lady, discovered on a suburban playground at age ten, he became a U.S. citizen on the eve of his coronation.

"What would you say to these kids who want to be you," I asked him, "these kids in Washington who are freaking out right now because they're playing on the same fields where you started out four years ago?"

"Have fun!" Freddy said, ignoring the forward urgings of his handler. "Just play. I learned by kicking balls of paper around, you know? Anything round, it didn't matter. A tennis ball, whatever. I drove my mother crazy with it, and I just got better and better at it, and then all of this just sort of happened to me. I never had a trainer or a coach. I just played. What can I say? What could anybody say? I'm just a kid, just like them."

"A very rich kid," I interjected. (Adu had already been signed to a million-dollar Nike endorsement deal.)

"A very *lucky* kid," he corrected me. "I didn't ever think anything like this could happen to me. I just loved the game, and I never stopped playing, and one day it all just . . . I'm so happy right now." At this gush of unfiltered commentary, his chaperone edged between us and eased him toward the FOX TV soundstage.

"Just play, right?" I called after him.

"Yeah, tell them to just play!" Freddy said over his shoulder.

Moments later, he was drafted to the richest contract in U.S. Major League Soccer. Congratulating him on live TV was FOX soccer commentator John Harkes, the onetime wonder boy from Kearny, New Jersey, whose photo still graces the wall above the shuffleboard at the Scots-American Club. From one "natural" to another, Harkes presented Adu with his first pro jersey, closing the final circle. It was the number 9, the sacred flag, Mia's number.

13.

A BETTER WAY

THE MAGIC IS IN THE BALL

Last game of the Hornets' first "perfect season," a Thursday evening in late April 2003. The local press would ignore the event, and no one in town would remember it thirty days later, but for twenty-four nine-year-olds and scores of local soccer aficionados, this was the World Cup. Bowie was in tatters at the half, down 2–0, whipped at every position. With just twenty-five minutes left to play, the season was ending better than we had hoped: the Prince George's County Championship was very nearly won. Bowie—with a population twice the size of College Park and a storied tradition as one of the oldest clubs in the region—was the only true superpower in the county, the Galactic Empire of youth soccer in these parts, and we were spanking them. Undefeated for the first time, 2-0-4, the kids from College Park were on a roll, unbeatable.

Once again we were playing under the lights at Duvall Field. There were at least a couple of hundred people on the sidelines— up on their feet with excitement. The kids were ecstatic, their parents red-faced and froggy from cheering. The mayor was there. If the turnout didn't set a record, it sure came close. Three years in the making, three years of fits and starts, and the team finally seemed ready to claim its honors. Edward had shut out Bowie at goalkeeper through the first half. Ben, Bryan, and Kevin looked unstoppable. The hometown crowd was on its feet the entire time.

Within the first ten minutes of the game, Bryan had airmailed a twenty-yard pass from the backfield to Ben, who settled the ball on the run in a single touch, split the right defender and the midfielder, dribbled straight over the center of the field, and threw a move at the sweeper that tangled the kid's feet and spilled him. Bryan arrived a split second later at a dead sprint. Tick, tock, and two Hornets were in the box. The keeper charged Ben, and he improvised on the spot—throwing out his right arm, dropping his left shoulder, and cranking back his right foot. Everything about his body mechanics suggested that he was loading up for the shot. But as the goalie dove to block it Ben abruptly dug his toe into the turf, tilted himself over on the opposite tack, goosed the ball away with the outside of his left foot, and walked into the goal.

"Man, what the hell is that one called?" Terry said.

"A Rummenigge," I said laughing. "The kids call it a rutabaga. You know? Like a turnip."

"Yeah, well, he just rutabaga-ed that goalie right out of his shoes!"

Pronounced *Room-in-ayga*, the move was invented two decades earlier by a former German bank clerk named Karl-Heinz Rummenigge—twice voted European player of the year in the 1980s and now immortal as one of the greatest fake-out artists in the history of the game. Like the great Stanley Matthews before him, Karl was known to stroll into the net on occasion.

Six or seven minutes later, Bryan delivered another deep pass, this time to Kevin Guerrero. Stutter-stepping once to back up his opponent, the Salvadoran gunner pulled up on the right sideline and ripped a thirty-yard bomb that arced into the box and bounced off a defender's arm. He had by then made his rep as the hardest shooter in the division, and most kids did their best to get out of its way. This time he drew what must have been his ninth "hand ball" of the season. Kevin was the obvious player to take the penalty shot, but it wasn't our decision anymore. The kids grabbed Ben and pushed him to the penalty spot. The referee dropped his hand, and the team's leading scorer placed his tenth goal of the season past the keeper's splayed right leg. So ended the first half, 2–0.

The Hornets' acrobatics were the work of one man: Roy Dunshee. He had taught Ben and Bryan more about the game in seven weeks that spring than I had managed to impart to them in three years. The first time I met him, it was a charcoal evening in March on a practice field behind a YMCA in Silver Spring. He was the same age as I, with the same gangly build and the same faint trace of a Jersey accent and a Jersey boy's native gregariousness. But from his cabled calves and upright stride and the instinctual way that he carried himself over his center of gravity, you could tell that he was a soccer player. If there was any doubt, he gathered a bunch of balls at midfield and started firing a steady fusillade of shots at the crossbar from thirty-five yards out, pinging them off a spot no bigger than a dime, one after another. In nine or ten volleys, he might have missed twice. As they arrived for practice, the normally unruly Calverton Flames stopped on the hill leading down from the parking lot and watched. Some of them sat in the grass. It was the first time I had ever seen them hold still for anything.

"What do you think of our new trainer?" Jeff Kestner asked

me when he pulled up a couple of minutes later. "Is he the real deal?"

"Oh, yeah," I said. "I think it's safe to say he's the real deal."

"I hope so," he said. "There's a lot of wannabes trying to pass themselves off as trainers, and nobody has really heard of this guy."

The reason so few people had heard of Roy Dunshee was that Coerver Coaching had yet to take hold in the state of Maryland. We may have quit being a British colony more than three hundred years ago, but when it comes to youth soccer we're still dominated by the English. And, from the lowliest rec teams to the mightiest squads in the private travel leagues, English trainers and amateur coaches infuse the short-passing game into kids' heads as if it were the only way to play soccer: the punt-and-run defense; the midfield mash-and-trample; the endlessly overlapping three- and four-man diamond-and-triangle geodetics. But Dunshee's method of coaching, the Coerver Method, is Dutch, and you have to look far and wide to find anyone who teaches the Dutch or Brazilian way of doing things. You'd also be hard pressed to find anyone who proceeds from a baseline belief that kids' sports should, first and foremost, be fun for the kids. Dunshee was one of those rare guys.

A former University of South Carolina midfielder, he was part of a wave of "new school" trainers who took up their trade here in the mid-1990s. He had given up a career in law by then to acquire a landmark tavern on the gentrified waterfront of Annapolis, near the U.S. Naval Academy. It was his friend and former Carolina teammate Tom Reilly who brought him out of semiretirement and put the cleats back on his middle-aged feet. Reilly had bought the rights to teach the Dutch training method just as American youth soccer was beginning to show its strength of numbers.

Reilly was a self-described product of the "old-school, kick-and-chase, argy-bargy" style of play that had defined North Jersey soccer for a century. "We used to run laps, jump over barrels, bang around in pit drills, all that kind of stuff," Reilly told me. "It was a hard, physical style of play, very little finesse. The old Scottish way, you know?" Through these less-than-graceful tactics, Reilly and Dunshee became mortal rivals as kids, once coming to blows on a New Jersey soccer field and setting off a melee that shut down the game when spectators poured onto the field.

"Tommy was a dirty player," said Dunshee. "I had no choice. I had to sort him out."

"Dunshee kicked me and threw a couple of sucker punches when I was on the ground," Reilly later told me. "That's the kind of player Roy was. I never even saw his face. He barely registered in my memory—a blip on the radar. The reason he probably remembered me is because he had to endure so many bitter defeats from my team."

"The only problem with that story is that it's probably true." Dunshee said when I alerted him to Reilly's version of events.

Out of such stuff are lasting friendships made in the game. Particularly in the 1970s, when the tribe was still small, "Everybody in the sport knew everybody else," Reilly recalled. "As the years went by, if you stayed in it you would run into the same guys at tournaments and camps, that kind of thing. If you went at it with somebody in a game, it was only a matter of time before you'd see him again."

After graduating from their respective New Jersey high schools, the two former combatants were reunited in the red, black, and white colors of the Carolina Gamecocks—part of a second-year infusion of Jersey prospects on a team top-heavy with St. Louis recruits. With the towering Dunshee covering his back at midfield, the pint-size Reilly led the team in scoring in 1981. "Tommy got all the goals," Dunshee sneered. "And I got all the yellow cards. If they kept track of that stat at Carolina, I'm probably the all-time leader in fouls. But that's a midfielder's job, to control the flow. We do the dirty work while the little guys get all the glory."

By 1989 Reilly was teaching physical education and coaching high school soccer back in his home state when he first heard about a new approach to coaching kids invented by Dutch legend Weil Coerver. A friend lent Reilly an early videotape outlining the method, and he was sold. He set up a meeting with Coerver officials at Newark International Airport and convinced them that they should franchise their brainchild to coaches in the United States who had proven credentials and were willing to immerse themselves in the Dutch model and submit to Dutch supervision. "They didn't just let guys go off into the hinterlands and start teaching their method, because they didn't want it to get watered down or screwed up by some yokels calling themselves Coerver guys. They were very serious about maintaining the integrity of the program, and very serious about their mission."

Reilly earned the trust of the Dutch, and he called his former Carolina teammates around the country and enlisted them as trainers. Within a decade, he held the rights in six states from New Jersey to North Carolina and west to Colorado. Dunshee agreed to be his man in Maryland.

Weil Coerver's mission was nothing less than the transformation of kids' soccer—a campaign to get coaches out of the way and give the game back to the players, while producing enough success to keep parents satisfied and quiet on the sidelines. The same postwar baby boom that occurred in the states happened everywhere else at the same time, later to produce similar suburban land rushes and shopping malls and child worship. Where sports are concerned, parental narcissism has become a worldwide affliction, if not quite so severe as it is in the United States.

The Coerver Method was a quantum leap in the understanding of how kids learn, what motivates them, and why they do the crazy things they do. As the head coach of Holland's Feyenoord pro team, which won the prestigious European Club Championship in 1970, Coerver began experimenting with "modeling," the concept that players master mechanical processes best by watching a demonstration, then immediately trying it themselves. By slowing down game films, he broke up the distinctive moves of the world's greatest stars—their small tricks and foot movements—into teachable bits. He then developed a library of games built around each maneuver. Later, to spice up the process and get kids to learn some history, he named the moves after the players who invented them and wrote short biographies describing their greatest moments on the field. So when a Coerver coach "models" a move for his team, he also tells them a short fable about a Cruyff or a Rummenigge, a Marco van Basten or a David Beckham, a Ronaldo or a Hamm. Coerver also banished most of the traditional rote coaching methods—the mindless drilling and lecturing and standing around in lines; the running of laps; the heaping on of positive and negative reinforcement—in favor of the revolutionary notion that kids learn best from one another during active play.

"It just made perfect sense to me," Reilly recalled. "No team I coached after that ever ran a lap. My kids won the New Jersey State Cup without ever running a lap. It made my job as a head coach a lot easier, too, and more rewarding, because the kids pretty much teach themselves, which allows me to work on the fine points with them."

In a year of watching Roy Dunshee work with the Calverton Flames—in some 150 hours of practices—I would never see him use the same game twice. I never saw the Flames run a lap, because the fast pace of a typical Coerver scrimmage was more than enough physical conditioning. I never heard him lecture the team for more than thirty seconds. Not once did he raise his voice. This is not to say that there were no insurrections, because nine-year-old boys seldom stop plotting the overthrow of the world, but Dunshee calmly quashed every barracks coup with push-ups that literally reduced the ringleaders to groundlings. Even here, however, he was building in soccer assets: push-ups produce shoulder power, and shoulders are half the game.

Weil Coerver is not the only beacon of this troubled age. I have no idea whether he and Cal Ripken have ever met, but the Iron Man's crusade to save kids' baseball from overachieving boomer fathers sounds much the same. So do Len Oliver's tireless licensing speeches in Virginia: "The magic is in the ball. The game is the great teacher."

"Until the kids are older, there's really not all that much we can teach them," Lighthouse Boys Club alum A. J. DeLaurentis told me on a practice field outside Washington one night that spring. "The only thing a youth coach can really contribute at this age is strategic pointers. You can overload the left or overload the right, maybe add a defender or mark a man if the other team is stronger, or pull some stunt on the kickoff. It's all pretty simple. They pick up the rest of it from each other. . . . No coach wants to hear this, but we're mostly here for the parents."

Most of what amateur coaches do today is "reinvent the wheel," as Mike Sidlak put it. I met the Baltimore biologist and former University of Maryland player that spring, too. The instructor for a two-day licensing course I took, he told a roomful of skeptical suburban soccer commandos that we coach kids best when we coach them least. In its transcendental state, our job was the art of appearing to do nothing. Many months later, after dinner at his house, Sidlak wouldn't let me leave without an armful of pamphlets, manuals, and videotapes describing how to set up "small-sided" games that only loosely resembled soccer: games with four goals, or six, or eight; two versus four players, or three versus five; games of tag; games of kickball; relays; volleys. "Touches," he said, are all that really matter. Almost anything fun that kids can do with a ball that doesn't involve their hands is "good stuff for soccer."

"They can't begin to absorb the fine points until they're twelve or thirteen," Sidlak told me. "Play, they understand. Fun, they get. Make it fun, and they'll teach themselves." As I pulled up my collar for the twenty-yard dash to my car in the rain, he added, "Nobody learns this stuff overnight. Nobody just suddenly becomes a coach. You have to work at it." Driving home that night, I took some comfort in the fact that most of my errors were universal, as much a reaction to the impossible demands of the situation as they were a consequence of my own ignorance. To win games, to include everyone, to contend weekly with the sideline hubbub that now surrounds children's sports is hard enough. But a soccer coach also has to serve the mutually exclusive desires of boomer parents. The jocks and indies and geeks all want things done their way—and the mother club will have its say, too—and it must all somehow be made to fit within the game itself. Football and baseball have a hard time accomplishing this miracle, because a kid either has the physical chops to compete or he doesn't. Hence the mass defection of boomer parents over the past thirty years to the utopian socialism of soccer, and our resulting schizophrenia upon discovering that it can serve as a petunia garden for only so long.

There is much to love about the soccer life—its vitality and humor and tolerance for failure. It is the ultimate teacher of civic values, precisely because its aims are so hard to achieve. It requires patience. It demands focus. For the hyperactive child, the attention-deficit kid, the OCD cases—the obsessive compulsives—it is a dreamworld. I have seen these kids go from struggling C students to solid Bs and back again, with nothing in between to explain the change except a nine-game soccer season. Mostly, it is the sharing of common burdens that works the greatest wonders on the people who play the game. Soccerheads are resilient souls, because their sport is rough and seldom fair, except over the long haul. As in life, every bad break or calamity on the field is eventually rewarded with an undue windfall later on. Don't ask me why this is; it just seems to be the nature of the game.

For all the good it does, however, soccer cannot possibly bear the weight of all our expectations and hopes. We get out as much as we put in. Contrary to the rose-colored visions painted by a great many boomer boosters, soccer does not trump Darwin. It cannot cure obesity or absolve our worries about our children's self-esteem, not without our help. There is only so much that an amateur coach can do to manage the conflict once the little primates begin to sort themselves out, and only so much leveling in the name of fairness that a referee can accomplish under the rules. Burnout becomes a major occupational hazard for those who try. I was in too deep to make a graceful exit from the Hornets—and still too overwhelmed by the unfolding epiphanies of that spring to decide whether I had what it took to become a coach, the real thing. But after three years together the thought of leaving them felt like a minor form of death.

At halftime in the Bowie game, with the county championship on the line and a 2–0 lead, I looked out across Duvall Field and felt a twinge. Something was wrong, but I couldn't quite put my finger on it.

"Be careful now, guys," I told the kids as they huddled around me on the grass, slurping down water and struggling to contain their excitement. "This is Bowie we're playing here, and they're desperate. And we all know what happens when Bowie gets desperate."

"Yeah, they start pushing," said Bryan.

"And fouling," Ben said.

"I heard they put a girl in the hospital once," another kid piped in.

"No, that was Beltsville," Terry reminded them. "And it was a long time ago."

"And it was an accident," I quickly added. "The point is, they're going to come out banging in the second half. They're frustrated because they're from the best club in the county and you're making them look silly. They're going to throw everything they've got at us—especially you smaller guys, especially Shelby. They're going to go after her because she's the girl, and they think they can crush her like a paper cup."

The Mosquito smiled at that, but it was less than convincing. The animal glimmer was missing from her eyes, and the sideways grin hadn't been seen in a while—not since she fell headfirst a few weeks earlier while hanging upside down from a playground swing set before practice. The paramedics sent her home under her own power that day, but she had been tender ever since.

Across the midfield line, the coach from Bowie was trying to pump his team back up. Hunched over, down on one knee, he slapped his hand in the grass and drew lines with his finger, occasionally looking in our direction for emphasis—no doubt reminding his kids that no Bowie squad had lost to a team from College Park since the Protestant Reformation. Five minutes later, the ref blew the whistle to start the second half.

"Damn, Terry, I didn't notice it till just this second!" I said. "They have the downhill advantage!" Bowie was about to crash right through us. At the kickoff, the team's right wing bowled Shelby into the grass as he ran by her. Alone in the backfield, Bryan saved the shot, but the opposition was back twenty seconds later—and the wing, a stocky kid in wire-rimmed glasses, knocked Shelby down again. Then again. Then some more. Intentional or not, it was a textbook example of "fouling away from the ball."

"He's just knocking her down!" Terry said. "Every time she gets up, he knocks her down again!"

"Chill, man," I said. "That's soccer."

"It isn't legal!" Terry said.

"Everything is legal that the ref can't see, you know that," I replied. "And so does she."

Now the parents joined the din: "TRIP!" and "PUSH!" and "HEY, REF, WHERE'S THE FOUL?" Both teams were tiring and getting sloppy, grabbing one another's jerseys, elbowing, banging into their own teammates, then into their opponents. "Come on, Ref!" someone foghorned. "Are you going to call *anything*?" Just then we had bigger problems. Alex Corboy, playing substitute keeper, made a gorgeous diving save, only to punt the ball away straight up the middle and right into a Bowie midfielder's lap, not twenty paces from our goal. On instinct the kid took an off-balance hack at the bouncing ball and caught it square, ripping a shot that seemed to ride toward our goal on a wire. It was one of those moments when mind, eye, and foot all line up just so. Two years later, I can close my eyes and still see it. Alex fell to his knees and buried his forehead in the turf. He had violated one of the fundamental laws of goalkeeping—"Never, ever, ever kick the ball over the middle"—and he knew it. The Hornets' ace in the hole, the "supersub" who had played every position on the field, the kid who saved us at crucial minutes all season long, couldn't bear to look up.

"We gotta pull him out," Terry said.

"Now?" I said.

"Yeah, now," he replied. "He's in shock. They'll walk right over him."

With Edward in the goal again, Braulio struck back. Gathering up a loping cross from Ben, he fired a quick right-to-left shot that skipped past Bowie's keeper and into the net to regain the two-point advantage. It was to be the Hornets' last goal of the season. At that point we should have fallen back into a five-man defense and smothered them, but I was too distracted, too shocked by the sudden turn of fortune. On the left side of the defense, Shelby finally folded. Knocked down repeatedly by the opposing wing, she rolled her eyes when their coach sent in a trio of dozers, his "jumbo" offense. With Bryan resting on the sidelines and a scrub substitute in the stopper position, the timing was disastrous. As Bowie's entire midfield flew past Shelby in a classic "jailbreak" for the goal, she got windmilled to the ground again. Edward charged from the box and plowed into the left wing, blocking the kid's shot with his shin guards. But with no defenders to support him he couldn't collect the ricochet in time. Bowie's right-wing lined up on the open ball and teed off from five feet out, like punting a chicken.

A minute later the same play yielded the same result. Edward was used up by now. The score was 3–3. The Hornets were falling apart faster than Terry and I could identify the problems. Our defense had disappeared, yes, that much was clear. Our goalie was panting and panicked. Our offensive players were starting to look hollow—on the verge of gassing themselves out with downfield retreats to shore up their second-string defenders. We were doing way too much running. Looking down the sideline at the subs, I tried to read faces. Which one or two or three could save us? Mercifully, the ball went out-of-bounds that very second.

"Alex, GO!" I said. "Relieve Edward. Bryan, IN! Right-side defender. You gotta button it down, Bry, their left wing is killing us. You need to be all over that kid."

"I'll do my best," he called.

"Cody, IN, left-side defender. Matty, UP, you're in for Thomas. Whatever you do, buddy, hit them like they're hitting us."

Before the subs could even get into position, while Alex was still tugging on his gloves in the goal box, the ref resumed play. Braulio threw in the ball from out-of-bounds, and time once again slowed down to an agonizing montage of frozen images. Alex heard the thump of the shot before he saw it. Ben tore into the box and leaped. Alex launched himself into the air a split second behind him, one glove on and one half off, arms reaching for the crossbar. The ball rose as it bore toward them, skipped off the top of Ben's head, grazed the tips of Alex's fingers, and spun into the roof of the net.

"Roll BACK!" Bowie's coach yelled to his team, dousing their celebration. "Roll BACK! Everybody on DEFENSE! Everybody! Strikers BACK! Stay BACK! Get BACK!" He barely contained himself for the next five minutes as his kids whipped into a whirl of flying bodies and shoulder blocks. Most of the hits were "clean," but the ref called three fouls—gave us the ball three times—none of them anywhere near the box. The Hornets never got closer to the net than twenty yards out. This was soccer, the real thing, the game as bona fide sport, or as close as nine-year-olds could make it. Aesthetically, tactically, technically, Bowie was nearly flawless in the second half. One goal was all we ever needed to take the title, but Bowie found it first, with 306 seconds left to play.

The whistle blew. The perfect season ended, undone by a single goal, the goal we had been chasing since the end of March.

Like a curse, that goal haunted me for the next three months. If not for the flu, I thought, if not for Shelby almost breaking her neck, if not for the mud, if not for the ref, if not for spring vacations, if not for fast food, if not for the fact that my son was an inch too short. If not for a thousand things, the Hornets would have managed a tie and the game would have been decided by a PK shoot-out—five point-blank shots on a dead ball—and there wasn't a coach in the county who would have bet a nickel against the College Park kids. Every time Terry and I talked that summer, "the goal" was all we talked about, until we got sick of talking about it and stopped talking altogether. Had any coaches in the history of the game suffered as much as we did? Did *anybody* deserve that one goal more than we did?

It was July before I could laugh about it, and once I started laughing the ridiculousness of my obsession finally set in. All ambition requires some degree of mania, because all of life is accidental. Nothing is ever truly under our control, or we would never die. Joy and love and hope live in the moments between the hours of heartbreak and loss and fear. Every minute of every day, one-third of the people in the world are winning and one-third are losing and one-third are breaking even by the skin of their teeth. There is a God, I concluded, and he gave us soccer at the dawn of time so we would never forget who is in charge.

Determined to become something more closely resembling an actual coach, I changed everything by August. Borrowing heavily from Mike Sidlak and Roy Dunshee, I became a conscientious objector to old-school coaching—the only model I had ever known, the thing that had driven me and millions of other indies away from organized sports in the first place. When the kids returned to preseason practices, we did nothing but play games—weird games, some with no nets and some with four, some with two balls and some with ten.

We played Doctor, Doctor and Rob the Bank and Foxes and Chickens; Freeze Tag, Sharks and Minnows, and Hospital Ball. The players never ran laps. I did my best to shut up, which was much harder than I ever imagined. In homage to Beckenbauer, we played with an "attacking keeper" and "attacking defenders." That winter we entered an indoor league, where the game moved so fast that it sometimes made me dizzy. In all, the kids played more than twenty-five scrimmages and matches from September 2003 to May 2004—a lot of soccer, hundreds of touches.

They lost twice and tied once.

By that summer they each owned three championship trophies, including the undisputed, undefeated, untied Prince George's County crown. They beat every major club at least once, and some two or three times, and they won half their games by shutouts. Shelby Hammond got recruited in the spring to play for the Freestate Lightning girls' travel team in Bowie, and she became a standout utility player within a matter of weeks.

Kevin Guerrero and Braulio Linares, two of the youngest Hornets, were selected to play on rising travel teams in a development league for promising kids, and they were soon contending for a slot in the National Capital Soccer League. Alex Corboy, the gawky walk-on who was so cruelly tortured by fate in the Bowie game, quit soccer in the fall to play football, but he returned two weeks later. By the spring of 2004, he made the cut for the Calverton Flames just as Ben and Bryan were graduating to starters.

The Flames went on to win a pair of major East Coast youth tournaments and an indoor title at the Maryland SoccerPlex before advancing to Division Two of the NCSL—undefeated in nineteen games, thanks to Roy Dunshee, an elegant defense, and Jeff Kestner's good sense as head coach to get everyone else out of their way. They are now poised to break into the top rank of one of the premier youth soccer leagues in the nation. They are just as hyper and just as asthmatic as they ever were, and they have one kid with a blond bowl haircut who was recently diagnosed with major allergies to twelve different kinds of grass. But he can still play like a Brazilian.

When the United States finally wins the World Cup, it will be with Italians and Nigerians in the goal; Germans and Koreans in the backfield; Jordanians and Indians at the circle; and Brazilians and Latinos up front. Catholics, Muslims, Protestants, Jews, Baptists, and Hindus. For we are the only nation on earth that can possibly figure out how to meld it all together—and we will be attacking, ever advancing, in the name of all that is holy and good, because, as Dunshee put it, "We're Americans, it's who we are, it's what we're good at." In the words of Admiral Farragut, "Damn the torpedoes, full speed ahead!"

My 1991 Volvo wagon is in the shop again, this time with a blown ignition. It has 136,279 miles on the odometer and two bald tires, but the ghost of Erno Schwarz now rides beside me in the shotgun seat. Soccer is life. The quest continues.

SOURCE NOTES AND
ACKNOWLEDGMENTS

In the summer of 2002, I was invited to a backyard barbecue at the home of my longtime friend Scott Higham of *The Washington Post*. I arrived fresh from a soccer practice, dressed in my usual coach's costume. In Washington, a soccer coach is the object of instant curiosity because some fifty thousand kids here play the game. So a lively two-hour conversation ensued as the assembled suburban parents swapped one anecdote after another—some hilarious, some heartbreaking, others simply outrageous—about their sideline experiences. As a first-time father, Scott was fascinated. "Somebody really needs to write a book about all this," he finally said, and he decided it should be me, and he nagged me about it until I did.

Among colleagues and friends who aided and abetted his efforts were two of my then editors at *The Baltimore Sun*, Jim Asher and Jan Winburn; compatriot Jersey boy and then *Sun* writer Neal Thompson; friend and author Lauren Cowen; novelist Bill Morris; author Miles Harvey; and Ashley Halsey, April Witt, and Gabe Escobar at *The Washington Post*. All lent timely advice or moral support that kept me moving when I doubted whether a book on this subject was even possible.

I am equally indebted to a great many people who patiently gave of their time and hospitality to explain the game and the soccer culture to me: hometown youth coaches like Ray Fetterer, Dave Olfky, and Dave Pinchotti; the pros and semi-pros: Jake Bradley, Tony DiCicco, Adele Dolansky, Rafael Guerrero, Heather Schou, and Mike Sidlak, as well as Roy Dunshee and Tom Reilly of Coerver Coaching; and, of course, the elders: Hall of Famers Walter Bahr, George Brown, and Gene Olaff, who lent their irreplaceable personal papers and recollections. Harry Keough deserves special mention for agreeing to sit down for a four-hour interview in his hotel room in Charlotte while awaiting word of a death in his family. I met most of these people in a matter of months over the winter of 2003–2004, and it is probably safe to say that no amateur coach in any sport has ever had his misconceptions so abruptly corrected.

It is often said in soccer that there are only three or four degrees of separation between any two people in the game, and Jack Huckel at the U.S. Soccer Hall of Fame proved that point. He not only afforded me access to the Hall's trove of original documents and artifacts (dutifully cataloged and maintained by archivist Peg Brown) but also introduced me to many of the notable experts who appear in this book. It was through Jack that I met Herb Giobbi, then director of the U.S. Soccer Foundation, who opened other doors and extended innumerable favors, including very good seats at the Women's World Cup qualifiers in 2004 to witness Abby Wambach's incredible feats of heading (with which she bloodied the North Koreans).

Other organizations that provided aid, counsel, or useful publications were the American Youth Soccer Organization; U.S. Soccer Federation; the U.S. Youth Soccer Association; the National Soccer Coaches Association of America; the Sporting Goods Manufacturers Association; the National Women's Law Center; the Women's Sports Foundation; the National Collegiate Athletic Association; the National Association of Intercollegiate Athletics;

Montgomery Soccer Inc.; Washington Area Girls Soccer; the National Capital Soccer League; and, of couse, the College Park Boys & Girls Club.

Every author follows in footprints laid down by others, but soccer is still largely unexplored terrain in the United States, so I cannot overstate my gratitude to the few who came before me: Roger Allaway, Colin Jose, and David Litterer, whose efforts to preserve soccer's forgotten past in this country are contained in their exhaustive *Encyclopedia of American Soccer History*, without which this project would have taken years; Zander Hollander's *The American Encyclopedia of Soccer*; and *America's Soccer Heritage* by the late Sam Foulds. No soccer library is complete without a copy of *Offside: Soccer and American Exceptionalism*, by Andrei S. Markovits and Steven L. Hellerman.

One of the most daunting hurdles in writing a book about soccer is that the game has a literary tradition that is at least as rich as that of baseball. So many great stories have been told, by so many lyrical writers, that any author contemplating a book is ever mindful of the fact that he risks looking pale by comparison. So I steeped myself in the writing of the masters. If the book has a heartbeat, it owes to them. Whenever I borrowed anything from these works, I endeavored to provide direct citations to the original in the text. If I occasionally failed, the reader will please let the following be his or her guide:

The best soccer book ever written by an American is probably *The Girls of Summer*, by the *New York Times* sportswriter Jere Longman. I turned early and often to his account of the 1999 World Cup campaign by the U.S. Women's National Team in writing chapters two and nine.

Longman's editor at HarperCollins, David Hirshey—probably the most knowledgeable soccer guy in publishing—generously offered early advice on possible sources and pitfalls to avoid.

("It's very easy to get sentimental where kids are involved . . . If you can't show them as real people, go write about something else," he told me.)

For all things concerning Brazilian and Dutch soccer, I consulted *Futebol: Soccer the Brazilian Way*, by Alex Bellos, and *Brilliant Orange: The Neurotic Genius of Dutch Soccer*, by David Winner. Both are hallmarks of "new-style" soccer writing, full of wit, insight, and verve. For general historical background on the game, I relied on *Football Against the Enemy*, Simon Kuper's freewheeling 1994 travelogue; the essays of Eduardo Galeano in his incomparable *Soccer in Sun and Shadow*, and Australian historian Bill Murray's indispensable *The World's Game*. As for the obsessive attraction of the sport, I found plenty of grist in *The Miracle of Castel di Sangro* by Joe McGinnis; *Among the Thugs*, Bill Buford's dark take on English hooliganism; and Nick Hornby's brooding *Fever Pitch*, which traces the tragicomic consequences of his lifelong fixation on London's Arsenal team. I also highly recommend *How Soccer Explains the World*, by American Franklin Foer, and *Dynamo: Triumph and Tragedy in Nazi-Occupied Kiev*, the superb narrative by Scottish writer Andy Dougan about the Ukrainian National Team.

In chapters three, five, seven, and eight, I relied heavily for general contextual background and measures of contemporary attitudes on Harvard scholars David M. Kennedy and Robert D. Putnam, whose towering works, *Freedom From Fear* and *Bowling Alone*, respectively, are invaluable bookends to the American Century. Hardly a question that arose in writing about the rise and fall and resurrection of U.S. soccer during these times was left unanswered in these volumes. For information on the Labor Movement and reaction to it in chapter six, I turned to *From the Folks Who Brought You the Weekend*, by Priscilla Murolo and A. B. Chitty; *The Impossible H. L. Mencken*, edited by Marion E. Rodgers (arguably the most user-friendly compendium of the great columnist's work); and the Web site BoondocksNet.com, where editor Jim Zwick has compiled an impressive collection of original source material about the national campaign to end child labor, including an article from the 1912 *Literary Digest* on the Lawrence Children's Strike. For any and all general inquiries pertaining to nineteenth-century cotton production, textile manufacturing, European immigration, and the "War between the States," I consulted Shelby Foote's three-volume *Civil War* series.

All information concerning the Lighthouse Boys' Club and the American triumph at Belo Horizonte is derived from interviews, the club's annual reports, or contemporary press accounts in Walter Bahr's personal papers. In chapter six, all references to Sun Tzu's *The Art of War* are drawn from the 1971 paperback edition of the original 1963 Oxford University Press translation by the late Brig. Gen. Samuel B. Griffith (USMC), or from the foreword by Sir B. H. Liddell Hart. For a good background discussion of the Soccer War between Honduras and El Salvador, see the Web site OnWar.Com.

In attempting to diagnose the causes of the paranoid schizophrenia among modern parents, I found much statistical and anecdotal support in *Fat Land: How Americans Became the Fattest People in the World*, by Greg Critser; *Parents Who Think Too Much*, by Ann Cassidy; and *Stiffed*, by Susan Faludi, a book controversial among conservatives that nonetheless provides important benchmarks on the state of American fatherhood. For information on U.S. marriage and divorce rates, the Michigan Department of Community Health has done an excellent job of compiling U.S. Census data over time at www.michigan.gov/mdch. For anyone who still doubts that boomer parents are delusional, please see Caitlin Flanagan's illuminating article, "Bringing Up Baby," in the *Annals of Retail* report of the November 15, 2004, *New Yorker*. To find out more about how parental pressures lead kids to quit sports, I strongly recommend "The American Athlete, Age 10," by Alexander Wolff, in the October 6, 2003, edition of *Sports Illustrated*; the 1999 book *Why Johnny Hates Sports*, by Fred Engh; and "Fixing Kids' Sports," by Peter Cary, in the June 7, 2004, *U.S. News and World Report*. Much of the undergirding for chapter twelve is derived from these reports.

This book is informed by articles in a variety of magazines, most importantly *Sports Illustrated* and *Soccer America* magazine—especially its resident curmudgeon Paul Gardner, the emeritus dean of U.S. soccer writers and a champion of greater diversity in the sport. Race is still an uncomfortable subject for many in youth soccer, but as long as Gardner is around there will be no escaping it.

For an interesting comparative analysis of the role of television in promoting the sport in the United States and Europe, see "Sports Rights and the Broadcast Industry," by Martin Cave of Brunel University in West London and Robert W. Crandall at the Brookings Institute; and "The Global Business of Sports Television," by Rachael Church, in the February 2003 edition of *Screen Digest*.

If the reader senses a feminine touch in the book, it is the result of the hands of so many smart and persistent women in shaping the material, foremost my editors at Farrar, Straus and Giroux, Ayesha Pande and Sarah Crichton; Susan Raihofer, my agent at the David Black Agency, who has a soft spot for long shots; my friend and Socratic torturer Renee Milligan; and my chief collaborator and inspiration, Donna St. George of *The Washington Post*, who has been living with my obsessions for almost twenty years.

Special thanks are due to my brother, Kevin Haner, a long-suffering Las Vegas Little League coach who served as both sounding board and source in the field of contemporary youth sports; to former *Baltimore Sun* books page editor Michael Pakenham, who inspected the texts for signs of lard, laziness, and poor grammar; and to Len Oliver, fellow Temple University alum, historian, and Hall of Fame midfielder, who put heart and soul into more than two hundred margin notes and fact checks on the original manuscript for the "good of the game."

Finally, to my friends Nick and Cindy Waring, my appreciation for lending their library of video footage and photos to help reconstruct the games—and to the kids of the College Park Hornets for sticking with it until Terry Hammond and I figured out how to bring home the trophies.